100 Caterpillars

PORTRAITS FROM THE TROPICAL FORESTS OF COSTA RICA

THE BELKNAP PRESS OF HARVARD UNIVERSITY PRESS

Cambridge, Massachusetts ▪ London, England ▪ 2006

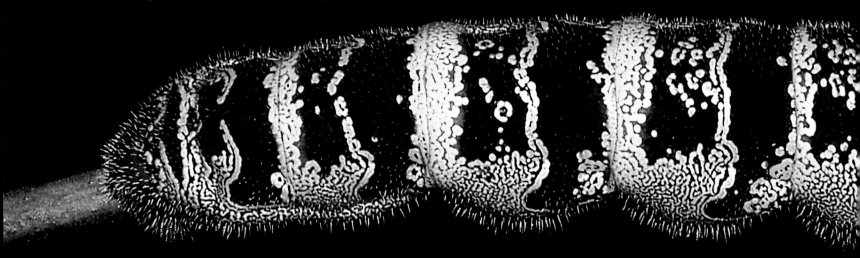

100 Caterpillars

JEFFREY C. MILLER ▪ DANIEL H. JANZEN ▪ WINIFRED HALLWACHS

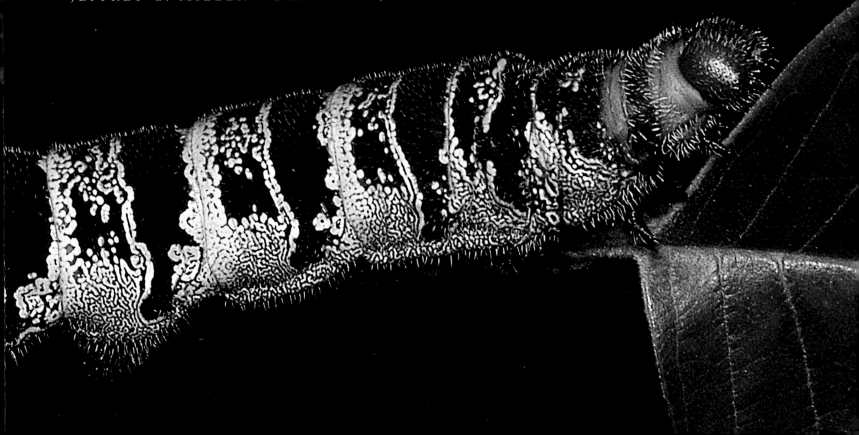

Image on pp. ii–iii: *Arsenura armida*

Library of Congress Cataloging-in-Publication Data

Miller, J. C. (Jeff C.)
100 caterpillars: portraits from the tropical forests of Costa Rica / Jeffrey C. Miller,
Daniel H. Janzen, Winifred Hallwachs.
p. cm.
Includes bibliographical references and index.
ISBN 0-674-02190-8 (cloth : alk. paper)
1. Caterpillars—Costa Rica—Pictorial works. I. Title: One hundred caterpillars.
II. Janzen, Daniel H. III. Hallwachs, Winifred. IV. Title.

QL553.C67M55 2006
595.78'139097286—dc22   2005059102

The parataxonomists are the wheels and engine of the ACG caterpillar inventory. To all the *gusaneros*, past, present, and future, we honor your dedication by dedicating this book to you.

Contents

A Caterpillar Natural History

*N*ature is a mosaic. The colors of life and death, and the mixing and juxtaposition of these colors, are in part the visible results of an ancient-to-modern process, the process of natural selection. The other part is serendipity. The same is true of body form. While functional, adaptive, and beautiful in simplicity and complexity, body form is also accidental and anachronistic. What we label as beauty in nature is testimony to the forces, opportunities, and histories that have molded what we see in a species today. A species is an ever-changing yet simultaneously long-static collection of genes confronting, surfing, and ignoring its environment. The convergences of colors, patterns, and forms among species that have a multitude of quite different histories compose an outline of one of nature's major webs of interconnectedness. The abiotic and biotic components of the environment nudge species along different paths as their members eat, sleep, avoid being eaten, and reproduce—over and over again. Some paths are long and boring. Some paths are short and ever so exciting. A vividly colored caterpillar may be a relatively short-lived evolutionary experiment. The organisms that achieve eat–sleep–avoid–reproduce—by whatever combination of an evolutionary past and present—are what we photograph.

Our book is intended to promote an awareness of the diversity displayed in the natural history of our extant biota, accompanied by snippets of our understanding of how their features tie into their behavior and ecology. Caterpillars are our subjects, a life stage that abounds with the beauty of nature. We present this book as an expression of art as well as a demonstration of science. In addition, it celebrates an ecological achievement—the success of the Area de Conservación Guanacaste, Costa Rica.

NATURAL SELECTION HAS CRAFTED caterpillars to convert a vast and diverse palate of vegetable matter, mostly leaves, into an even more vast and diverse array of butterflies and moths. The *mariposas* of the world consist of more than 225,000 species. Every single individual among all of those species existed as a caterpillar that for all but a fraction of its life span fed on a leaf, fruit, stem, or root of a plant. We can therefore fairly state that caterpillars are herbivores. Because caterpillars eat plants, they impact the dynamics of populations and communities of plants as well as ecosystem processes. In this context, working from small to large, from the ecology of one species to a global ecosystem, contemplate for a moment a world without caterpillars. Would it matter? Read on.

A world lacking caterpillars, and consequently butterflies and moths, would be a different place indeed. Start with the nature of herbivory. Caterpillars, as a whole, consume billions of tons of foliage. This foliage supports the function of the plants' photosynthetic factory—the source of energy and refined products. A loss of foliage generally translates into a change for the worse, lowering growth rates and reserves, and reducing competitive vigor. Paradoxically, this does not mean the loss of all caterpillars would lead to a change for the better. Without caterpillars, the status quo among plants would be altered, affecting nutrient cycling, plant succession, and other ecosystem processes. The diversity of phyto-biochemicals would be altered as well. Plant metabolic factories and chemical warehouses involve a diverse array of simple and complex molecules serving a role in protecting the plant. Plant physiology just wouldn't be the same if caterpillars were removed from their (co)evolutionary history. Whether the alterations resulting from the lack of caterpillars would result in a "good" or "bad" event depends on the human perspective—good if the plant is a crop, bad if the plant is a weed. Although caterpillars are not pollinators, the adults, moths and butterflies, often are. Imagine eliminating the particular species of moth on which a plant species depends for pollination. Deprived of the pollinators, the plant would produce no seeds and thus the species would have no future.

Similarly, the thousands of species that are insectivorous—invertebrates and vertebrates alike—rely heavily, if not exclusively, on caterpillars as food. If the world were to lose its caterpillars, these secondary consumers would feel the consequences. A world without caterpillars would also imply a world without the moths and butterflies so prized for their beauty and respected for the complexity of their natural history.

THE LIFE CYCLE

The life cycle of every species of butterfly and moth follows a basic routine typical of insects expressing holometabolous development, or complete metamorphosis: egg, caterpillar (larva), pupa (sometimes in a silk cocoon), adult. Each time the population passes through one cycle of this four-staged life it has completed one generation. Some species are typically, or absolutely, univoltine, meaning that they pass through only one generation per year, and the timing (phenology) of each life stage is synchronized to the vagaries and opportunities offered by the environment, in particular, availability of food and avoidance of harsh weather. Other species may be multivoltine, exhibiting two or more generations per year.

The challenges of food shortage and environmental harshness are met by a multitude of life history tactics. Mortality is high. Probably not more than a few percent of the eggs make it to the adult stage on account of predators, parasitoids, pathogens, inclement weather, and insufficient food. Traits such as fecundity, competitive nature, feeding tactics, phenology, developmental rates, dispersal behavior, and solitary versus group living can confer advantages to some species. The nuances in life history tactics are diverse and are an expression of natural selection past and present. The best way to illustrate some of the complexities of becoming a caterpillar, passing through adolescence as a caterpillar, and perhaps achieving adulthood is to share some of what we know about natural history in the context of Costa Rica—its flora, fauna, and conservation efforts.

THE CYCLE BEGINS

A virgin female moth or butterfly "calls" not vocally but with chemistry. She is releasing a perfume, molecules of which can be detected by males in the parts per million and less. The antennae of certain moths are very feathery (see the image for the adult *Automeris zugana*, portrait #3). These plumose male antennae provide a large surface area that houses the array of sensilla that perceive the airborne pheromone molecules emitted by the female. The male will then follow the chemical trail to the waiting female. They mate. Eggs are laid, and the eggs hatch, perhaps in four to six days or perhaps in ten months. For instance, one ACG species, *Hylesia lineata*, passes the six-month-long dry season as dormant eggs. Timing depends on the ingrained life history pattern that is followed by the species and the presence of certain environmental cues, in particular, moisture and temperature, to awaken the genes responsible for development. A moth's typical egg load may be 80 to 250. Some species can deposit over 900 eggs. Species that deposit high numbers of eggs often do so in a cluster. Typically, eggs are laid on a plant chosen by the adult female, but in some species the eggs may be placed on any substrate, including rocks, buildings, and vehicles. Once the eggs hatch, the caterpillars begin to feed, typically at or near where the eggs were laid.

The caterpillar eats and grows, shedding its skin every few days to few weeks, until it has gone through five molts. In entomological jargon, the caterpillar just described molted its cuticle while developing through five instars. An instar is the body of the caterpillar between molts. The last instar, usually the fifth, transforms into a pupa after passing through a prepupal phase. The prepupal phase is not marked by a molt, but noted by other distinctive behavior: ceasing feeding, voiding its gut contents, perhaps changing its color, and wandering in search of a pupation site.

Pupae come in many forms. As with the eggs, development into the ensuing life stage may occur in a short time—three weeks for a pupa—or a long time—eight to ten months in the pupal stage. The pupa of a butterfly is called a chrysalis. A chrysalis is typically attached to a substrate, such as a twig, hooked into a pad of silk by its rear end. It may also be supported by a "waist" belt, a strand of silk wrapped around the body of the chrysalis, strapping it to the substrate. The pupa of moths is usually one of two types. Some pupae are naked in a cell formed by the prepupal caterpillar among leaves or soil. Others are in a silk or silk-and-leaf cocoon spun by the prepupal caterpillar.

To illustrate the events preceding and following metamorphosis, we provide the example of *Agrias amydon* because the actual emergence of the adult, a butterfly, occurs out in the open. In the prepupal phase, the *A. amydon* caterpillar changes appear-

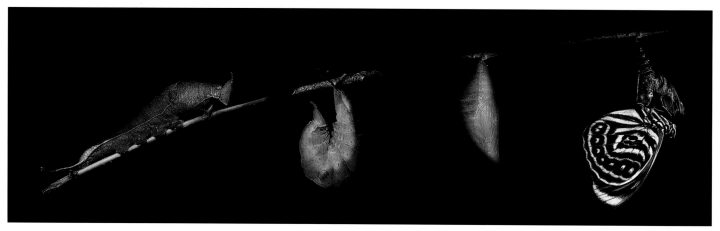

The later stages in the life cycle of *Agrias amydon:* the fully developed caterpillar, prepupa, pupa, and emerging adult.

ance from a cryptic brown dead leaf to a hanging green leaf. The hindmost proleg crochets are firmly hooked into a silken pad, the gut has voided all it can void, and now the tissues are reorganizing. Old tissues are breaking down and new tissues are building up. Then, just as it does in molting from instar to instar, the caterpillar splits its cuticle at the head end and the pupa wiggles out. Somewhat miraculously, the crochet-bearing rear end of the pupa, the cremaster, pulls out of the skin and hooks itself into the same silk pad from which the prepupa was hanging. A few weeks later, or months later if there is pupal dormancy, the transformed butterfly splits the pupal skin and is equipped to conduct much of its life based on the resources acquired as a caterpillar. The butterfly hangs for a few hours from the empty pupal skin or a twig, expanding and hardening its wings. Once this period is complete, the adult is off to an aerial life of avoiding danger (predation), courtship, feeding (in some species), and ovipositing. Many species of feeding adult moths and but-terflies live two to six months, and some may live much longer, but those that do not feed as adults live only five to ten days.

THE CATERPILLAR LIFE STAGE

Since we are particularly interested in the caterpillar stage in the life history of butterflies and moths, we have devoted a section of this chapter to comments about caterpillar development, diet, behavior, and enemies. Caterpillars are the vegetative phase of a butterfly or moth, and in carrying this floristic analogy further, the eggs are the seeds. Out of the egg the newly hatched caterpillar, typically two to five millimeters in length and one to six milligrams in weight, has only two duties: eating and avoiding being eaten. The eating starts at the front end with the head and its mouthparts. Digestion and excretion are inevitable consequences of consumption, occurring in the midgut and hindgut, respectively. The head is not filled with a relatively enormous brain but rather with enormous muscles that drive a pair of mandibles. The mandibles are hard, with grinding and cutting surfaces. They open and close with a scissors- or pliers-like action. They snip and grind off tiny piece after tiny piece of leaf blade. The pieces of leaf are swallowed, along with the plant juices, into a crop in the foregut, similar to the function and design of a chicken's crop. At intervals the fragments of leaf are shunted out of the foregut and with deliberate manipulation passed into the midgut. This is a midgut unlike any component of the digestive system found among vertebrates. Inside the midgut is a peritrophic membrane, a thin membrane like a sausage casing into which passes the chipped or mushed leaf parts. This part of the digestive system is something like an intestine within an intestine, or in a more simplistic analogy, a Christmas stocking into which all the "goodies" are placed.

Caterpillar food is a leaf on a plant in a tropical forest, at least in Costa Rica. These leaves are filthy, splattered and covered with secretions and excretions of all sorts, subjected to dust, dirt, mud, and regurgitations, along with anything else you can think of that would entice sickness and disease. Thus, the intake diet of a caterpillar includes not only the leaf and its contained nutrients, but also a film of slime containing hordes of bacteria that for the most part are a health risk. The last thing a caterpillar needs while growing big is to get sick or have undesirable microbes settle in and usurp nutrients, let alone express a fondness for caterpillar tissue. Natural selection has reinforced the presence of a system creating one of the single most extreme and inhospitable living environments on Earth. That environment is inside a caterpillar midgut—more precisely, inside the peri-trophic membrane inside the caterpillar midgut. The pH inside the cavity enveloped by the peritrophic membrane is about 10–12, making that microenvironment extremely basic. The food moves through the gut without fermenting (in contrast to the fermentation in our own small intestine or a cow rumen). The soluble nutrients in the leaf, as well as some of the nasty defensive chemicals plants possess that confer defenses against herbivores, including caterpillars, ooze through the peritrophic membrane into the space between it and the caterpillar's midgut wall. There the caterpillar's mutualistic bacteria and the caterpillar itself work their digestive magic, providing the building blocks for more caterpillar energy and tissues. In the meantime, the food bolus moves on down the channel within the peri-trophic membrane and into the hindgut. In the hindgut the remaining mass of plant material is neatly pressed into cylindrical pellets for eventual expulsion. Additionally, water is recovered in the hindgut with the aid of the Malphigian tubules. Because some adults lack functional mouthparts and can't feed, the water obtained and retained in the last instar is all the water that will be available for functions through metamorphosis, adult eclosion, and other adult activities, including flight and oviposition. A specific example regarding the gut microenvironment of a caterpillar can be found in our account of *Rothschildia lebeau*, portrait #82.

As the young caterpillar grows, it puts essentially all of its energy into getting bigger. While the little *gusano* is racing toward the last instar, which is indeed an eating machine, it faces a major problem. Its soft body is flexible and stretchable. The cylindrical caterpillar expands in size as its muscles and tissues accumulate, but the hard head is a fixed size. The way to acquire a bigger head along with a bigger body is to stop feeding for a day or less, literally grow a new head inside the neck area behind the old head (see *Chrysoplectrum* BURNS01, portrait #90, showing the initial growth of a new head), and at the same time synthesize a new skin underneath the old one. The molt into the next instar is completed by the old skin splitting at the head. A newly cloaked caterpillar emerges by wiggling and walking out of the previous cuticle. The shed skin may be left behind for only a few moments in some species. In many cases the newly emerged caterpillar eats the molted skin, perhaps recovering valuable nutrients (see *Acharia hyperoche,* portrait #44). The newly eclosed caterpillar is very soft, and for a few minutes to hours, before the new head and skin have hardened their protein-sugar cuticular structure, they expand to a much larger size than that of the previous instar. Typically, the molting cycle is repeated four times during the life of a caterpillar. Successful execution of the molting process depends on the chemistry of hormones, proteins, and fatty acids. Caterpillar physiology leading up and into each molt involves a well-timed, highly synchronized chain of events involving a variety of enzymes and hormones.

The accumulated amount of food eaten by the first through fourth instars is only a minor fraction of what is consumed by the largest and last instar, typically the fifth. For all species, a caterpillar in the last instar is the largest eating machine the insect will ever benefit from. The last instar is no longer eating to molt into a yet bigger caterpillar, but eating to store the water, fat, and protein that will carry it through the pupal stage and into a full-sized adult. Notably, for those many moth and few butterfly species that do not feed as adults, the fifth instar is the last effort to build the energy (water and nutrient) reserves that will carry it through metamorphosis and into all adult activities of escape, courtship, egg maturation, and oviposition. Even for adults that do feed on flower nectar and pollen, rotting fruit, slime fluxes, blood, sandbank minerals, and other such foods imbibed through the straw-like tongue of adult lepidopterans, the reserves gathered in the last instar are much of the insect's crucial energy endowment needed for completing its life cycle.

MORPHOLOGY

Morphology is, by definition, form and function. The basic insect body plan consists of three major body parts: head, thorax, and abdomen. Overall, the expression of form in these body parts is diverse and the functions are specialized. The caterpillar has a huge head and a small (but quite muscular) thorax bearing the classical and diagnostic hexapod plan of six thoracic "true" legs placed to assist in positioning the head while biting off leaf parts. A caterpillar has six tiny stemmata, each being a single lens eye, on the lower front of each side of the head, and it certainly can determine light intensity and whether a shadow is passing over. It does not appear to be able to form an image, however. The abdomen consists of ten segments and the huge gut, where all that leafy material is being processed.

A set of thick and very muscular prolegs (not true jointed legs as on the thorax) are tipped with many tiny fishhook-like crochets and serve as the "feet" that move this great harvesting machine around and keep it from falling off the plant. There is one pair of prolegs per segment in some primitive sense, but over evolutionary time, half or more have been lost. With the exception of certain primitive taxa, the typical proleg arrangement is one pair on each mid-abdominal segment (three through six), and one pair on the tenth, anal segment. The arrangement of the prolegs is used in part to classify and identify Lepidoptera. Different families of caterpillars have different numbers of prolegs. For instance, the Geometridae, the so-called inch-worms or geometers, have just two pairs—one pair on the sixth abdominal segment and the other pair on the anal segment. This is a family-level diagnostic trait that allows us to discriminate inch-worms from those species of Noctuidae caterpillars that have converged on the inch-worm walking pattern, but have three or four pairs of abdominal prolegs. Although a predator can be quite successful at dislodging the caterpillar's three single-point tipped pairs of thoracic legs, the prolegs are much more difficult to get to release their grip. The multi-crocheted prolegs are extraordinarily adept at holding tightly to a leaf, twig, or silk resting pad, to the salvation of many a caterpillar in a windstorm or when under attack.

Respiration, the exchange of oxygen and carbon dioxide, is performed by an insect through a complex system of valves and tubes. This is a very different way of moving oxygen to all the needy parts than how we do it with lungs and red blood cells. The valves at the outer end of the tubes are spiracles, obvious in many caterpillars as the colored oval openings occurring on most segments located along each side of the caterpillar. There is a spiracle on each side of the first thoracic segment and then on

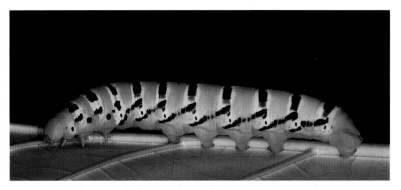

A typical caterpillar, *Oryba kadeni*, showing the head, thorax, abdomen, true legs, and prolegs.

both sides of each of the first eight abdominal segments. For instance, the spiracles are white in *Eacles imperialis* (portrait #14), turquoise in *Adeloneivaia jason* (portrait #39), and black in *Cocytius lucifer* (portrait #55). The adaptive function of colored spiracles is anyone's guess. The tubes are structured like vacuum-cleaner hoses complete with circumtubular reinforcement to prevent collapse. These tubes are called trachea and transport oxygen in and carbon dioxide out. A superb view of the tracheal system can be seen through the thin transparent cuticle of *Talides* BURNS 01, portrait #21.

BEHAVIOR

Many species of caterpillars live solitarily, while others live in groups. In fact, many solitary caterpillars are belligerent toward other caterpillars and especially toward individuals of their own species. The outcome may even result in cannibalism. Caterpillars of some species that lay eggs in a cluster, however, are gregarious and highly tolerant of one another even when in

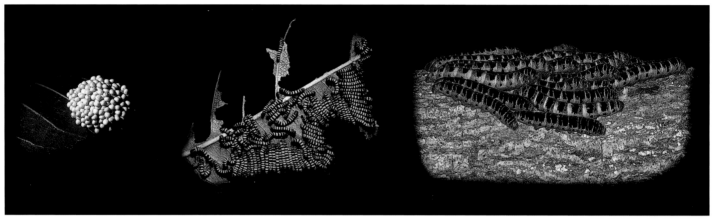

The early stages in the life cycle of *Arsenura armida:* a cluster of eggs, an aggregation of young caterpillars, and an aggregation of fully developed caterpillars.

constant physical contact. An excellent example of a species whose caterpillars live in a cohesive group is *Arsenura armida* (portrait #18). Fifth instars of *A. armida* remain grouped together during the day on the lower trunk of a tree. The foliage of the tree is their food, but during the day the caterpillars roost on the lower trunk, not feeding, not moving. At night the caterpillars, in procession, file up the tree trunk and out onto the leaves to eat. They will follow this circadian pattern of behavior from the day they eclose from their cluster of eggs placed on a leaf of the tree.

How do caterpillars stay together? Only recently, in 2004, did J. T. Costa and colleagues find an answer. As the caterpillar walks, the cuticle produces an odorant that results in the deposition of a chemical track, a trail pheromone, that each can follow and thus maintain group cohesion. As early instars they occur in a mass of tightly clustered caterpillars with black and yellow rings. These caterpillars, with their aposematic warning color-

ation, are toxic to trogons, brilliant tropical birds that are some of the most dedicated toxic-caterpillar hunters among all vertebrates. As last instars, each caterpillar is the diameter of a human ring finger but longer, yet they still retain the tightly bound family unit. Collectively they create a massive warning display of pale greenish yellow and black rings between "caps" of red heads and tail ends. This is just the right set of colors to evoke an avoidance response in a bird or monkey. Natural selection has genetically programmed certain predators to avoid preying on organisms with this appearance, such as a coral snake. These caterpillars still face danger, however. Living in a group and forming a larger visual display does have the disadvantage of creating a large and easily located target for the parasitoid wasps and flies that lay their eggs in and on these caterpillars. Some species of caterpillars even go off and pupate together in groups. In the case of *Arsenura,* the caterpillars split up and go their own way to find a place to burrow into the soil to make a pupal chamber.

Despite the many techniques that caterpillars use to avoid being eaten, there are no caterpillars with a venomous bite. Toxic caterpillars, some displaying bright colors as discussed above, may do disagreeable things to your physiology if eaten. There are also many with urticating spines, from which, if you handle them roughly, you will feel sharp pain. Yet you can fearlessly let these caterpillars walk on you.

PARASITOIDS

Parasitoids are major and omnipresent killers and consumers of caterpillars. Insects that are parasitic on other insects are termed "parasitoids" because they kill their host. In contrast, most true parasites do not kill their host, at least not directly, and if so, not for a very long time from the moment of infection. Most parasitoids of caterpillars belong to a single family of flies, Tachinidae, and various families of parasitic wasps, or for the pedant, parasitoid wasps.

Although this varies among ecosystems and among families of caterpillars, about 5 to 10 percent of caterpillars are killed by tachinid flies and 1 to 4 percent by parasitoid wasps. There are some species of caterpillars that have no parasitoids at all. A few species may be parasitized at a frequency as high as 20 to 40 percent. The parasitoid wasps—mostly Ichneumonidae, Braconidae, and Eulophidae—are extremely specific to a certain species of caterpillar, or to a genus, family, or particular caterpillar lifestyle. Most tachinid flies are host-specific, but there are a few species that parasitize an enormous variety of species, genera, and families of caterpillars.

The female parasitoid may locate a host using cues such as plant volatiles emitted from damaged leaf tissues and caterpillar volatiles emitted from saliva, excrement, and the cuticle itself. Many tachinid flies glue their eggs to the caterpillar cuticle or a nearby leaf. If the eggs have been glued onto the host, the maggot parasitoid drills directly into the host from underneath the egg shell. If the eggs have been glued to the foliage, then they must be swallowed by a caterpillar as the leaf is eaten. Other species of tachinids give birth to maggot-like larvae that then locate the host on their own. Most parasitoid wasps penetrate the caterpillar cuticle with an ovipositor and place the eggs inside. These are known as endoparasitoids. The ovipositor may be able to determine if the host is already parasitized, or otherwise unsuitable, and the wasp then leaves (without ovipositing) in search of another host. Other parasitoid species may lay an egg in a parasitized host, setting up a competitive conflict. Solitary parasitoids are those species in which there is one individual parasitoid per host. To persist in the host they may have to fend off intruders, including conspecifics. Gregarious parasitoids are those species in which there are many individuals per host. In either case, solitary or gregarious, rarely does more than one species successfully parasitize an individual host. The larvae of some species of parasitoid wasps live on the outside of the host. These are known as ectoparasitoids.

Different species of parasitoids attack different stages—eggs, caterpillars, or pupae. Many species are obligate egg parasitoids, attacking and emerging only from the host egg. Tens of thousands of species attack only the larva or the pupa. Many species that oviposit in caterpillars may delay their development, however, until the caterpillar has accumulated most of its reserves or even pupated before eating the caterpillar or pupa. The timing of a parasitoid's life events must be synchronized with those of the host. Female parasitoids must be active at the time their "preferred" host life stage is present. Temperature and seasonal events act as cues to trigger parasitoid activity. For instance, through numerous studies in the 1980s and 1990s, Janzen observed that in the dry forest the rains brought new foliage and the lowest density of predators and parasitoids in the yearly cycle, but as the season progressed, parasitoid density and diversity increased.

A major caterpillar defense against parasitoids is encapsulation of the egg. The caterpillar employs cells in the blood to suffocate the parasitoid egg or first instar. Some species of parasitoids counter this defensive mechanism by injecting a polydnavirus into the host at the time of oviposition. The polydnavirus neutralizes the host's ability to encapsulate foreign bodies.

THE AREA DE CONSERVACIÓN GUANACASTE AND THE ACG INVENTORY

The inventory of caterpillars of the Area de Conservación Guanacaste (ACG) is only a part of the bigger picture of what this conservation area is all about. The geography of Central America 85 million years ago would have the present-day western region of the ACG as an island out in the Pacific amid a lot of blue ocean. Some 16 million years ago that island slid into an emerging archipelago to become the Santa Elena Peninsula, pro-

jecting west from the newly forming Central America. About 1.5 million years ago, the huge volcano that perched on the east side of the then much larger Lake Nicaragua, extending south to today's Liberia, blew up. In a matter of hours, the entire area was a moonscape, a veritable land-bound Krakatoa 200 meters deep in what had been a huge volcano. The Costa Rican part of the lake was obliterated and the floral and faunal restoration through immigration from the remainder of the Central American tropics began. Then 20,000 to 50,000 years ago the young volcanoes—Orosi, Cacao, and the massive complex around Rincon de la Vieja—emerged to make a wall blocking the moisture-laden trade winds off the Caribbean. The result was dry forest on the rain-shadowed Pacific (west) side—Sector Santa Rosa, Sector Santa Elena, Sector Murcielago, and Sector Pocosol. Today, this dry forest extends north to the mountains behind Mazatlan and into the Caribbean lowlands from Tampico to Veracruz, Mexico, and south into Bolivia and Venezuela, with a few rain-forest barriers along the way. Plate tectonics also created the cloud-forested northern end of the Andean highlands, stopping with the Nicaraguan lowlands. To their north is the bottom end of the Rocky Mountains. Another result was the present-day rain-forested slopes and eastern piedmont of the Cordillera Guanacaste—the entire set of volcanoes residing within the ACG—extending across the Caribbean lowland rain forest, north to Veracruz and south to Bolivia.

In all of the New World tropics, the ACG—a UNESCO World Heritage site—is the only property designated as conserved that ranges from the Pacific to the Atlantic ecosystems. All four major tropical ecosystems—marine, dry, cloud, and rain

Area de Conservación Guanacaste - World Heritage Site

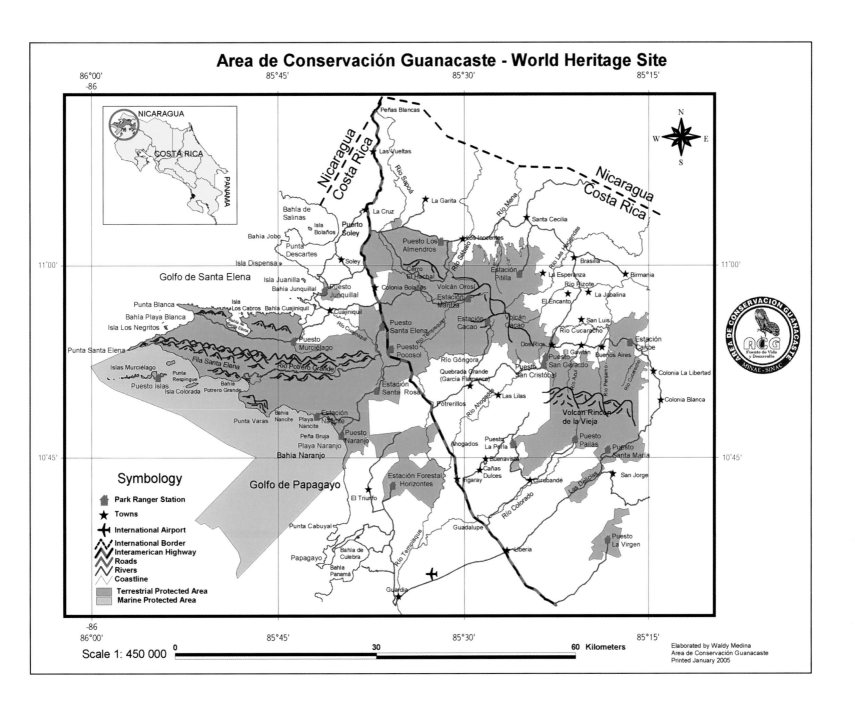

NICARAGUA
COSTA RICA
PANAMA

Nicaragua
Costa Rica

Nicaragua
Costa Rica

Peñas Blancas

Las Vueltas

Río Sapoá

La Garita

La Cruz

Santa Cecilia

Río Mena

Bahía de Salinas

Isla Bolaños

Puerto Soley

Los Inocentes

Puesto Los Almendros

Río Las Inocentes

Brasilia

Bahía Jobo

Punta Descartes

Soley

Cerro El Hachal

Estación Pitilla

La Esperanza

Birmania

Isla Dispensa

Volcán Orosí

Río Pizote

Golfo de Santa Elena

Isla Juanilla

Puesto Junquillal

Colonia Bolaños

Estación Mariza

El Encanto

La Jabalina

Bahía Junquillal

Punta Blanca

Isla Los Cabros

Bahía Cuajiniquil

Cuajiniquil

Río Cuajiniquil

Puesto Santa Elena

Estación Cacao

Volcán Cacao

San Luis

Río Cucaracho

Bahía Playa Blanca

Isla Los Negritos

Estación Cabe

Punta Santa Elena

Puesto Murciélago

Puesto Pocosol

Río Góngora

Dos Ríos

El Gavilán

Puesto San Gerardo

Buenos Aires

Fila Santa Elena

Río Potrero Grande

Quebrada Grande (García Flamenco)

Puesto San Cristóbal

Río Pizamo

Río Azul

Colonia La Libertad

Islas Murciélago

Punta Respingue

Bahía Potrero Grande

Estación Santa Rosa

Río Cucaracho

Colonia Blanca

Puesto Islas

Isla Colorada

Potrerillos

Río Ahogados

Las Lilas

Volcán Rincón de la Vieja

Punta Varas

Bahía Nancite

Playa Nancite

Estación Nancite

Ahogados

Puesto La Perla

Puesto Pailas

Puesto Santa María

Peña Bruja

Puesto Naranjo

Playa Naranjo

Buenavista

Cañas Dulces

Bahía Naranjo

Golfo de Papagayo

El Triunfo

Estación Forestal Horizontes

Trigaray

Curubandé

Los Delicias

San Jorge

Punta Cabuyal

Río Colorado

Guadalupe

Puesto La Virgen

Papagayo

Bahía de Culebra

Río Tempisque

Liberia

Bahía Panamá

Guardia

Symbology

- Park Ranger Station
- ★ Towns
- ✈ International Airport
- International Border
- Interamerican Highway
- Roads
- Rivers
- Coastline
- Terrestrial Protected Area
- Marine Protected Area

AREA DE CONSERVACION GUANACASTE
ACG
Fuente de Vida y Desarrollo
MINAE - SINAC

86°00'
-86
85°45'
85°30'
85°15'

11°00'

10°45'

Scale 1: 450 000

0   30   60 Kilometers

Elaborated by Waldy Medina
Area de Conservación Guanacaste
Printed January 2005

Top: The Area de Conservación Guanacaste (ACG) is a mosaic of recently abandoned ancient pastures *(yellow grass in center),* old-growth original forest *(foreground),* and secondary successional forest up to 400 years old. The view is from Cerro Pedregal on the upper Pacific side of Volcan Cacao, looking northwest across Cerro El Hacha in the early dry season.

A fifty-year-old secondary successional ACG dry forest in Sector Santa Rosa, 300 meters elevation. Such deciduous forest occupies many tens of thousands of hectares of Pacific lowlands in the ACG, and will eventually give way to a mix of evergreen and deciduous species over the next thousand years of natural forest restoration. *Left:* Late April, just before the rainy season begins. *Right:* Early June, two weeks after the beginning of the rainy season.

Top left: An assortment of deciduous and evergreen dry forests cover much of the ACG lowlands: a young, woody invasion of abandoned fields *(foreground);* an evergreen tall forest along a permanent water-course *(midground);* and a deciduous forest dotted with evergreens on the rocky volcanic slopes *(background).* In the rainy season it all turns bright green, and much of the environmental heterogeneity is not nearly so visible.

Top right: Caribbean intermediate-elevation rain forest clothes the eastern portion of the ACG at over 200 meters, extending up the slopes of the Cordillera Guanacaste to the cloud forest–covered tops at 2,000 meters. This image was taken on a rare clear day.

Bottom left: A cloud-free day in the ACG cloud forest reveals old-growth forest *(upper left)* and newly abandoned young pastures *(right),* pastures that will slowly fill with young forest as the decades pass.

forest—are contained in the 153,000 hectares that comprise the ACG. The area also contains about as many species as are in all of North America north of Mexico, all packed into an area about the size of New York and its suburbs. Every species arrived after the volcanic blast laid down a clean slate 1.5 million years ago. The flora and fauna did not evolve in place, but rather, take their form largely through ecological fitting together of species evolved elsewhere.

Inferring from the caterpillar inventory and the adults caught with light traps (lights set out at night to which some adults are attracted), we currently estimate that there are 9,500 species of macrocaterpillars in the 1,150 square kilometers of land in the ACG. There are probably another several thousand species of leaf-mining Lepidoptera larvae, but our inventory does not search for them because their rearing and their taxonomy require a quite different set of specialized activities.

Caterpillars are found by looking carefully at foliage. The diversity of life in the Costa Rican forest can make a single caterpillar difficult to spot. The largest ACG caterpillars weigh fifteen to twenty-five grams, about the same as a small mouse or small bird, and much more than a hummingbird. Leaf damage and fresh droppings provide a hint that a caterpillar is in the area. At night, the beam of a flashlight is reflected by the skin of the caterpillar, causing it to shine and be seen easily. Another technique used for observing caterpillars is to capture an adult female and keep her in a container until she lays eggs, let the eggs hatch, and then feed the caterpillars. The complication is knowing what species of plant the caterpillar will eat.

The ACG Inventory's rearing barn is simple but effective.

Each caterpillar is put in its own plastic bag with fresh foliage by a parataxonomist, or *gusanero*. The bag is hung with a clothespin on a clothesline. The caterpillar's unique voucher code is written on the bag with a magic marker. From the very beginning, in 1978, each caterpillar has had its own unique code in the project database. This code is applied to all events following the bagging and feeding of the caterpillar in the rearing barn, in particular, the specimen and emergence data for an adult, and photographs. Even parasitoids that emerge from the field-collected caterpillar are given their victim's code as well as their own.

Some caterpillars develop quickly, whereas others develop slowly. The growth rate of a caterpillar depends on many factors. Three of the most influential of these factors are nutrition, genetics, and temperature. For instance, within tolerable ranges, warmer temperatures promote faster growth than cooler temperatures; growth rates of siblings feeding on the same diet may differ according to their maternal source; and the nitrogen content in some plant parts is so low that growth is extremely prolonged if such parts are the sole dietary component. Put into practical terms, the caterpillars collected by the *gusaneros* may remain in the barn for quite a long time. Although some species of small caterpillars feeding on flowers or very new foliage can develop from a newly hatched first instar to the day of pupation in as little as seven days, a more typical caterpillar life is fourteen to thirty days, depending on the species. The opposite extreme for the caterpillar life cycle is eight to eleven months from first instar to pupation for a large caterpillar feeding on shaded foliage in high-elevation cloud forest, a notably cool environment.

As many as half of the caterpillar species within the ACG

(Clockwise from upper left): The ACG *gusaneros*, 2005; a black light placed in front of a sheet to collect moths at night; a caterpillar rearing barn featuring rows of bags, each with an identifying number code and containing a single field-collected caterpillar with foliage of its food plant.

feed only on a single plant species or several very closely related plant species. Another quarter have several food plants that do not appear to be very related to each other, yet they are found feeding on them over and over and apparently ignoring the thousands of other species that are available. The last quarter have quite long lists of known food plants, but even these are clearly not feeding on the great majority of species available. Most species of ACG caterpillars need to eat something within twenty-four hours. If starved longer than that, they may not recover even when given food. Many of these "generalists" are restricted to a particular life form of plant, plant part, or micro-habitat. The longer the food plant list of a species of caterpillar, however, the longer it can starve without noticeable conse-quences. Aside from the many tiny species that mine inside of leaves, there are a small number of species that eat flowers, seeds, fruits, rotting leaves, fungi, ant larvae, and other very strange foods. Caterpillars can feed for hours at a time, so they eventu-ally can eat quite a bit of leaf in a day. A large caterpillar in its last instar might consume six to eight square inches of leaf in one day. Over a lifetime, that could add up to twenty to forty-eight square inches. Some species of caterpillars feed in daylight hours, but a very large number perch motionless, not feeding, during the day and feed only at night. Presumably the daytime inactivity is to avoid being seen by predators.

CATERPILLAR PORTRAITS

This book is, first and foremost, an effort to portray caterpil-lars as beautiful objects unto themselves. Since we are diurnal color-vision mammals, the photographs we chose tend to be those of ostentatious caterpillars, set against a black, velvety background to further emphasize their brilliance and color. As a result, the particular ledger of species we chose is biased in favor of aposematic caterpillars, those that warn the potential predator to stay away, and their mimics. The individual species accounts following the portraits make frequent refer-ence to this aspect of their biology. The irony is that while it is easy to know that the bright colors and complex patterns and shapes were selected for in caterpillars as a result of predation, so little experimentation has been done that we do not know which are poisonous or distasteful, and which are merely mimics. We do have a more direct understanding of those that are painful to the touch. More confusing yet, we have only the slightest trace of an idea regarding which caterpillars are avoided because the predator has had an unpleasant experi-ence with them or a look-alike, and which are avoided because the predator is genetically hard-wired to avoid that color or color pattern.

We have chosen just 100 species on the concept that less is more, and because an individual book has its limits. The final portfolio was set, in part, by luck-of-the-draw serendipity. The species that appear in the book are those that were available at the time the book was being prepared. If your favorite or desired caterpillar did not make it into the book, perhaps it will appear in our next book, in which we will present another 100 ACG species of adult Lepidoptera and their caterpillars. A second vol-ume of ACG Lepidoptera is justified by the fact that the gor-geous caterpillars in this volume do not necessarily have a gorgeous adult. The next book will emphasize species with ostentatious adults.

In this book 27 percent of the featured species are caterpillars of skippers (Hesperiidae: eleven species) and butterflies (mostly Nymphalidae: thirteen species; others, three species). This translates into the Rhopalocera, or butterflies and skippers, being represented over five times more frequently than they are represented in a list of species in the ACG. It just happened that those caterpillars were considered by us to be colorful and ecologically interesting. About 95 percent of the ACG macrocaterpillar species are moths, mostly Saturniidae (twenty-two species) or Sphingidae (twenty-one species), and they received their share of attention in this book's portraits.

Unofficial interim names rather than formally described species names have been used for eight of the portraits. This is because these species are undescribed, or in a few cases they cannot be matched with a described species and are therefore strongly suspected to be undescribed. In other words, from the results of the inventory we know that there is a population of that species in the ACG, but the taxasphere has not yet had the time or resources to formally describe it and baptize it with a name. They eventually will be described, and their names and rearing records updated on the project Web site. Such new species are commonly revealed by the caterpillar inventory because it offers a data set largely new to the taxasphere for these species—food plants, seasonal timing, microgeographic location, behavior, and parasitoids. When these data are combined with more classical morphological and macrogeographic information about adults, the patterns that emerge may point to the existence of several species that were previously thought to be just one. During the past decade, DNA information, most recently termed "DNA barcoding," is adding yet another dimension to the elucidation of species boundaries and is an essential tool in systematics. In fact, recently, in 2004, P. D. Hebert and colleagues found one of the caterpillars we display, *Astraptes* LOHAMP, can be discriminated reliably only from its look-alike species by knowing its caterpillar food plant in conjunction with certain segments of its DNA.

If a group of interested biologists or ecotourists walked up to one of us with a certain caterpillar species in hand, they would likely hear a version of one of the species accounts that follow the portraits in this book. Our strategy for each species account was to focus on a theme relevant to the natural history of that species. A more complete discussion of their behavior and ecology will be possible only after the secrets of their lives are fully revealed to future generations of biologists.

A Gallery of Caterpillars

1. *Automeris postalbida*

3. *Automeris zugana*

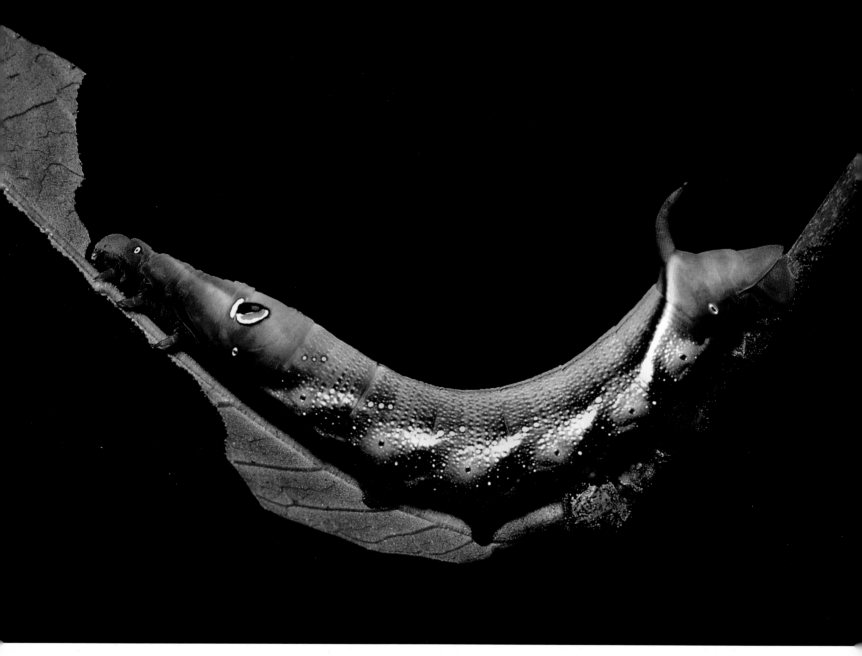

5. *Xylophanes juanita*

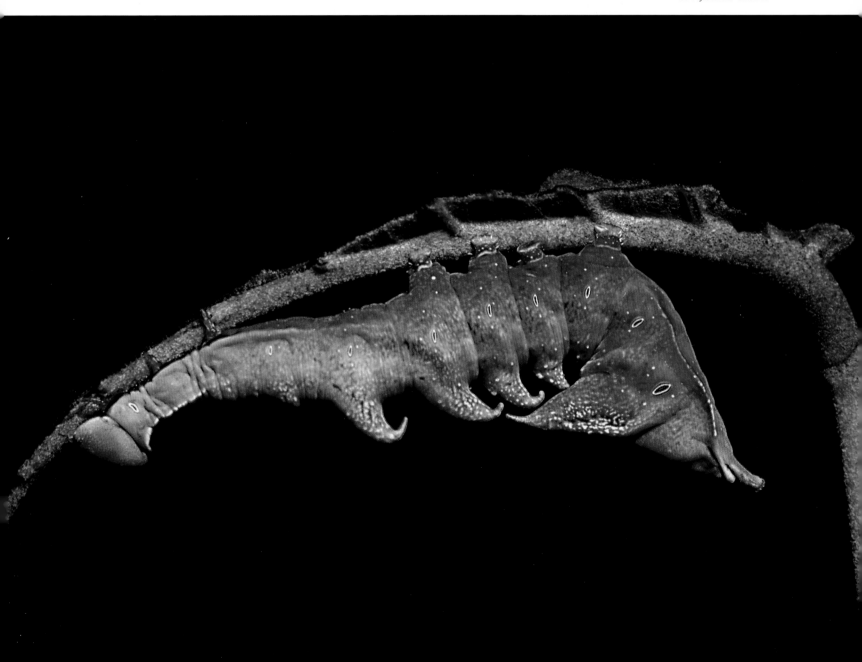

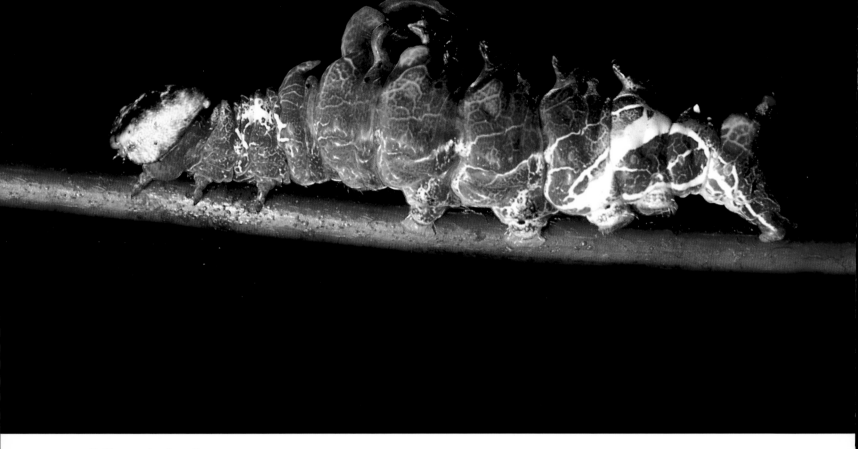

7. *Navarcostes limnatis*

8. *Morpho polyphemus*

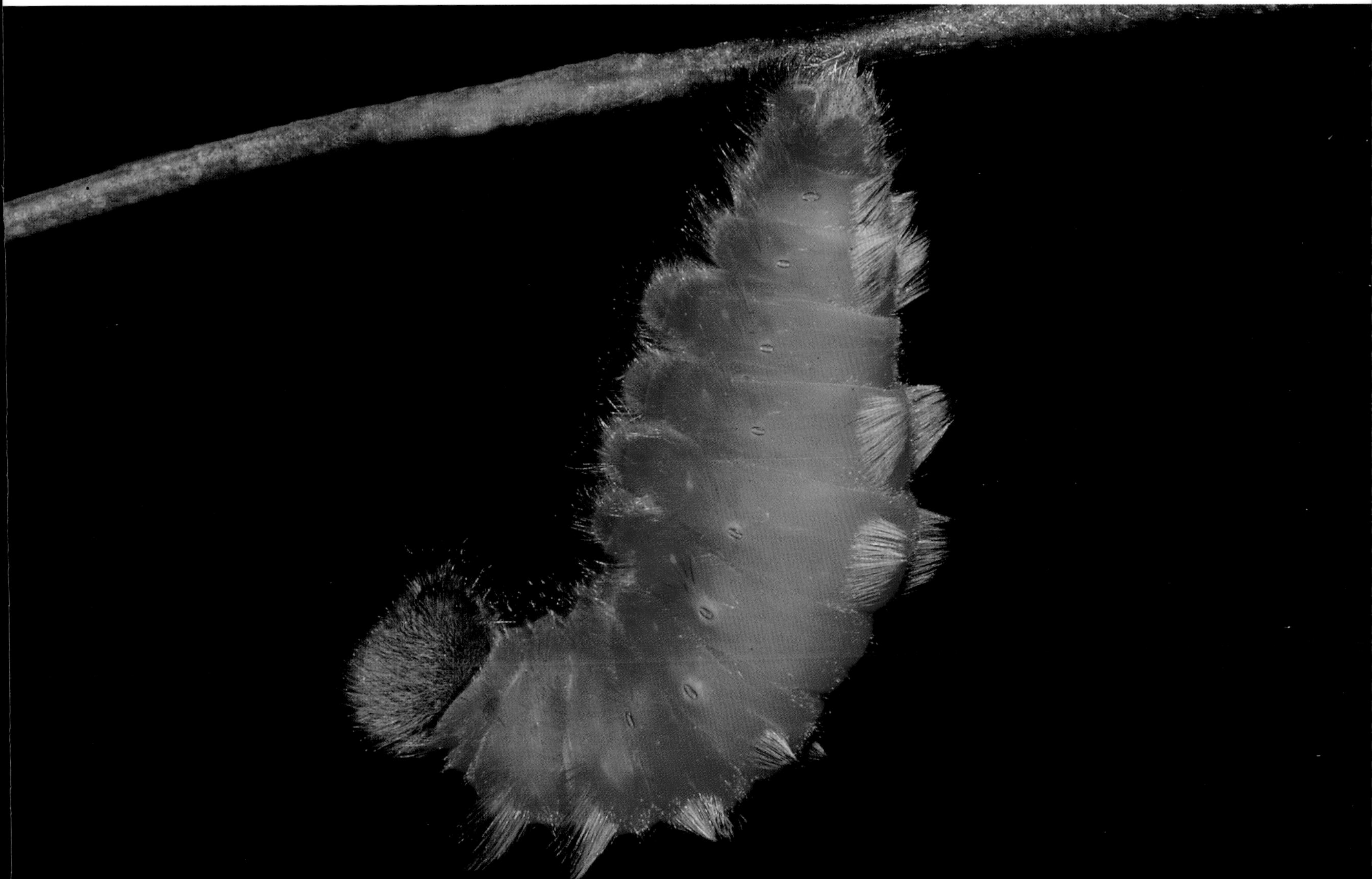

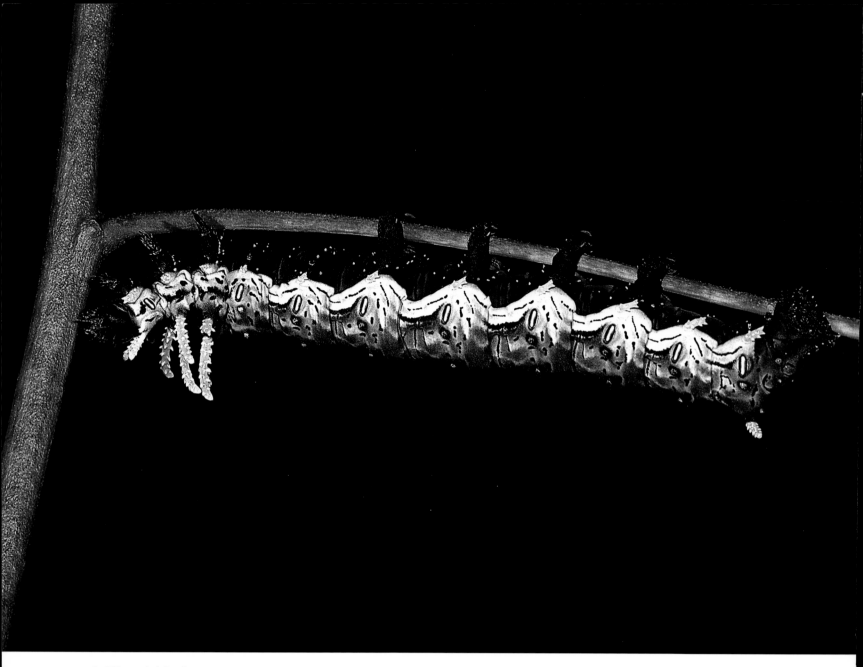

9. *Citheronia lobesis*

11. *Opsiphanes zelotes*

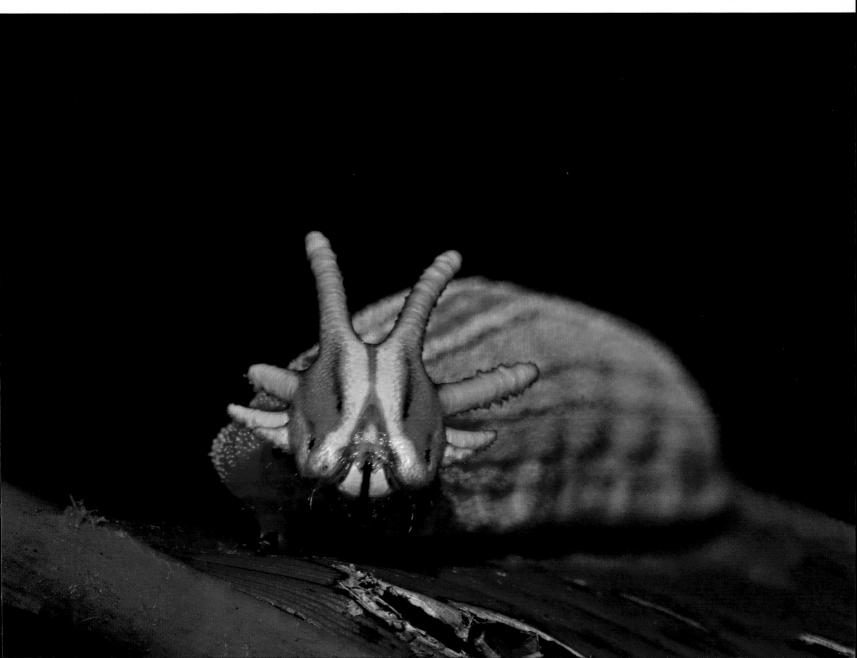

13. *Xylophanes guianensis*

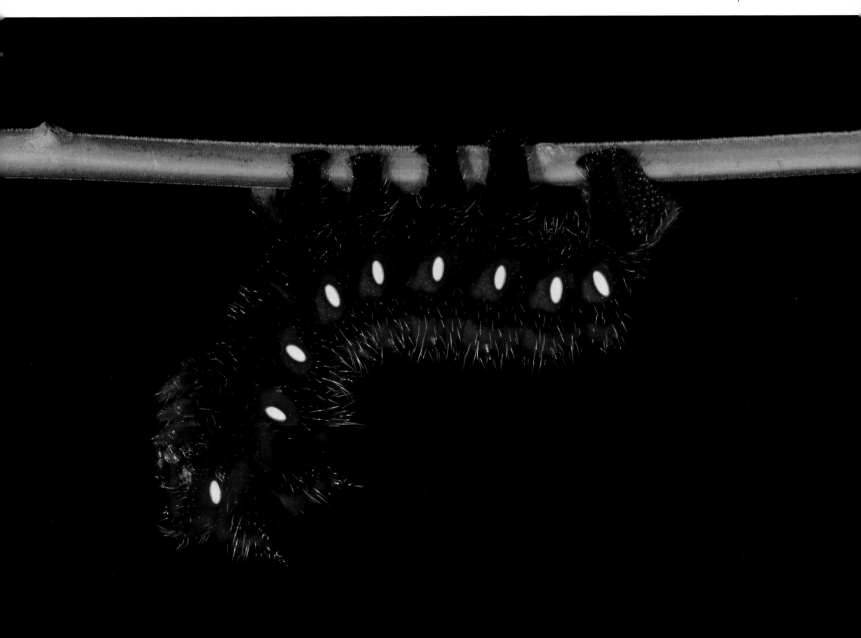

15. *Othorene purpurascens*

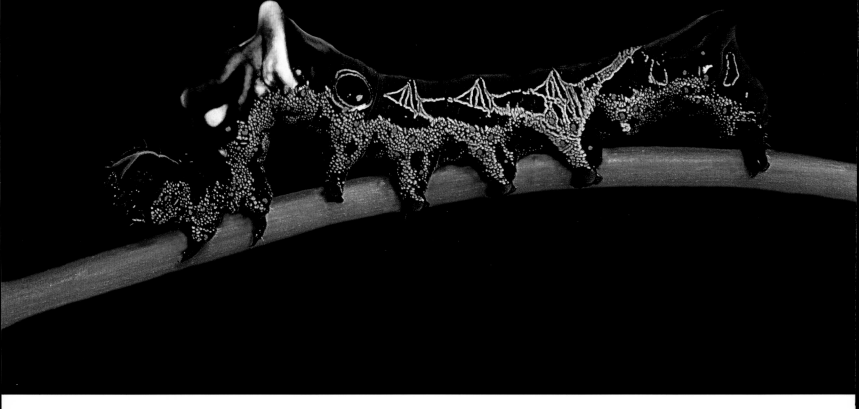

17. *Eudocima colubra*

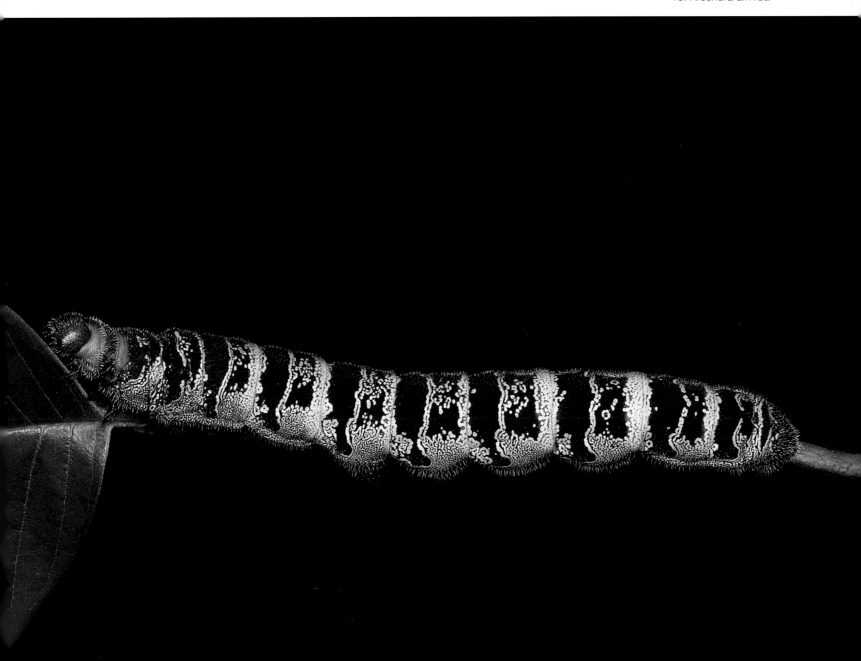

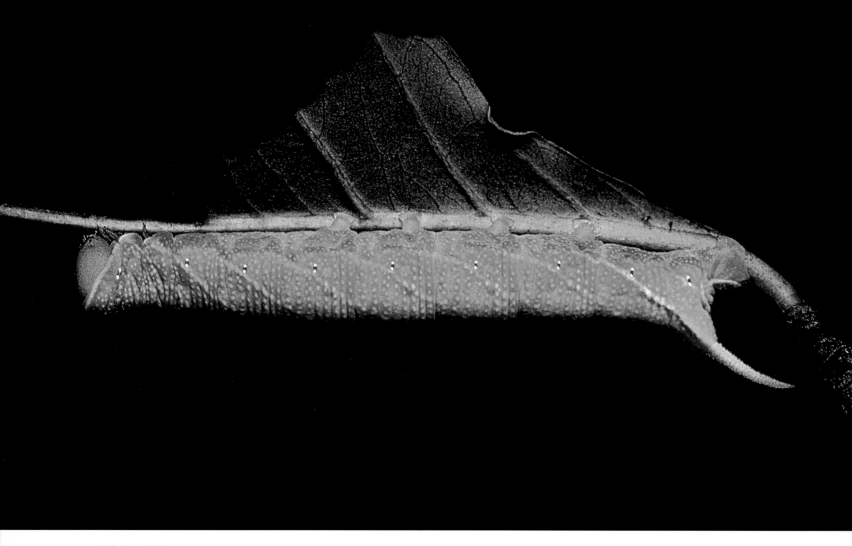

19. *Perigonia ilus*

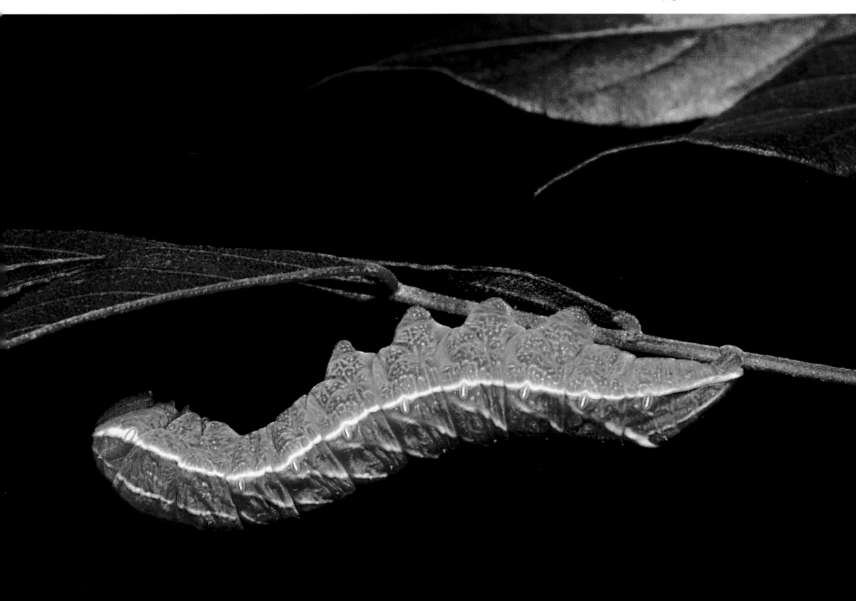

21. *Talides* BURNS01

22. *Phocides lilea*

25. *Euselasia eubule*

27. *Phobetron hipparchia*

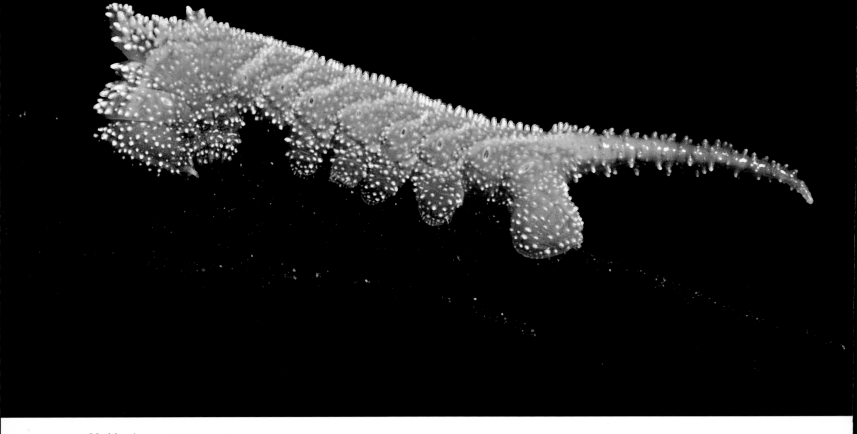

29. *Manduca muscosa*

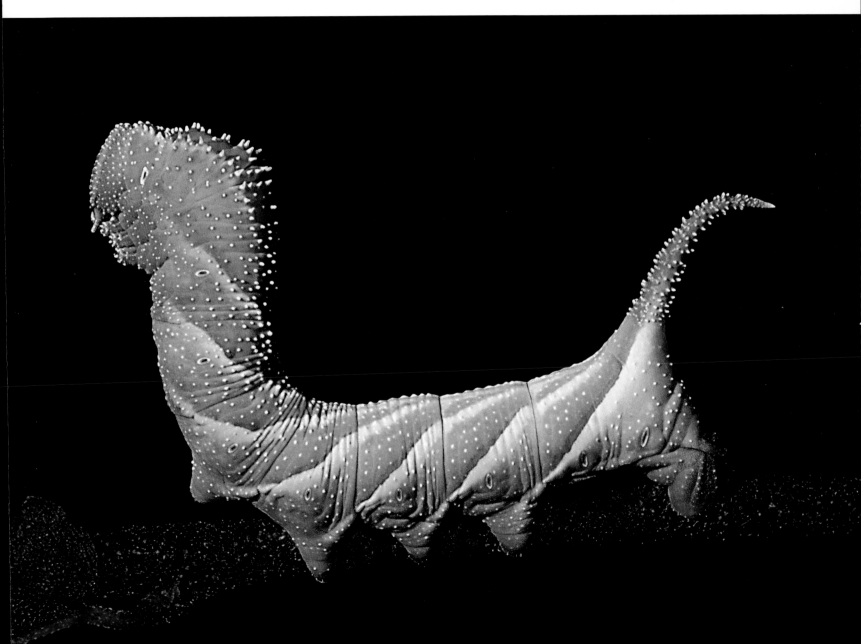

31. *Colax apulus*

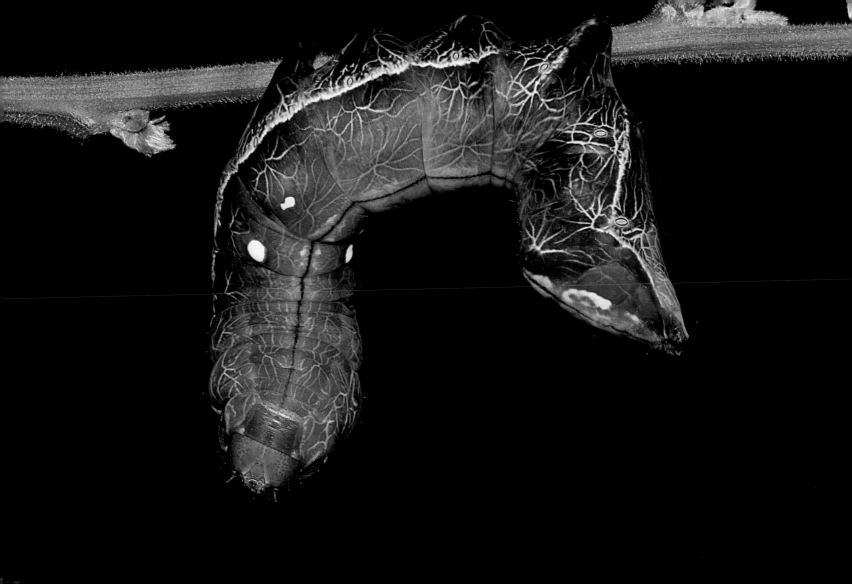

33. *Dyscophellus* BURNS01

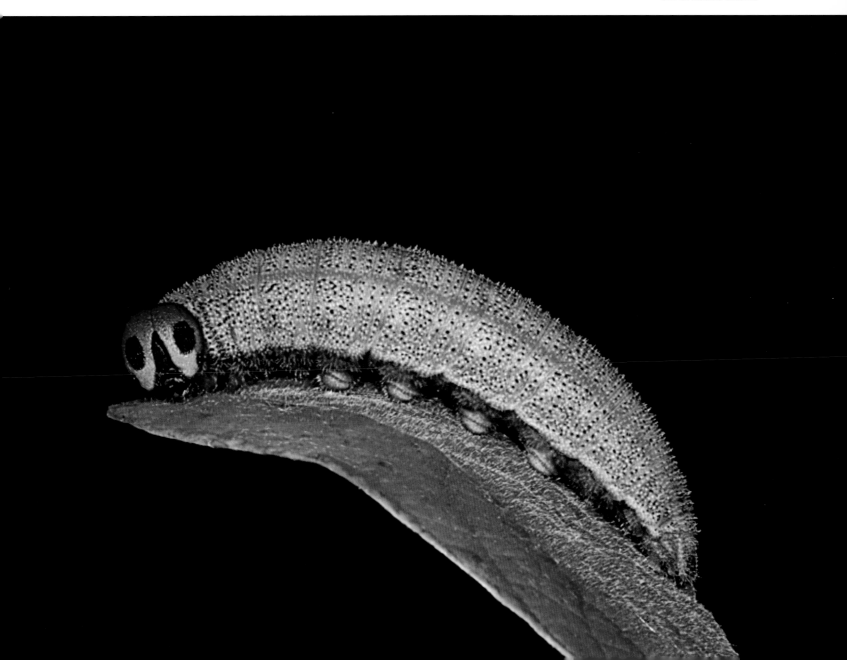

35. *Narope* JANZEN01

36. *Archaeoprepona meander*

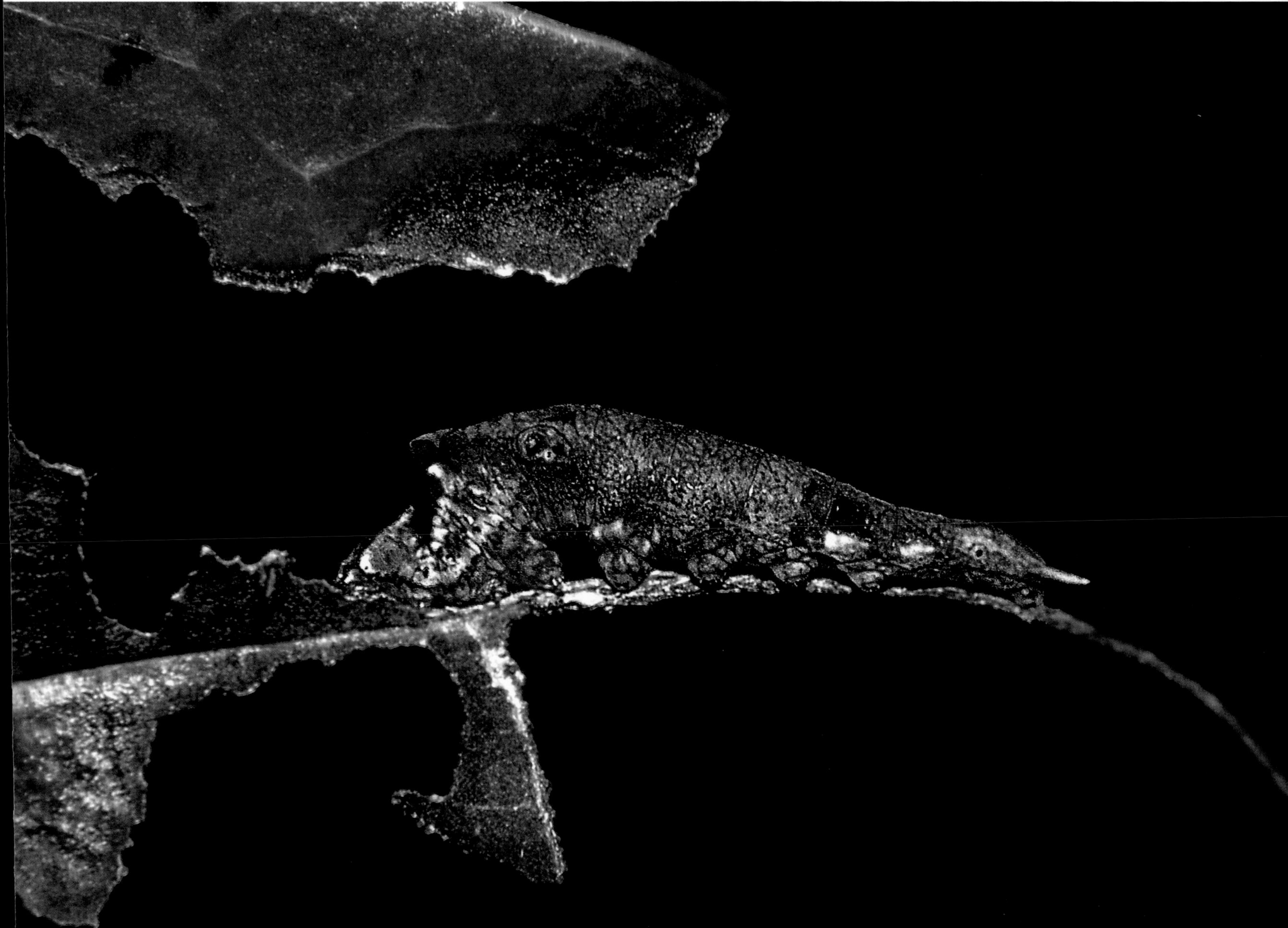

37. *Erinnyis crameri*

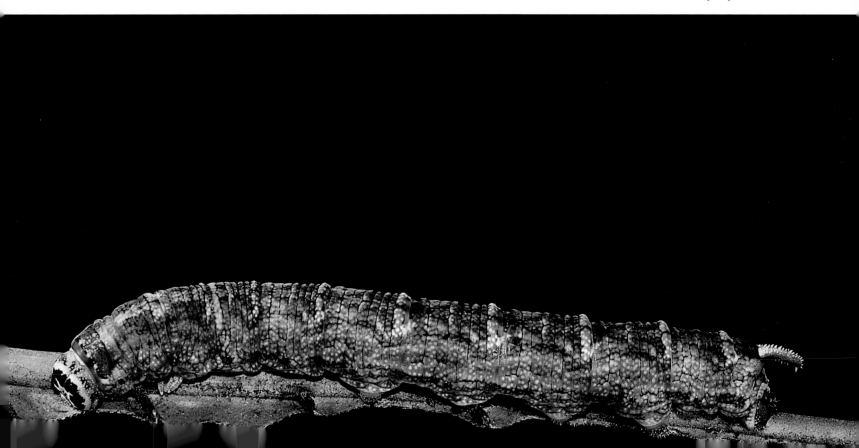

39. *Adeloneivaia jason*

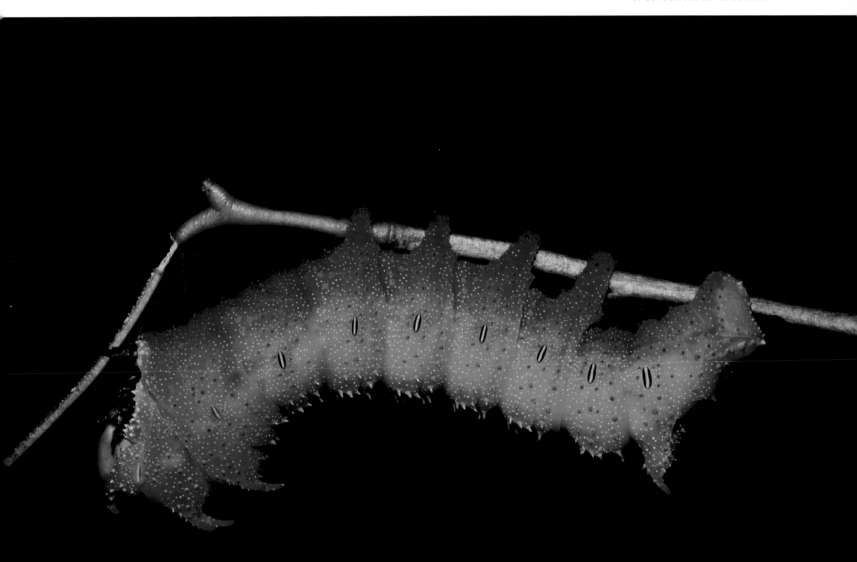

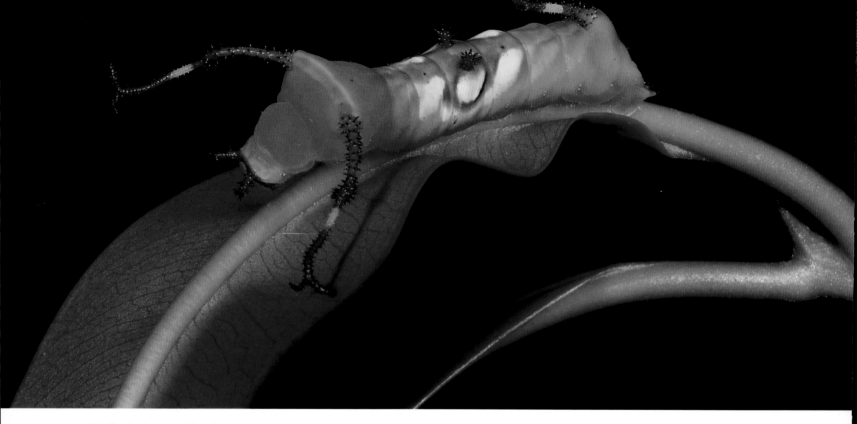

41. *Copiopteryx semiramis*

42. *Arsenura batesii*

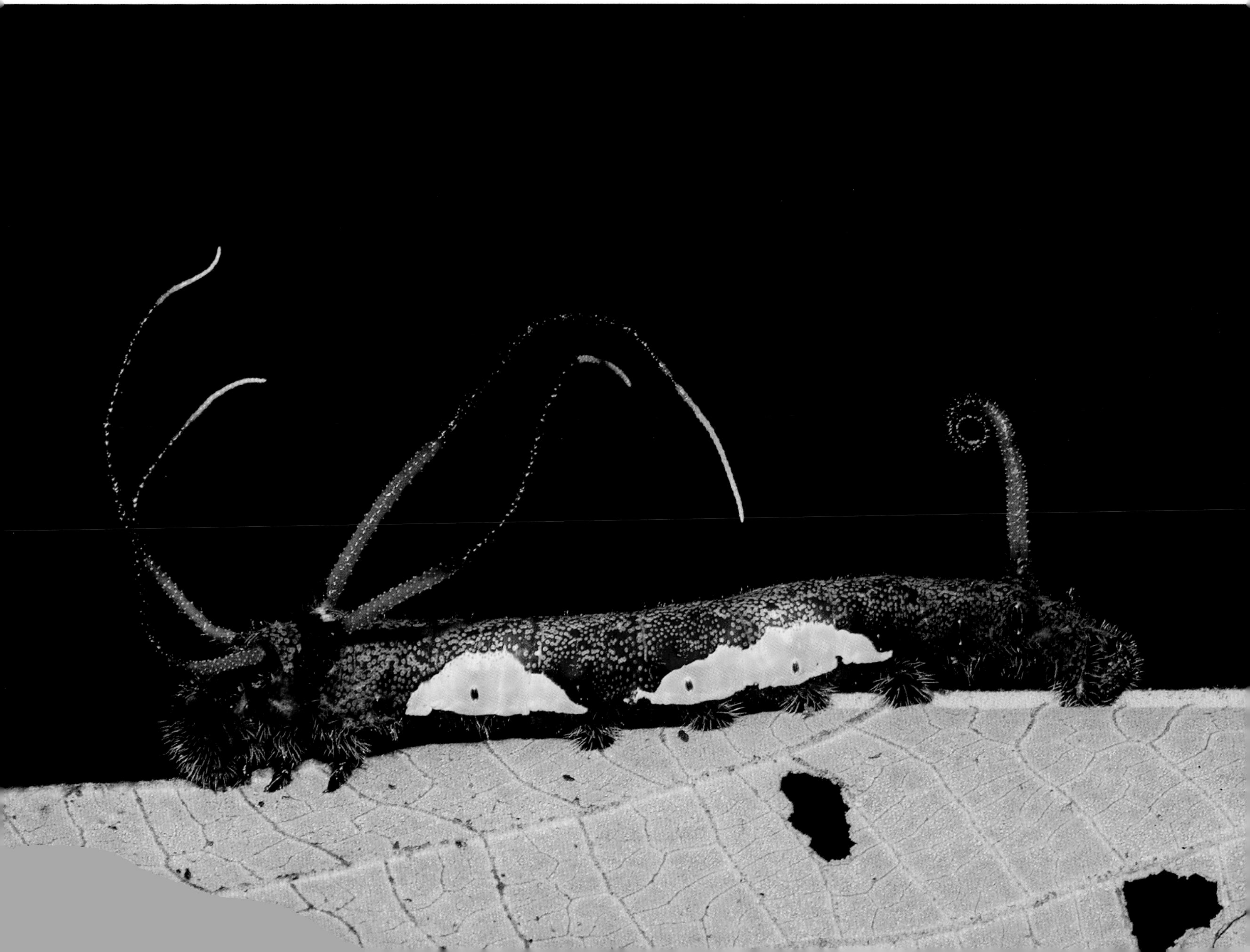

43. *Adelpha celerio*

45. *Anurocampa mingens*

47. *Sosxetra grata*

48. *Yanguna cosyra*

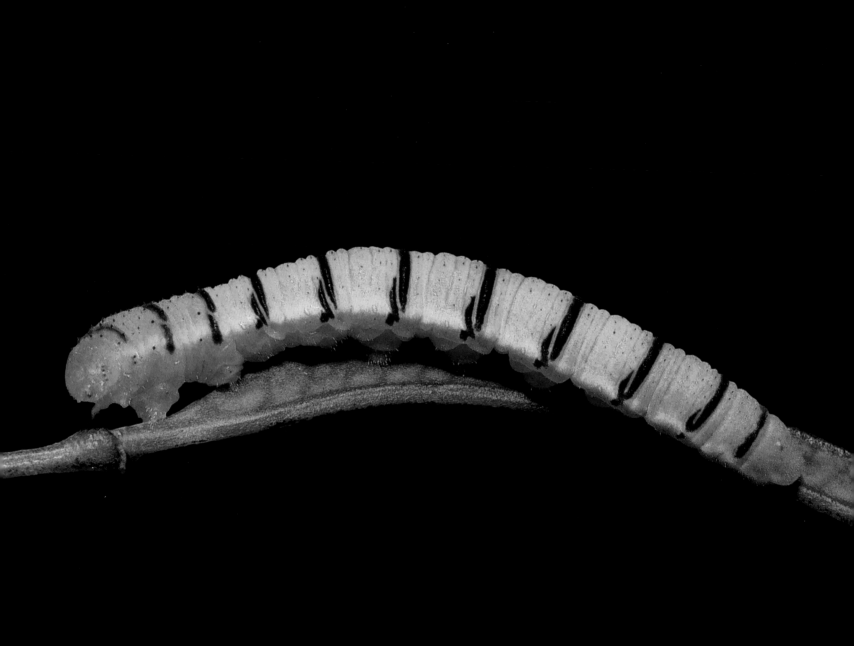

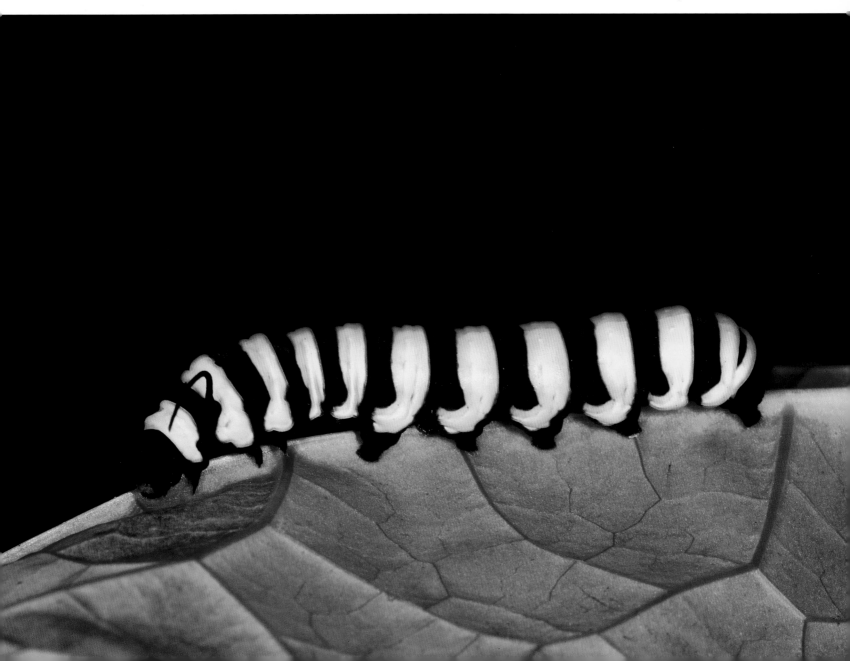

51. *Xylophanes chiron*

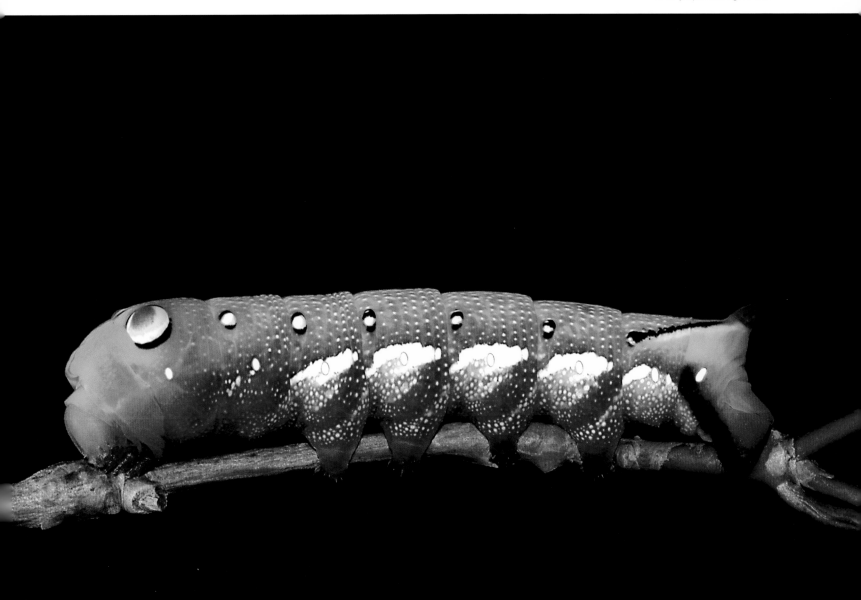

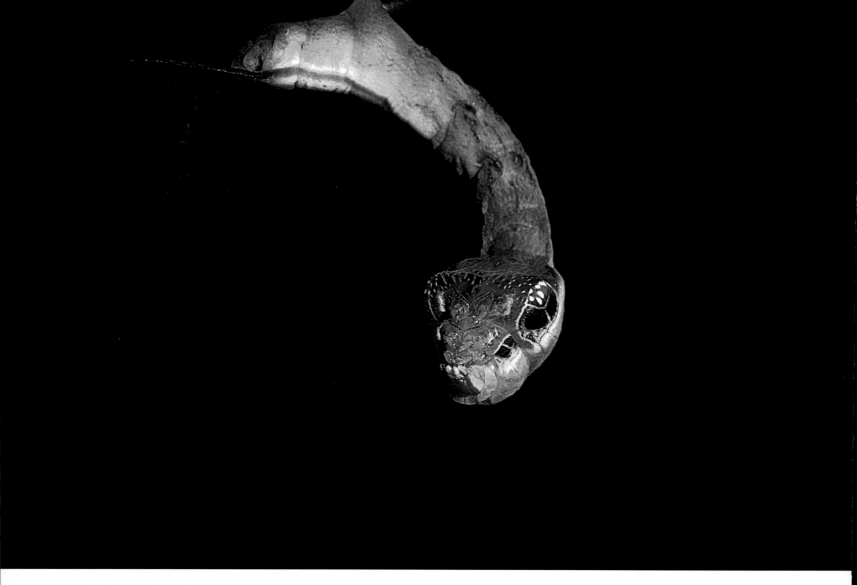

53. *Hemeroplanes triptolemus*

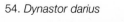

54. *Dynastor darius*

57. *Phiditia lucernaria*

59. *Dyscophellus* BURNS02

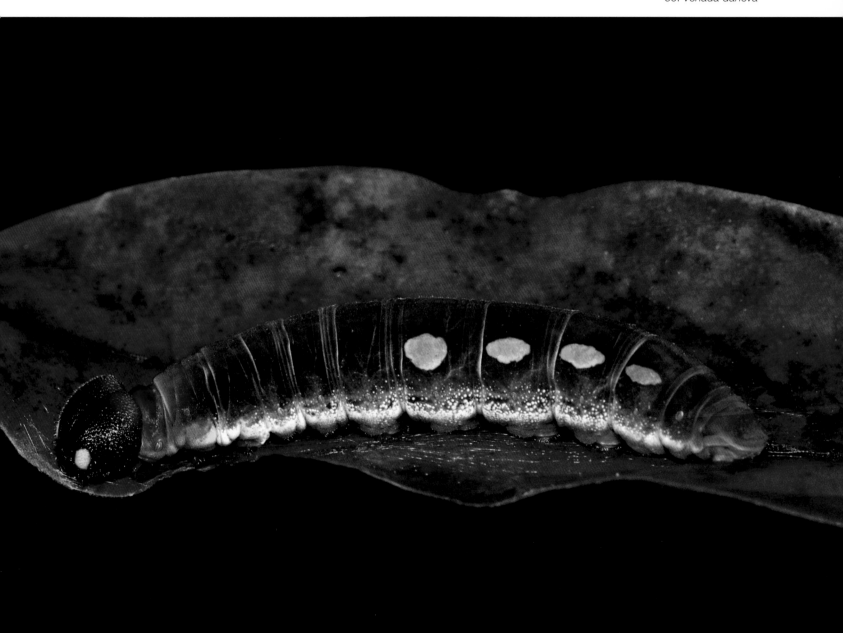

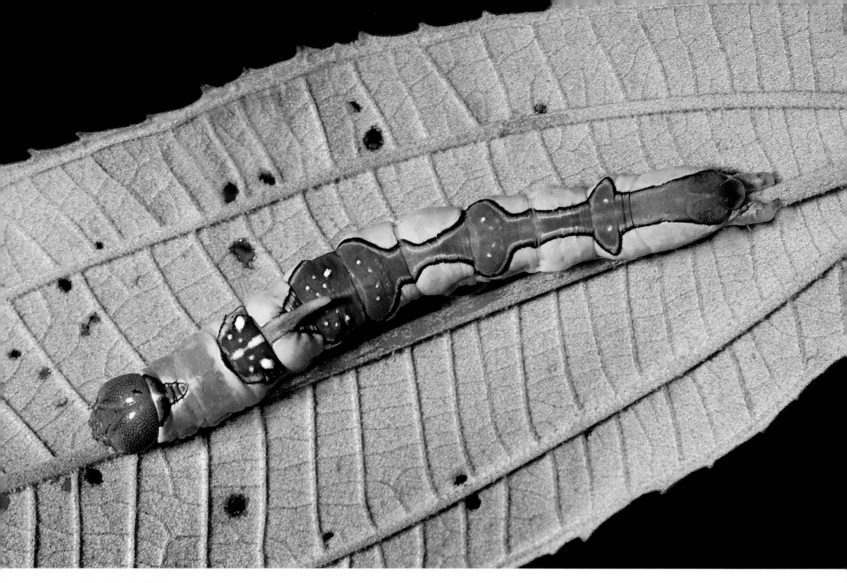

61. *Rhuda dificilis*

63. *Erinnyis ello*

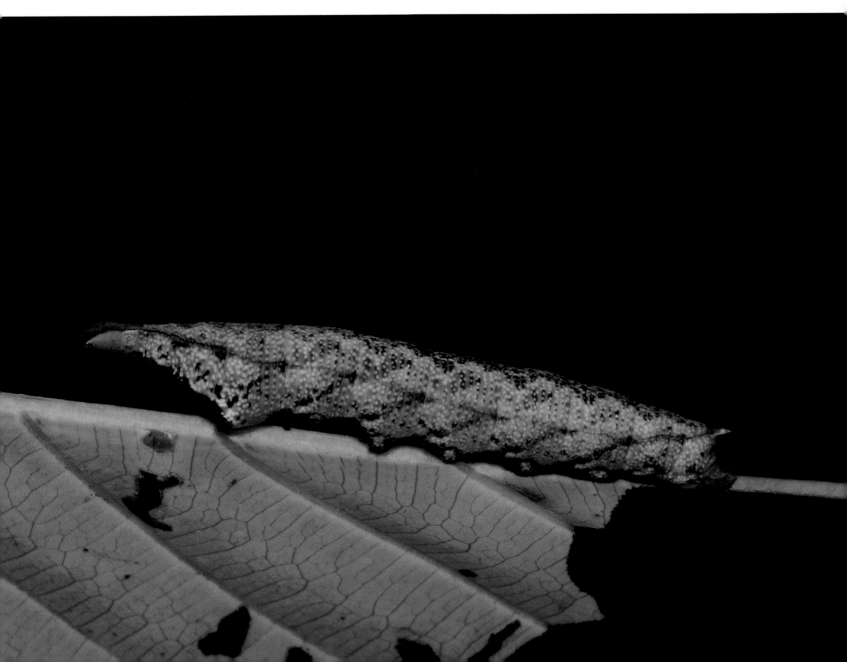

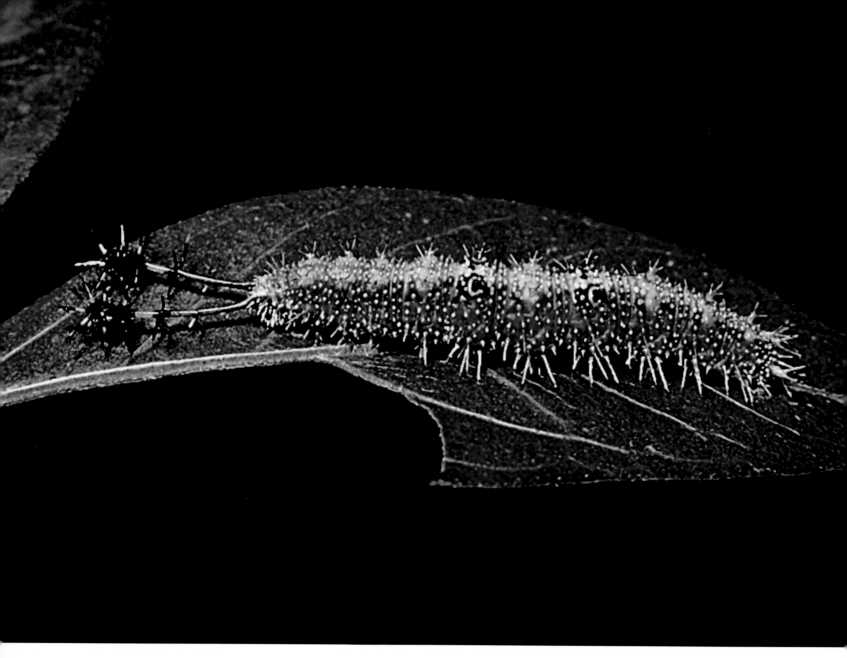

65. *Callicore pitheas*

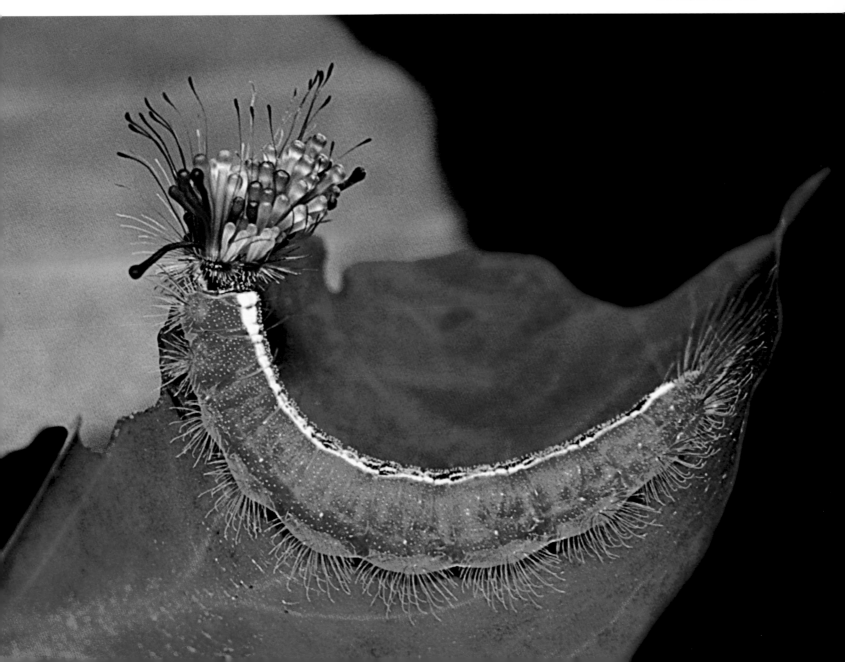

66. *Calydna sturnula*

67. *Syssphinx mexicana*

69. *Archaeoprepona demophoon*

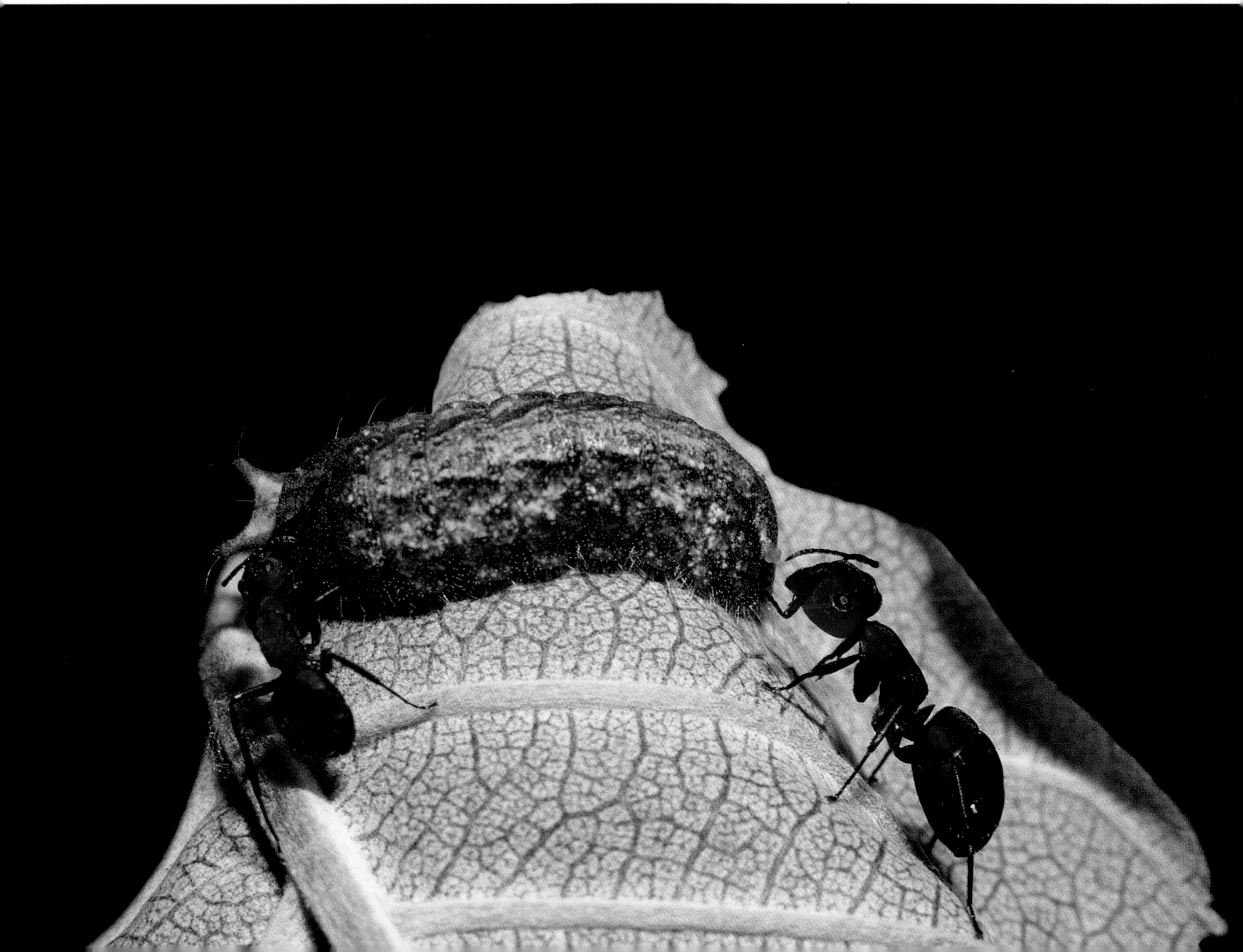

70. *Synargis mycone*

71. *Protambulyx strigilis*

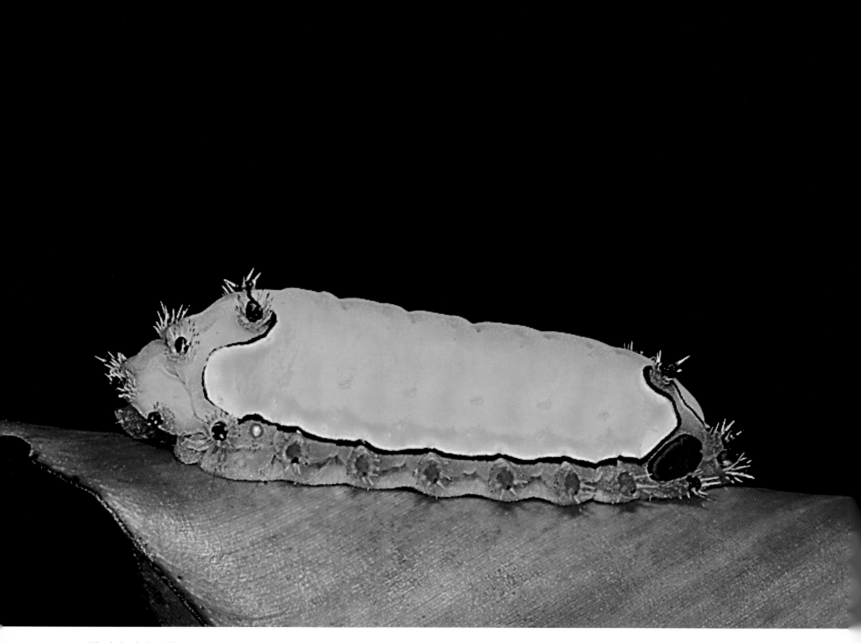

73. *Acharia horrida*

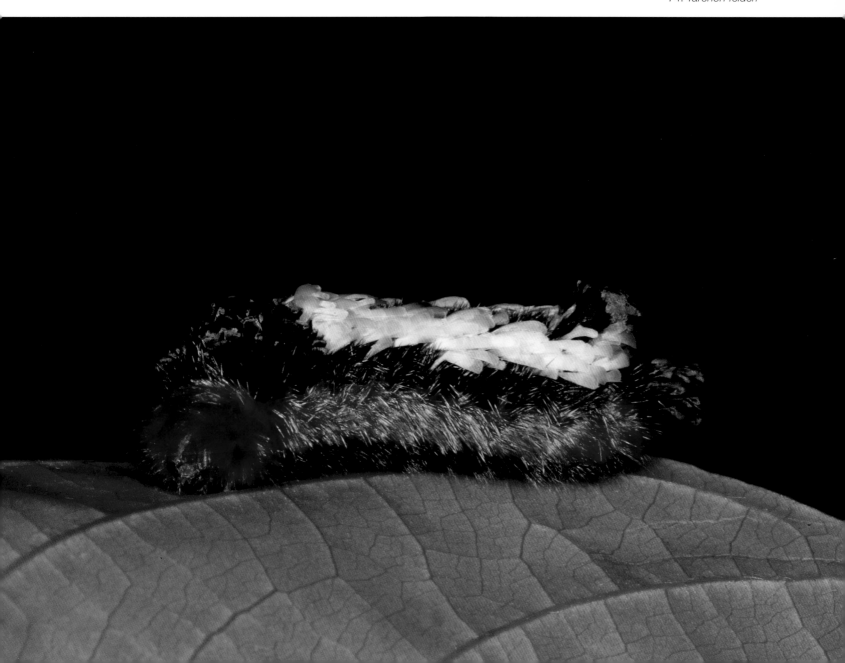

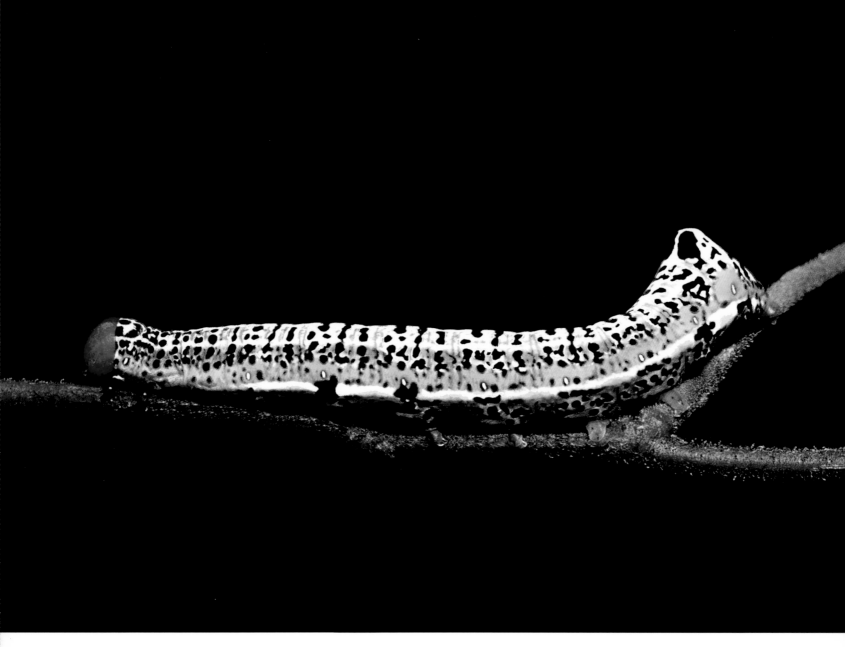

75. *Dipterygia ordinarius*

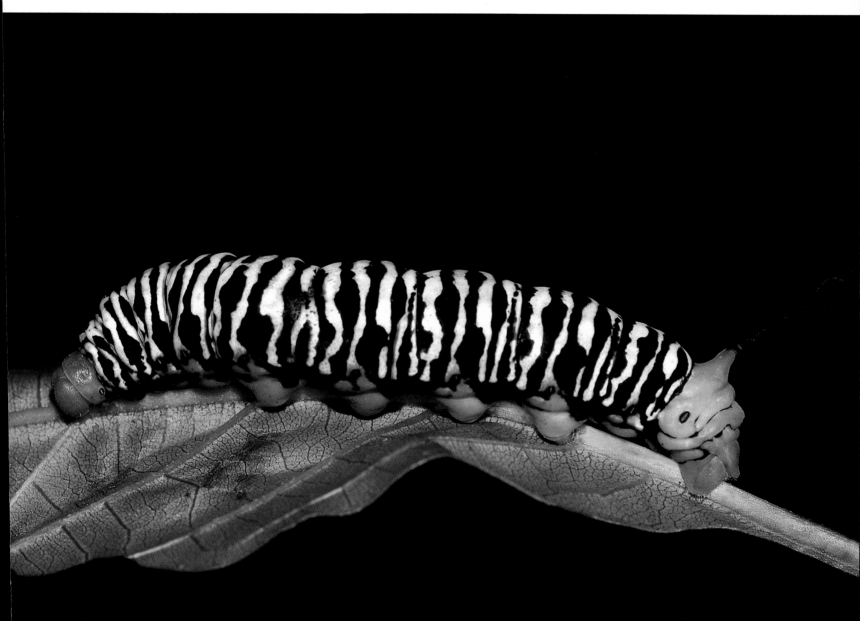

77. *Parasa sandrae*

78. *Acraga hamata*

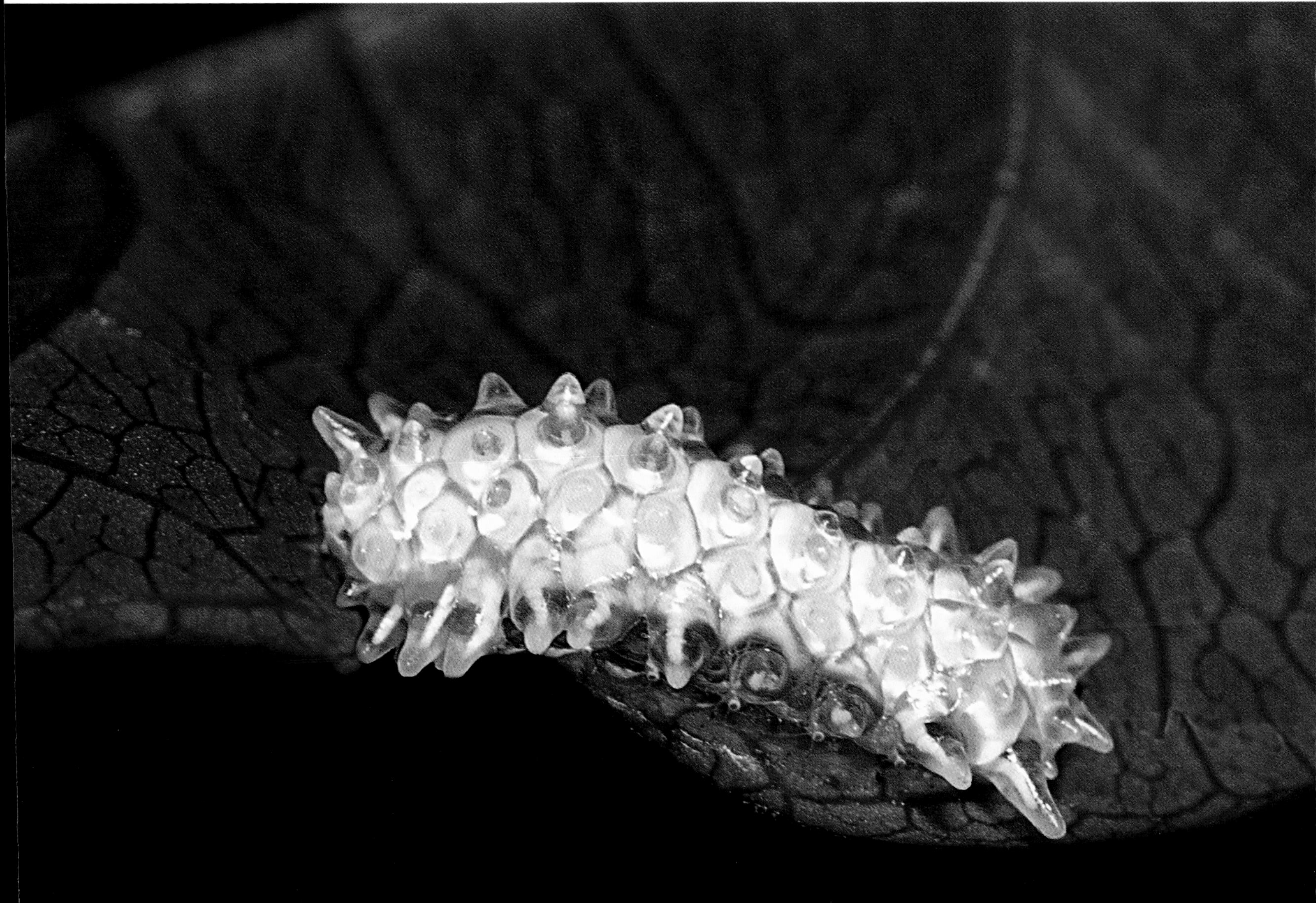

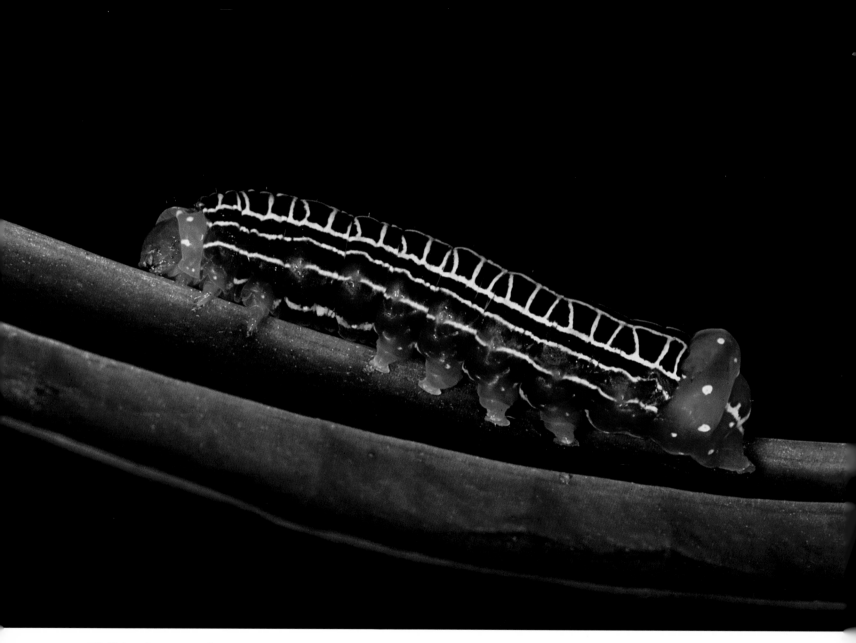

79. *Heterochroma sarepta*

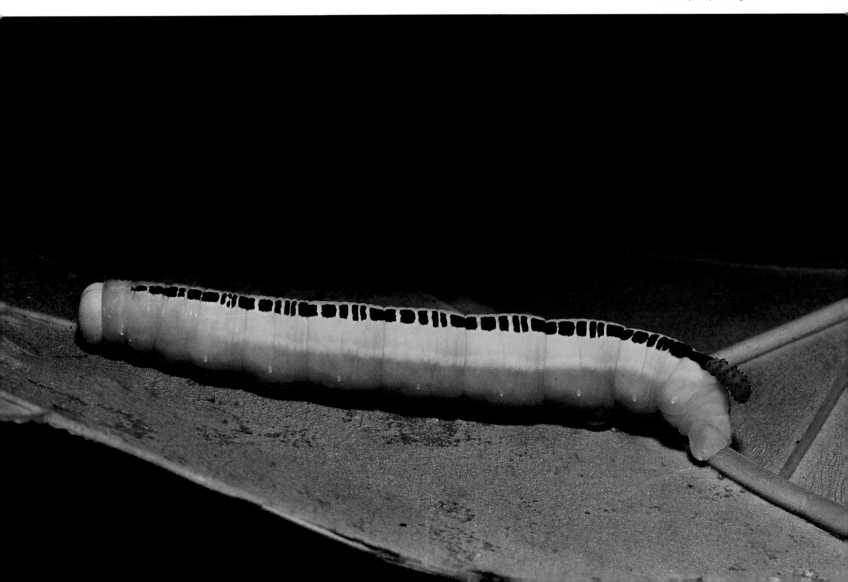

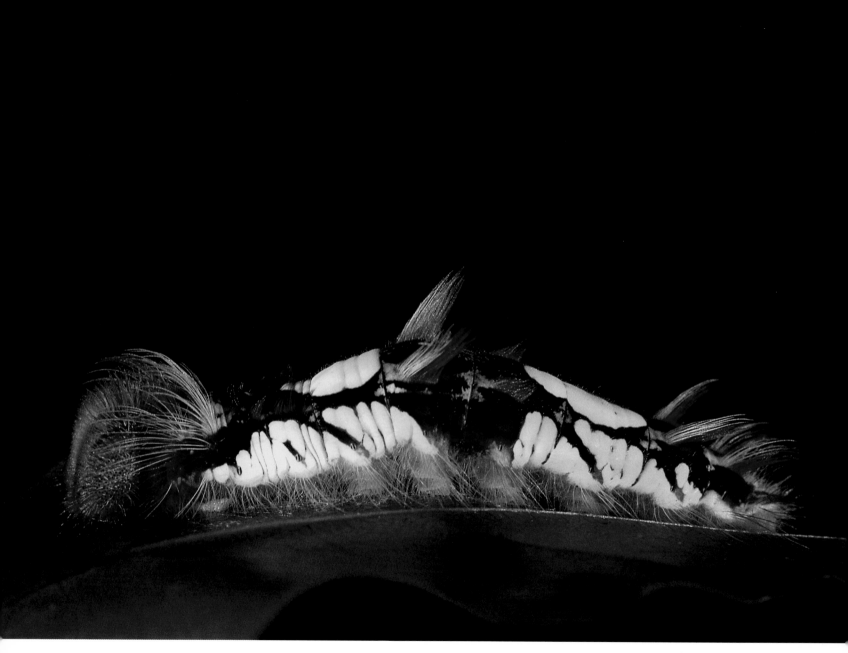

81. *Morpho peleides*

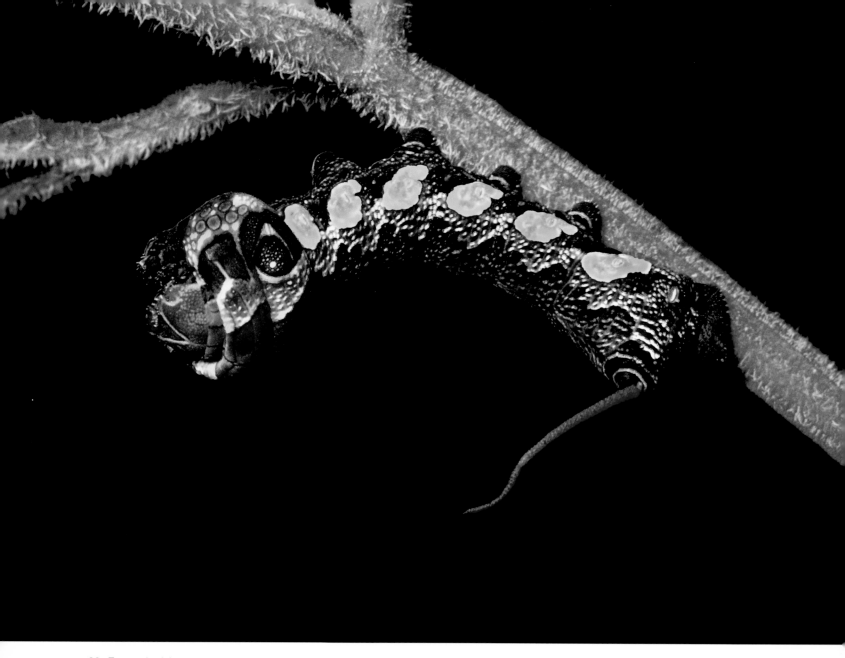

83. *Eumorpha labruscae*

85. *Jemadia pseudognetus*

87. *Copaxa rufinans*

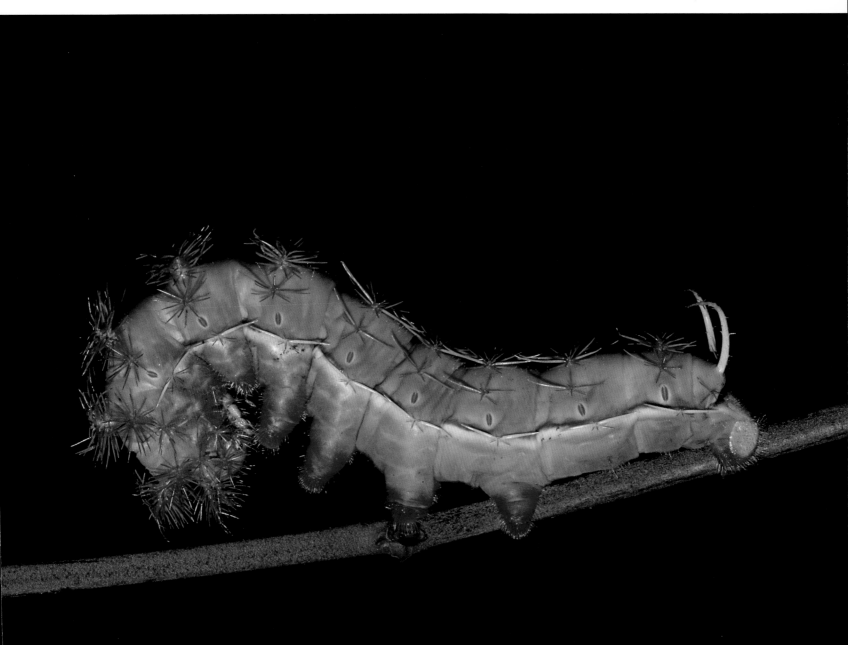

89. *Astraptes* LOHAMP

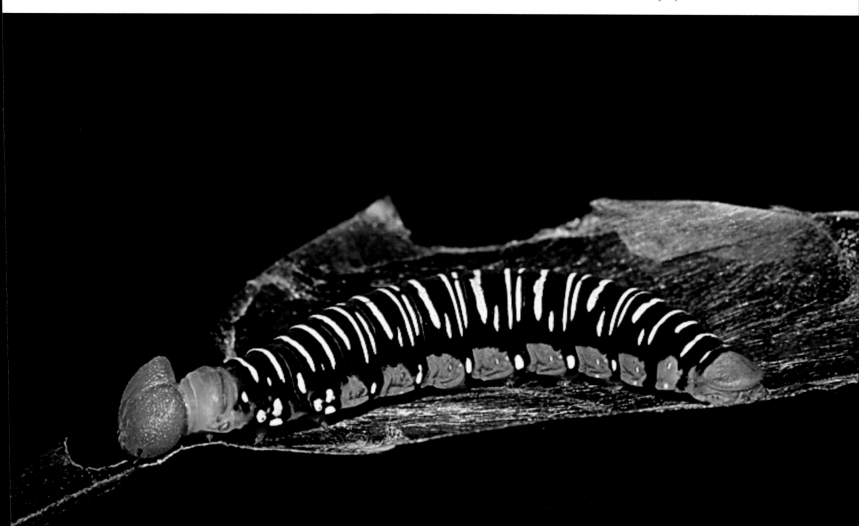

91. *Munona iridescens*

93. *Caio championi*

94. *Eumorpha satellitia*

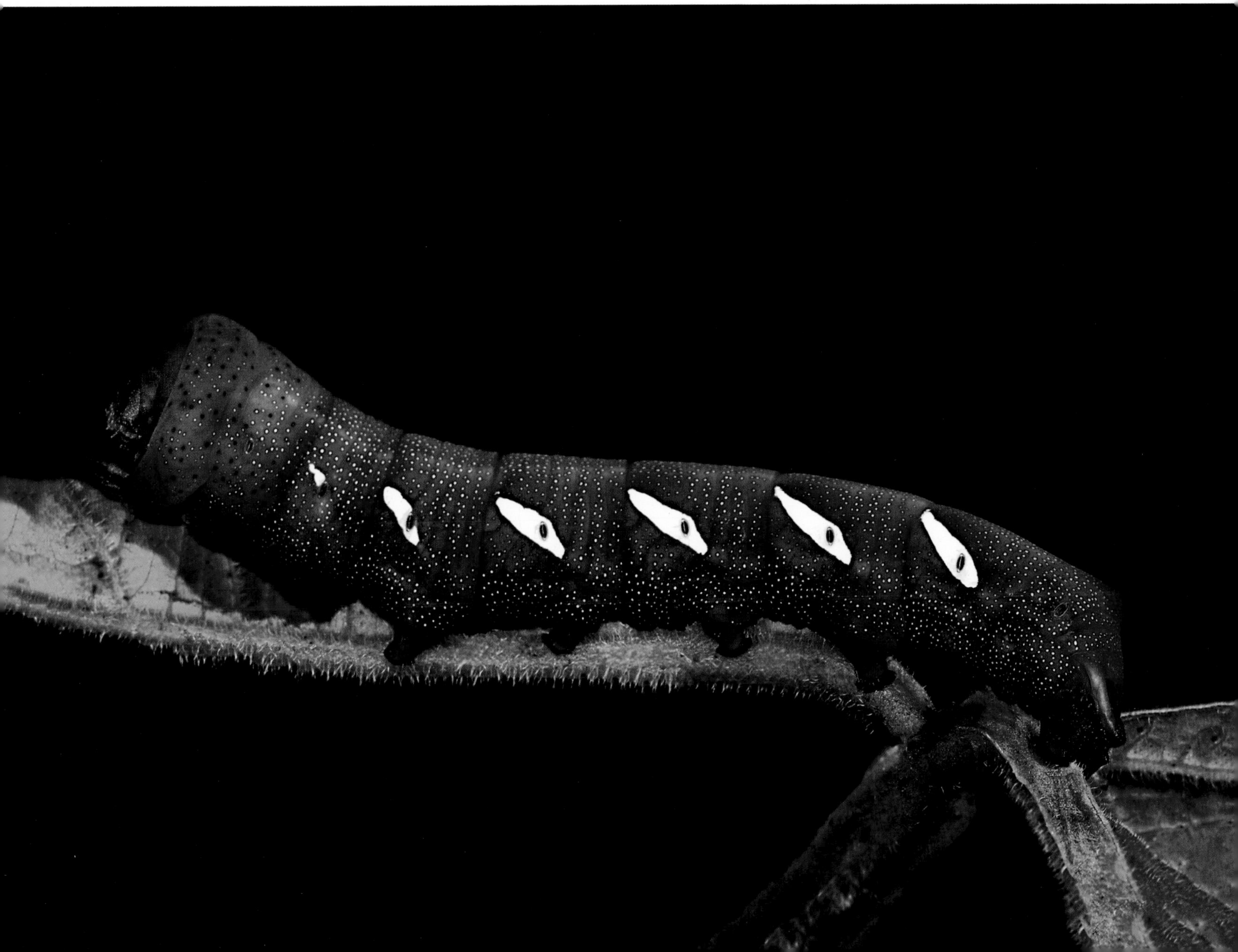

95. *Syssphinx molina*

96. *Manduca florestan*

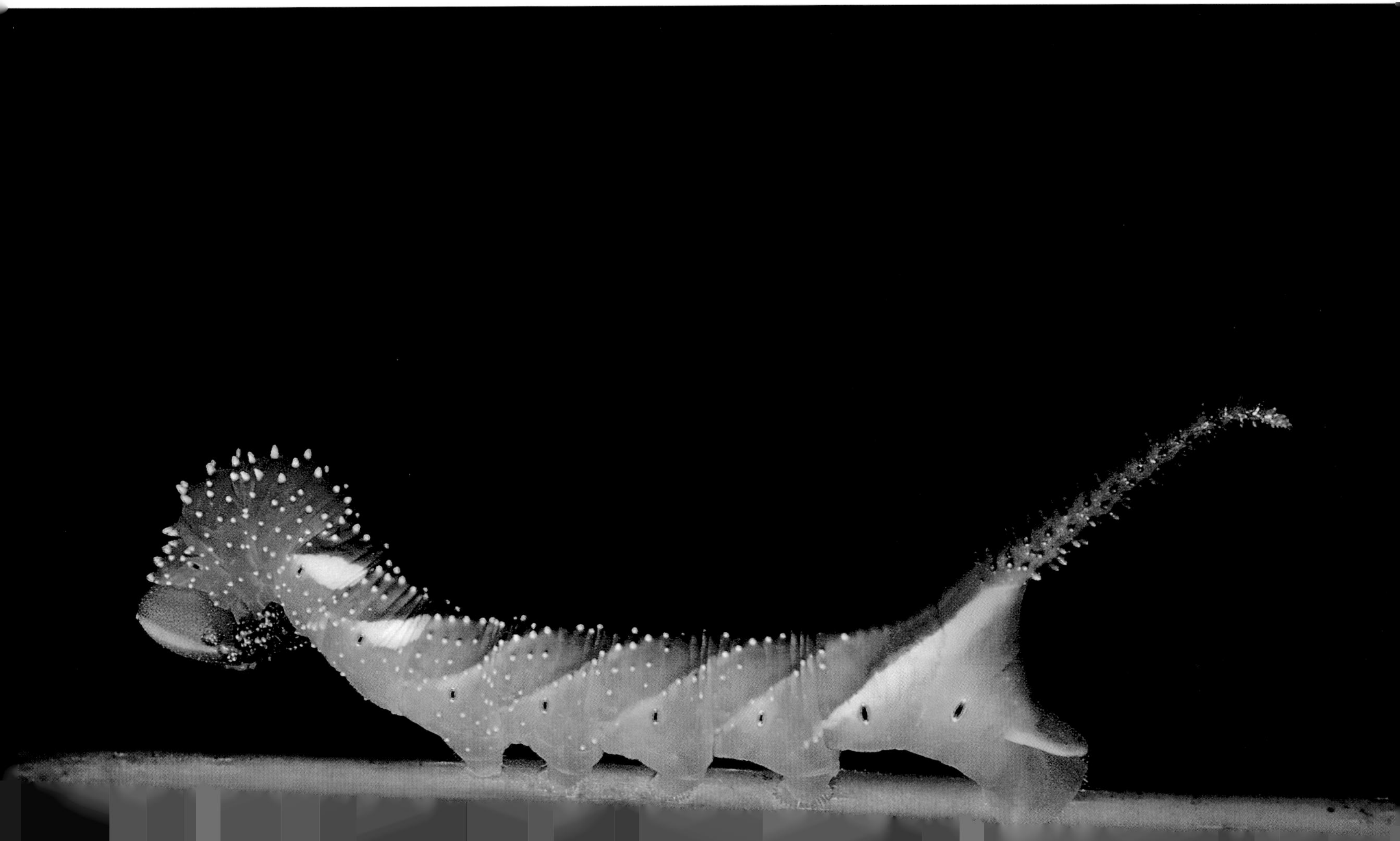

97. *Lirimiris gigantea*

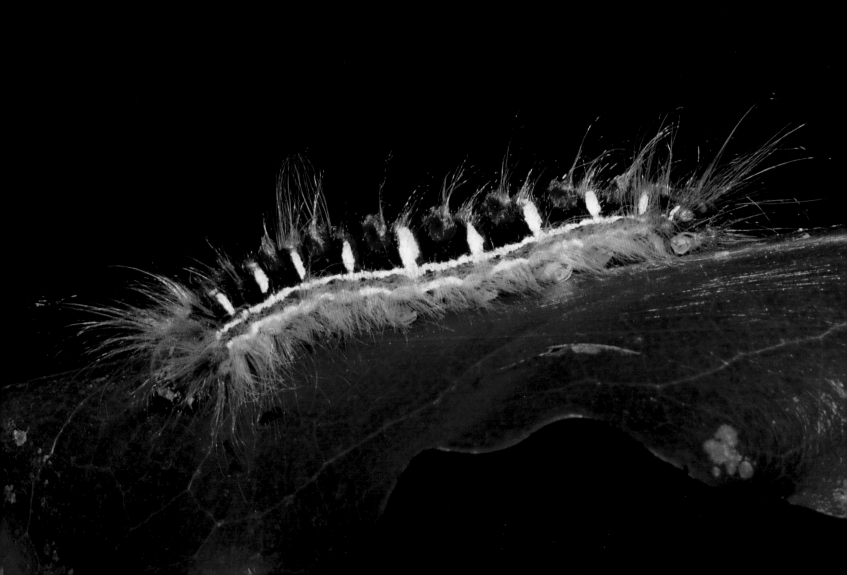

99. *Elymiotis alata*

Behavior, Ecology, and Adult Images

1. *AUTOMERIS POSTALBIDA* – SATURNIIDAE

Automeris postalbida is the largest of the spiny and urticating saturniid caterpillars in the ACG rain forest. Just about everyone that walks trails will eventually find or back into this caterpillar, reacting with a grimace as the long urticating spines find their way through a shirt. Identification is easy. It appears that the large black spot between the bases of the very long, pink, posterior spiny scoli is absolutely diagnostic among the known ACG species. A caveat is necessary regarding this description, however. The unknown large caterpillar of the extremely rare, sympatric within the ACG, and adult look-alike, *Automeris larra*, might also have the size and coloration of A. postalbida. There is a reason why *A. postalbida* is so frequently encountered by the forest-wandering naturalist and the caterpillar-collecting parataxonomist. Not only is it large and ostentatious, but it also tends to perch in full view on twigs below the leaves it has recently eaten.

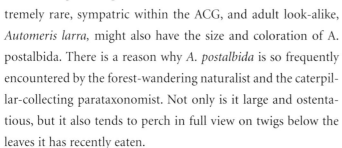

For unclear reasons *A. postalbida* does not enter dry forest nor penetrate cloud forest for any significant distance, though it does reach the cloud forest. Although not an ecosystem generalist, it has the longest list of food plants of any ACG rain-forest saturniid. Based on over 750 rearing records of field-collected caterpillars, it is known to feed on more than 120 species of plants in forty-five families. The list will continue to increase for many years as the caterpillar ACG inventory continues. The eggs are laid in small clusters of twenty to thirty. The caterpillars remain feeding side by side for the first three instars and then, in the fourth instar, wander from the plant of their mother's oviposition choice. In the fourth and fifth instars they probably change individual food plants and species frequently, both by explicit wandering and by dropping off plants when startled or attacked. Dropping off the plant is a commonplace defensive move among hemileucine saturniid caterpillars, and for that matter among many other urticating caterpillars in other families.

Not surprising for its large size, *A. postalbida* can require as many as three months from egg to pupation. It then remains a dormant pupa in the cocoon for two to twelve months or even longer. The long larval period is not merely the consequence of large size. Large sphingids, such as *Eumorpha triangulum, Pachylia ficus, Manduca rustica* (#30), and *Oryba achemenides,* can reach the same final caterpillar body weight in as little as a month. The difference is that *A. postalbida,* like other Saturniidae, snips off pieces of leaves and swallows them nearly whole (Bernays and Janzen 1988). Thus, the caterpillar obtains only a very small portion of the nutrients present in the leaves. Sphingids, however, crush the leaf fragments as they bite them off, thereby releasing a much greater portion of the leaf's nutrients and at the same time being exposed to many more of the chemical defenses of the leaf. In this vein, *A. postalbida* caterpillars, like other saturniids, do not appear to get any of their chemical defenses directly from the foliage of the food plant. The nasty painful soup of histamine and acetylcholine, a neurotransmitter, is injected by a penetrating spine and appears to be synthesized *de novo* by the caterpillar. The chemicals present in caterpillars' urticating spines may also be more diverse than is presently recognized, however.

CATERPILLAR VOUCHER: 04-SRNP-4967; JCM
ADULT VOUCHER: 98-SRNP-3710; JCM

2. *AUTOMERIS TRIDENS* – SATURNIIDAE

This lovely apple-green caterpillar, the diameter of your little finger and nearly as long when full grown, is quite invisible at any distance, such as that of a bird flying by. But up close, the lateral white racing stripe signals to the potential predator, "All those spines hurt like crazy." And the spines really do hurt. Each is a hollow tube with a tiny fragile tip, sharp as the sharpest pin. Brush it with your hand, or worse, the tender tissues of your mouth, and each spine is like a miniature syringe. The penetrating tip breaks off and the contained liquid, under pressure, is injected. The liquid consists of a mixture of acetylcholine and histamine, both intensely reactive with vertebrate nerves. In fact, it is the same chemical soup, obviously evolved independently, that the stinging nettle plant, *Urtica,* injects into your bare leg on a camping trip. The threatened caterpillar also curls into an approximation of a hedgehog or sea urchin, a position that enhances the visual signal of the white racing stripe. This mini-

mizes the chance of being grabbed by the head by a vertebrate that can and will penetrate this urticating defense (see the species account of *Automeris zugana,* #3). Present an experienced white-face monkey, *Cebus capucinus,* with an *A. tridens* caterpillar and the monkey goes into a fit of avoidance and alarm. Just to remind the reader that no defense is perfect, however, Janzen also watched an old female spider monkey, *Ateles geoffreyi,* in the San Jose (Costa Rica) zoo wrap an *A. tridens* caterpillar in a large leaf, crush it, and eat it.

These marvelous defenses against vertebrates are largely irrelevant when pitted against parasitoid wasps and flies. Because of the physical barrier of the spines, one kind of tachinid fly, *Carcelia,* cannot get its abdomen neatly down against the caterpillar cuticle to glue an egg onto it, so it glues eggs, each on a stalk, to any part of the caterpillar that it can reach with its long ovipositor. A few hours later the newly eclosed parasitoid maggots burrow through the cuticle to hide somewhere as tiny and developmentally arrested larvae within the host body. Perhaps they are in a salivary gland, where the caterpillar's defensive encapsulating cells cannot get to it. There they wait until the caterpillar has fed long enough to become a last instar, a fully sized package of high-quality food for the fly maggot, and spins a cocoon. At this point in the life cycle of the host the maggot initiates development. The maggot eats the "goodies," tissues such as fat and muscle, within the caterpillar, punches through the cuticle of the dead body, and pupates in the caterpillar-spun cocoon or drops to the litter below to pupate there instead.

Automeris tridens (also known as *Automeris rubrescens* in older literature) is typically a wide-ranging dry-forest moth (Lemaire 2002). Within the ACG, however, there are a few captures of adults in the Atlantic rain-forest lowlands. This suggests that this species may be one of the many dry-forest species that have followed the clearing of rain forests for pastures and fields, making them drier, hotter, and richer in fast-growing food plants. In dry forest, *A. tridens* passes the six-month dry season as a dormant pupa in a strong but thin-walled silk cocoon inside a dry leaf. The adult ecloses about the second week after the first rains in May. The heavy-bodied rosy-red female hangs by her cocoon, luring the males with pheromones late at night. She is mated that same night by one of the fast and frantically flying

yellow males. She lays several hundred eggs in long strings glued to leaves during the second and third nights. Even with their very short and nonfeeding adult lives, only five to ten days in duration, the adults are conspicuously protected from vertebrate predators. They look like a pendant dead leaf when at rest, but when approached by a predator, they abruptly display magnificent false eyes on the hind wings and somewhat less complex eyespots on the undersides.

CATERPILLAR VOUCHER: 83-SRNP-1358; DHJ
ADULT VOUCHER: 93-SRNP-2614; JCM

3. *AUTOMERIS ZUGANA* – SATURNIIDAE

Although the thumb-sized *Automeris postalbida* (#1) is the first rain-forest *Automeris* caterpillar that most hikers encounter, the slightly smaller *Automeris zugana* fills this niche in the ACG dry forest. At present, *A. zugana* may be a name that represents a complex of species. DNA barcoding (e.g., Hebert et al. 2004) has revealed that this common moth in the ACG is at least three species. There is a smaller dry-forest species and two larger and darker species in the rain forest. One occurs in the lowlands and the other occurs at over 600 meters on the Caribbean side of Volcan Cacao.

The caterpillar is green and blurry at a distance of more than a few meters, but close up it is decked in a red, white, and black gaudy pattern on a turquoise thorax that is not leaf green. The spines are a warning flag and mean what they say—ouch to those who dare to touch. Just as with *A. postalbida*, *A. zugana* does not hide among the leaves but perches conspicuously on twigs and feeds and moves in the daytime. When approached it will, however, make the concession to being a caterpillar after all. It stops feeding and draws its blue-turquoise head under the coiled and very spiny urticatious thorax, but it does not go into the full-circle ring-shaped defense of large *A. tridens* (#2) caterpillars.

The urticating spines on *Automeris* species are probably very good defenses against many vertebrate predators, but they certainly do not appear to work with absolute perfection against all medium-sized birds. Trogons (*Trogon elegans* and *Trogon melanocephala*) and squirrel cuckoos *(Piaya cayana)* are known for their appetite for noxious caterpillars. The gizzard of a road-kill lesser ground cuckoo *(Morococcyx erythropygius)* found on the road between Quebrada Grande and Gongora on the lower slopes of Volcan Cacao was stuffed with last-instar *A. zugana* caterpillars. Nestling squirrel cuckoos were brought *A. zugana* caterpillars in the Cafetal in Sector Santa Rosa, along with cicadas, *Crinodes besckei* (#32), and other large insects, and small *Anolis* lizards. Trogons will soon be even better known as predators of noxious caterpillars once the results of an ongoing study documenting which caterpillars are brought to the nestlings in the ACG is published (Janzen et al. in prep.). Eighty-three of 4,515 caterpillars and other large insects brought to nestling *T. elegans* and *T. melanocephala* in Santa Rosa were *A. zugana*, along with the occasional *Automeris tridens*.

The heavy-bodied female *A. zugana* lays several hundred eggs in two neat side-by-side rows along the underside margin of a leaf from which she is hanging, on any one of about ten species of plants. The first three instars feed as a group and soon construct a flimsy nest by spinning silk to tie a pair of overlapping leaves together. They feed day and night, returning to the nest after a feeding bout. Near the end of the third instar, or after they have molted into a new fourth instar, they leave the natal food plant and disband as solitary feeders, utilizing any

one of over 100 species of dry-forest trees, shrubs, and vines (Janzen 2003). Except for the occasional grass, herbs are not part of the food-plant list. This long list of food plants should not be interpreted to mean that they eat everything and do not have preferences. There are many more records from certain plants than others. For instance, *Inga vera* (Fabaceae, Mimosoidea), *Cydista heterophylla* (Bignoniaceae), *Annona purpurea* (Annonaceae), *Andira inermis* (Fabaceae, Papilionoidea), and *Trigonia rugosa* (Trigoniaceae) have far more records of *A. zugana* caterpillars than all the other species on the food-plant list put together.

CATERPILLAR VOUCHER: 01-SRNP-2348; DHJ
ADULT VOUCHER: 81-SRNP-20308; JCM

4. *DIRPHIA AVIA* – SATURNIIDAE

The beige and uncomplicated leafy brown adults of *Dirphia avia* are the first saturniids to greet an ACG light trap at the beginning of the dry-forest rainy season in mid-May (Janzen 1993a). They sometimes anticipate the rains by as much as two weeks. The fragrant adults have a quite odoriferous garlic-like odor, and are so well protected chemically that if one is dropped in an *Eciton burchelli* army ant swarm, there is immediately an ant-free area around the moth. This type of chemical defense, though not necessarily the particular chemical, is also possessed by adult *Periphoba arcaei* (#88), another leaf-colored ACG hemileucine saturniid that when grabbed or otherwise disturbed becomes motionless ("plays dead") while displaying its banded abdomen. *Periphoba arcaei* also repels army ants. This simple example is not meant to imply that army ants are a major threat to these two species of moths, but rather that the ant response is indicative of the effectiveness of the adult moths' defenses against invertebrates. Whether their very distinctive odor repels vertebrates is unknown, but there must be some reason why birds foraging at a light trap at dawn leave the *D. avia* adults sleeping peacefully on the white sheet.

The very visible bone-white spherical eggs are laid in a neat packet of about fifteen, glued in a tight triangle to the trunk of the food-plant tree. Each has a tiny black dot at the apex that looks like the exit hole of a wasp egg parasitoid and, perhaps, was selected precisely to appear to be that. Hatching about fifteen days later, hemileucine eggs take two to three times as long to hatch as do the other three ACG saturniid subfamilies. The caterpillars feed as a group for their entire lives unless forced apart by a predator or windstorm. This is why our image of *D. avia* shows two prepupal last instars on the same twig. They may even spin their cocoons in the litter side by side when they descend from the tree after finishing larval growth.

During the day the last instars rest in a tight group, presenting a dense patch of urticating spines only a meter or so above the ground. At night they ascend twenty to thirty meters into the tree canopy to eat leaf after leaf of mature and old evergreen plastic-like *Hymenaea courbaril* (Fabaceae) leaves. This tree is the well-known source of the 40-million-year-old fossilized resin otherwise known as New World amber. Caterpillars of *D. avia* also feed on the mature leaves of *Cedrela odorata* (Meliaceae) and *Quercus oleoides* (Fagaceae). All of these leaves are resin- and tannin-rich, and *D. avia* are classical snippers of leaves. As a test, if you squash the caterpillar's pellet-like droppings between your fingers, they break up into what appears to be hardly more than separate leaf pieces rather than something that had dissolved as it passed through a digestive system (Bernays and Janzen 1988).

When species of cryptic caterpillars reach the prepupal stage, they often change from their beige, gray, green, brown, ringed, or other color patterns into pink or maroon all over, or perhaps just a maroon stripe down the back. This is when they are wandering off the food plant to find a pupation site or spin a cocoon, and it is assumed that this rather obvious color pattern offers some aposematic (warning) value. *Dirphia avia* has a white-gray caterpillar with a fine black pattern that first turns a rosy pink-lavender dorsally (showing as a pinkish cast in our image), scoli and all. Then it turns lavender all over the body when it is ready to leave the tree and spin its tough silk cocoon in the litter. What we do not know is whether it descends to the litter thirty meters below with a fall and a plop, as do *Schausiella santarosensis* (#40) saturniids feeding in the crowns of the same *H. courbaril* trees, or whether they walk in single file sedately down the trunk head to rear as they have for the previous month or more of circadian treks. Once into the litter, and the commencement of pupation has occurred, this insect appears to have chemical protection well before an adult ecloses. Pupae offered to mice, *Liomys salvini* (Heteromyiidae), champion predators on seeds and pupae in the ACG dry-forest litter, are rejected. This protection is not enjoyed by most other large saturniid pupae.

CATERPILLAR VOUCHER: 80-SRNP-235; DHJ
ADULT VOUCHER: 89-SRNP-5762; JCM

5. *XYLOPHANES JUANITA* – SPHINGIDAE

When the caterpillar inventory of the ACG dry forest started in 1978, it soon encountered the caterpillars of *Xylophanes porcus* eating *Hamelia patens* and *Psychotria microdon* (Rubiaceae). Had the inventory begun in the rain forest, it would have as easily encountered the same species of caterpillar eating *Palicourea guianensis* (Rubiaceae). Anytime we have placed lights in a mountain pass between the two ecosystems, or at a high point in one of them, the adults of *X. porcus* are almost guaranteed to appear at the lights. Well, one day after many days of rearing the caterpillar, an adult *Xylophanes* that looked very much like *X. porcus* appeared in its rearing bag, but it just did not seem quite right. Spread and dried, it still looked not quite right. Shortly before, Jean-Marie Cadiou, the first-rate Belgian sphingid aficionado, had very kindly visited Philadelphia to identify our blossoming collection of sphingid voucher specimens. He was also keen to see if, by any miracle, we had encountered the much sought and excruciatingly rare *Kloneus babyaga,* which the ACG inventory did not find until 2004, some two decades later. So, Janzen called him. He asked Cadiou if he knew of a variation in

X. porcus that would account for slightly shorter forewings. The pause from the other end of the phone could not have been more than about two seconds when his voice from the other side of the world said, "Oh my god, William Schaus described that from Veracruz a hundred years ago. It has to be *Xylophanes juanita;* they are almost unknown." Cadiou has in his head the world sphingid fauna consisting of nearly 2,000 species and what is known about them. Until the ACG inventory found it, this animal was known from the holotype (the single specimen that serves as the model for the identification of the species) and perhaps a few other specimens in the British Museum, today known as The Natural History Museum, in London.

This species is rare in collections but not in ACG nature. We have reared over 450 *X. juanita* caterpillars from the four species of dry-forest *Psychotria* (*P. horizontalis, P. microdon, P. nervosa,* and *P. pubescens*), from a smattering of other *Psychotria* from the dry-forest/rain-forest interface, and even once from *Faramea occidentalis* (Rubiaceae), the usual food plant of *Xylophanes tyndarus. Xylophanes juanita* is a marvelous example of a common dry-forest sphingid moth whose adults simply do not come to lights (Janzen 1984a). In thousands of trap-nights, there have been exactly two specimens found at the Santa Rosa light trap.

Certain species, such as *X. juanita* and many other sphingids, have caterpillars that may come in two very distinct colors.

In the case of *X. juanita,* the green form is the more common and the purple-black form that we portray in our image occurs occasionally. Usually the presence of a dark caterpillar suggests that its food plant was occupied by another *X. juanita.* When they encountered each other, one turned to a different color at the molt from penultimate to ultimate instar (see *Eacles imperialis,* #14). This caterpillar's thoracic false eyespot is, as is the case with the false eyespot of the apparently quite unrelated *Xylophanes adalia,* composed of two separate components. The two together give a striking three-dimensional depth to the eyes' appearance when viewed from the front or front-above, as well as when the head is drawn in and the thorax expanded.

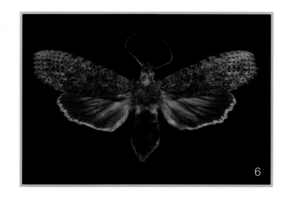

6

The paired false eyespots serve in a defensive role by mimicking the face of a small vertebrate, such as a snake (see *Hemeroplanes triptolemus,* #53).

CATERPILLAR VOUCHER: 89-SRNP-486; DHJ
ADULT VOUCHER: 99-SRNP-2884; JCM

6. *NYSTALEA COLLARIS* – NOTODONTIDAE

Introduced guava trees, *Psidium guajava* (Myrtaceae), are everywhere and it seems like any careful search of one, be it in rain forest or dry forest, produces a *Nystalea collaris* caterpillar. Appearing to be a pink-brown, rotted and torn leaf edge, or a jagged piece of bark, this caterpillar is one of the classical notodontid caterpillar life forms—a big rear end, small head, and a grotesquely modified dorsum. Any caterpillar that looks even vaguely like this is likely to be one of the many species of Costa Rican *Nystalea* or a close relative, such as *Poresta* or *Calledema.* No other family of Costa Rica caterpillars does it the same way, though there are a few geometrids (e.g., *Nemoria*) that also have evolutionarily taken their cryptic appearance in the direction of distorted body shapes.

Prior to the introduction of guava trees from somewhere in the Neotropics (they are not native to Costa Rica), the population of *N. collaris* caterpillars was sustained by leaves of native Myrtaceae, such as the many species of *Eugenia* and even *Psidium guineense.* The thing is, people and horses love to eat guava fruits. The seeds are therefore abundantly dispersed around dwellings and pastures. Guava trees are common, particularly in old pastures that are being allowed to regenerate back to young secondary successional forest. Presently, these trees clearly sustain a high density of *N. collaris* caterpillars, giving the impression that the adult moths are quite abundant (at lights), when, in fact, before human intervention, the species was probably quite scarce. *Nystalea collaris* is only one of tens of thousands of species of Costa Rican animals and plants that have such a human-influenced element to their demography. All of the Costa Rican countryside is quite populated with such species. A serious thought exercise is to imagine what must have been the densities and relationships of the common species of plants in a national park, such as Sector Santa Rosa of the ACG, prior to massive human perturbation. This also leads one to realize that once the ACG has regenerated back to a moderately "natural" state, it will be a very different place, and as nearly as we can tell, there will be no guava trees.

About the time we thought we really understood *N. collaris*, the *gusaneros* found eighteen caterpillars of them on two species of Combretaceae—the two combretaceous mangrove trees, *Laguncularia racemosa* and *Conocarpus erectus*. There is no particular defensive chemical relationship between Combretaceae and Myrtaceae, so one really wonders if the *N. collaris* feeding on these two coastal mangroves really are the same as the inland *N. collaris*. Such a situation is ideal for DNA sequencing, otherwise known as barcoding in current popular biological slang, to see if they really are the same species as those found feeding on Myrtaceae. To make things worse, there is another species of *Nystalea* with extraordinarily similar adults, but with unknown caterpillars. It is so similar to *N. collaris* that we cannot tell the adults of the two species apart. The Combretaceae-eater just might be this other species of *Nystalea*.

Four species of parasitoids use *N. collaris*. One species of tachinid fly parasitoid is apparently monophagous, *Winthemia* sp. 08b, with eight rearings out of 223 wild-caught caterpillars. Although a rare occurrence, *N. collaris* also suffers parasitism by a generalist tachinid, *Patelloa xanthura*. Furthermore, it is attacked by two undescribed species of small black braconid wasps in the genera *Glyptapanteles* and *Hypomicrogaster*. The *Hypomicrogaster* is clearly a specialist on several species of *Nystalea* and a few other medium-sized notodontid caterpillars while the jury is still out on the degree of specialization of the *Glyptapanteles*.

CATERPILLAR VOUCHER: 80-SRNP-195; DHJ
ADULT VOUCHER: 01-SRNP-22187; JCM

7. *NAVARCOSTES LIMNATIS* – NOTODONTIDAE

A *Navarcostes limnatis* caterpillar exemplifies the "sick leaf syndrome." At any distance other than the end of your nose, this enigmatic notodontid simply appears to be a very sick, still green, fungus-ridden leaf, stuck lightly to a thin diseased stem. The caterpillar even rocks slowly from side to side as if blowing lightly in a breeze. It would be quite interesting to see just how many species of foliage-gleaning birds would be fooled by this combination of morphology and behavior. The distinctive dorsal broken-saw-tooth morphology, especially of the penultimate and ultimate instars, appears to have phylogenetic ties to *Nystalea* caterpillars, which have all evolved in the direction of the dead browns, pinks, grays, and other nongreen pastels. The adult, however, is quite a stretch to be in the *Nystalea* morphology group. In fact, the adult of *N. limnatis* does not seem to be related to any moth, even to those of its own family, the Notodontidae. Even experienced moth taxonomists puzzle over its taxonomic affinities when they see it for the first time. The genus name is also unique; as of 2006 there is just one publication, the one presenting its description.

We probably will never understand the caterpillars of *N. limnatis* very well, even though it is now evident that its usual food plants are the widespread rain-forest vine *Dioclea malacocarpa*, several species of the tree *Lonchocarpus*, and several other woody Fabaceae. This is because the caterpillars occur at extremely low numbers. Only fifty-two caterpillars of *N. limnatis* have been found in many years of searching their rain-forest food plants in hundreds of hours of exploration by the *gusaneros*. This assertion of low density needs to be tempered, however, by noting that the *gusaneros* may well be occasionally fooled, especially at a distance, by this caterpillar's crypsis. Evidence to date suggests that the female lays only a single egg per oviposition event, and this may be in the crown of large plants as well as on saplings and low-hanging parts of large, woody vines.

This is one of the many species of ACG caterpillars that appear to have no host-specific wasp or fly parasitoids. Although a sample of fifty-two caterpillars producing no parasitoids may seem quite small, it has been our experience that when there are host-specific parasitoids, they are found within the first ten to thirty wild caterpillars encountered. Additional rearings may well reveal some cases of *N. limnatis* being attacked by parasitoids, in particular the more "generalist" tachinid flies. This may be said for virtually all of the species of caterpillars in the ACG, however.

CATERPILLAR VOUCHER: 01-SRNP-2090; DHJ
ADULT VOUCHER: 04-SRNP-23053; JCM

8. *MORPHO POLYPHEMUS* – NYMPHALIDAE

The caterpillar of *Morpho polyphemus* constructs a loose and sloppy nest of leaves and silk in which it rests, an extraordinary behavior for a noncharaxine nymphalid butterfly. This behavior is quite different from the caterpillars of its blue brethren of adult butterflies, who as caterpillars look like various kinds of rotting brown to yellow twigs as they perch against stems and twigs when not feeding, which is most of the day, or when pressed to the undersides of leaves. Caterpillars of *M. polyphemus* are quite cryptic in their bright green and gray-brown body color with gray hair tufts, but they are most cryptic against a tangled leafy background rather than the gray to brown and black twig colors. These caterpillars spend much of their lives hidden inside their cloud-forest nests, which are just one to three meters above the ground where the insectivorous monkeys, *Cebus cebucinus*, never seem to forage. Their color pattern appears to have been evolutionarily designed to avoid being noticed by a bird that has hastily torn into the mass of leaves and silk in search of any type of prey (spiders, small caterpillars, resting beetles). When entering the prepupal phase (as in our image), the caterpillar turns an overall bright apple green, a preview of the pupal color, and looks like a small section of a torn leaf dangling from a twig.

The huge adults flapping and soaring high in the canopy on sunny days look like sheets of flying white paper. We have never seen a bird chase them and the wings are notable for lacking beak marks and tears. It is likely that they, like the large, blue ACG morphos—*M. peleides*, *M. amathonte*, and *M. granadensis*—are far too agile to be captured on the wing by anything but the specialist butterfly predators (see Langham 2004). The female butterfly lays its solitary eggs on *Inga* and *Zygia* (Fabaceae) or the totally unrelated *Forchhammeria trifoliata* (Capparidaceae) in late August or September in the gradually disappearing ACG cloud forest. The caterpillar grows until June and pupates for six weeks, after which the adult emerges. Why a ten-month journey as a caterpillar? First, the leaves of its food plant are in the deep shade of old-growth forest understory, where nutrient content is minimal. Second, it lives in a forest at 800–1,400 meters elevation, where it is like living in a refrigerator. The cloud forest never freezes but only rarely really warms up, that is, at least until global warming destroys the cloudy and cold volcano-top climate. It shares this very slow development time with other large cloud-forest caterpillars such as the large, hairy orange *Coloradia marathusa* (Eupterotidae) and *Creonpyge creon* (Hesperiidae), though *M. polyphemus* does appear to be the record-holder for prolonged larval development.

A lone species of an undescribed tachinid parasitoid, *Hyphantrophaga* sp. 05, is shared with caterpillars of both *M. polyphemus* and *M. peleides*. The latter is the common iridescent blue *Morpho* found in lowlands to cloud forest and dry forest to rain forest that every tourist sees and that appears so commonly in ecotourism brochures. This tachinid is also the sole fly parasitoid of *M. peleides*, though out of many hundreds of *M. peleides* caterpillars we have only three records from generalist tachinids, such as *Patelloa xanthura*.

CATERPILLAR VOUCHER: 04-SRNP-35612; JCM
ADULT VOUCHER: 99-SRNP-42; JCM

9. *CITHERONIA LOBESIS* – SATURNIIDAE

Citheronia lobesis is a tropical dry-forest relative of the North American hickory horned devil, *Citheronia regalis* (see Boettner et al. 2000), and is a rarity in moth collections. *Citheronia lobesis* is quite common at lights in the last two weeks of May, however, following the end of the six-month dry season. These adults have just eclosed from pupae that have been dormant a few centimeters below ground since the middle or end of the previous rainy season. The huge caterpillars seem curiously out of place on one of their "favorite" food plants. Patterned gray, purple, and white against a dark-brown ventral side with "fearsome" thoracic scoli, they are quite visible as they perch on the long, naked petioles of the large (and few) leaves of *Cochlospermum viti-*

folium (Cochlospermaceae), as is the one we show. Perhaps this is not its favorite food plant, but the caterpillars are frequently discovered on such plants because they are so visible there. This food plant is a fast-growing, spindly, sparsely leafed tree that is common throughout the early stages of succession in the ACG dry forest. For reasons not obvious, this moth does not range into the adjacent ACG rain forest, even though its sibling species *Citheronia bellavista* is common there. The latter is occasionally found in dry forest, though with the increasing dryness and heating from global warming, it appears to be disappearing from the ACG dry forest. Eggs of *C. lobesis* are placed singly on a small number of dry-forest trees: *Spondias mombin* (Anacardiaceae), *Calycophyllum candissimum* (Rubiaceae), and *Bombacopsis quinatum* (Bombacaceae). They are also found on the common woody perennial and nearly evergreen true parasitic plant, the mistletoe *Phorodendron quadrangulare* (Viscaceae, Loranthaceae of older literature).

The cigar-sized caterpillars look fearsome but are quite harmless. They are commonly brought to nestling *Trogon melanocephalus*. The adult bird bashes the caterpillar against a branch repeatedly and even masticates it with its bill, reducing it to a size that a nestling can swallow.

A large black and yellow tachinid fly, *Belvosia* sp. 10, is a frequently reared parasitoid of *C. lobesis* caterpillars. This fly glues its single eggs onto a few leaves in the vicinity of the caterpillar. The eggs are swallowed by the caterpillar as it eats the leaves. Once swallowed, the egg hatches and the maggot hides somewhere in the caterpillar (location unknown) and waits one to nine months to initiate development. The maggot development does not initiate until the caterpillar has completed its development and pupated (see Ichiki and Shima 2003). Then it eats the pupal contents and forms a puparium inside the dead host pupa. The adult fly ecloses a few weeks later. There can be one to eight *Belvosia* puparia in a single *C. lobesis* pupa. Very strikingly, when the flies have finished feeding on the pupa, the remaining tissue does not rot. The fly larva is undoubtedly synthesizing a strong antibiotic so that the location of the pupa and its contained puparia are not revealed to mammalian predators, such as armadillos and *Liomys salvini* mice, as they search for prey in the soil and litter. There is also a *Belvosia* sp. 09 in the same habitat with the same life cycle, except that it attacks only the ceratocampine saturniid *Eacles imperialis*, a close relative of *C. lobesis*. When the first set of thirteen species of reared *Belvosia* was sent to Norm Woodley, a fly taxonomist in the National Museum of Natural History in Washington, D.C., to begin the identification process, he separated all but one group of specimens with relative ease. Each grouping turned out to be very specific to a particular species or ecological class of host caterpillars. He determined that there was one group of somewhat variable flies that he did not want to attempt to sort into species. It was requested that he sort them anyway. He called a few days later with his two tentatively designated groups of extremely similar flies and read their rearing codes. One group turned out to parasitize only *C. lobesis* and the other only *E. imperialis*. This specialization is particularly impressive since *C. vitifolium* is commonly used as a food plant by *E. imperialis* caterpillars as well.

CATERPILLAR VOUCHER: 03-SRNP-13337; JCM
ADULT VOUCHER: 02-SRNP-12701; JCM

10. *LEUCANELLA HOSMERA* – SATURNIIDAE

This elegant black caterpillar with its striking yellow and white starburst of highly urticating spines illustrates the complexities of mimicry. *Leucanella hosmera* is a medium- to upper-elevation cloud-forest denizen. It is aposematic, diurnal in feeding behavior, and marches around and feeds in large, ostentatious groups, even in the last instar. It is hardly something a predator can fail to notice and, if inclined to experiment, learn not to pick up with hands or beak. This is standard fare in the biol-

ogy of mimicry. On a larger geographic scale, however, the upper slopes and tops of mountains are only a small part of the Central American experience. The individual birds that live and hunt there, as well as the monkeys, for the most part stay (though there is some degree of seasonal migration at least by the birds up and down the side of the mountain). The lowlands of Central American rain forests and even the evergreen riparian vegetation of dry forests are clothed with *Cecropia* spp. trees (Cecropiaceae), those spindly fast-growing trees with the raised rings at each node up the trunk and the huge, palmate, com-

pound leaves. The *Cecropia* are frequently fed on by a black, harmless, nymphalid butterfly caterpillar, *Colobura dirce,* with bright yellow-white starburst spines, giving it the perfect appearance of a half-sized *L. hosmera* caterpillar. It is certainly tempting to think of the caterpillar of *C. dirce* as a Batesian mimic of the *L. hosmera* caterpillar. We have no idea, of course, what avian foragers might encounter this potential mimic of *L. hosmera,* or when. Yet if it is to be a mimic, there would have to be at least some of the lowland tropical birds circulating up into the mid-high elevation cloud forest, learning a painful lesson, remembering it, and then circulating back into the lowlands over enormous stretches of ecosystem to provide the selection to maintain this mimicry. This is not a parsimonious explanation, and not likely. It is more likely that these two caterpillars have fortuitously hit on the same aposematic coloration—*L. hosmera* aposematic in its own right and *C. dirce* simply tapping into a general, genetically programmed behavior to avoid brightly colored spiny caterpillars. This resembles the case of birds being genetically programmed to avoid coral snake–colored caterpillars and the real snakes as well (Smith 1975). To complicate matters, *C. dirce* ranges from tropical Mexico to central South America. It is very much a stretch to imagine that there are *Leucanella* caterpillars throughout this range and that they are models maintaining a specific mimetic advantage to the color and form of *C. dirce* caterpillars. It is much more likely that *C. dirce* caterpillars will remain genetically locked into this color pattern until there is some strong population-encompassing selection against it, highly unlikely except to a small isolated population.

CATERPILLAR VOUCHER: 98-SRNP-15668; DHJ
ADULT VOUCHER: 00-SRNP-23645; JCM

11. *OPSIPHANES ZELOTES* – NYMPHALIDAE

Phil DeVries, a most astute tropical butterfly specialist, invested many years of his life in Costa Rica finding, observing, and otherwise documenting nearly all within-country species of nymphalid butterflies (DeVries 1987). To our knowledge, he did not document only one large species of butterfly among hundreds, and that is this species, *Opsiphanes zelotes*. The very distinctive caterpillar matches up with a very distinctive adult. Why was it never collected in all the centuries of butterfly collecting in Costa Rica? First, throughout its range (it was previously known just from Colombia) it is very scarce in collections. There is just one specimen in the Natural History Museum in London. When the first one reared in the ACG was shown to Dick Vane-Wright at that museum, he initially was inclined to agree that perhaps it was an undescribed species. Then, after several hours of careful search, he found the single specimen from Colombia, an old specimen badly faded from its original dark background

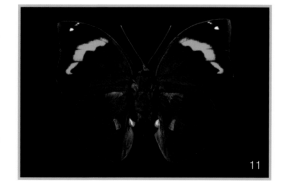

11

color. Second, since traps baited with fermenting bananas or other fruit are famous for attracting the three other ACG species of *Opsiphanes,* all common and with very wide geographic ranges, it appears that *O. zelotes* does not come to fruit bait, causing one to wonder just what the robust adults do feed on. Third, being conspicuously darker in color than the other *Opsiphanes,* perhaps it is the most nocturnal of the four species, out of the range of diurnal butterfly collectors, yet not going to lights as do moths. Fourth, even knowing the food plant, the caterpillar rearing inventory has only been able to find eleven *O. zelotes* caterpillars, in striking contrast to more than 1,500 caterpillars of the other three *Opsiphanes.* Furthermore, all eleven are from an area of mid-elevation rain forest about thirty square kilometers in area. Since it has been reared from four different species of palms—*Prestoea decurrens, Desmoncus schippii, Bactris hondurensis,* and an unidentified species—it does not appear that its scarcity is linked to being a specialist on a rare food plant. *Opsiphanes zelotes* is simply a very low-density species.

The reasons why there is not an *O. zelotes* caterpillar on one out of every thirty understory palms, a density that can sometimes seem to be the case with *O. quiteria* in the same habitat, will remain unknown until someone focuses on the natural history of this species and contrasts that with the natural history of its three sympatric congeners.

The caterpillar of *O. zelotes,* the most beautiful of the five species of ACG *Opsiphanes,* is a highly cryptic green with longitudinal stripes to match the long, straight veins of the large-leafed, monocot food plants. The adult is beautiful as well, though experience suggests that its scarcity definitely raises the perception of beauty. This in turn tells us that part of our criterion for beauty is indeed scarcity, which in turn tells us that another criterion for beauty is value in the eyes of competitors, which certainly links tightly with scarcity. It is perhaps ironic that what is thought of as a physical trait—color, pattern, and size—is actually a perception issue in our primate minds, one that directs foraging and measures fitness with the same variables as do all other organisms.

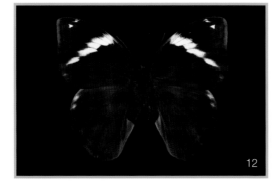

CATERPILLAR VOUCHER: 03-SRNP-34935; DHJ
ADULT VOUCHER: 00-SRNP-869; JCM

12. *OPSIPHANES BOGOTANUS* – NYMPHALIDAE

Five species of *Opsiphanes* occur within the ACG. *Opsiphanes tamarindi* is the *Opsiphanes* that is most common and often seen eating banana plant leaves everywhere in Costa Rica, be it rain forest (common) or dry forest (rare). You also find it if you search wild bananas, *Heliconia* (Heliconiaceae); gingers, *Renealmia* (Costaceae); and Marantaceae for large green nymphalid caterpillars with straight head horns. The much scarcer *Opsiphanes bogotanus* is an *O. tamarindi* look-alike that feeds almost entirely on wild *Heliconia* in the rain forest, with

only very few records from *Calathea lutea* (Marantaceae) and banana, *Musa cavendishii.* The caterpillars of *O. bogotanus* should never be confused with those of *O. tamarindi* because the former has a bright red stripe, bordered by robin's-egg blue bands, down the middle of its back. The stripe is just visible behind the head horns in our image. In contrast, *O. tamarindi* caterpillars have a green central stripe down their back bordered by a very fine red line on each side and a green stripe to the outside. The central stripe of *O. zelotes* is green, bordered by a yellow stripe. While it is an easy assumption that these strong linear stripes are meant to render the caterpillar cryptic against the straight linear venation of its large-leaf, monocot food plants, what selected for the distinctive stripes that allow discrimination of the species of caterpillars is perhaps a selective pressure lost in evolutionary and historical time.

The adult of *O. bogotanus* is so similar to that of *O. tamarindi* that DeVries (1987) was prompted to wonder if it was just a color morph of *O. tamarindi.* The adults of these two species are just as easily distinguished as are the caterpillars, however. There is no trace of reddish hues on the upper side of the hind wings for *O. bogotanus,* while both sexes of *O. tamarindi* have a strong to faint reddish-cherry-burgundy wash on the posterior portion of the upper side of the hind wing. There are also very subtle details of pattern on the complex underside that differ between these two species, but this is best learned by comparing the undersides of a specimen of each.

In contrast to *O. tamarindi,* which occasionally is parasitized by tachinid flies, there are no records of Tachinidae attacking thirty-seven wild-caught *O. bogotanus,* and only one record of a braconid wasp, *Glyptapanteles*, of a species that usually feeds on *O. tamarindi.* Likewise exceptional, the *O. bogotanus* caterpillar was feeding on banana and the wasp probably confused it with *O. tamarindi.* Whether this absence of tachinids parasitizing *O. bogotanus* caterpillars is a sampling artifact remains to be seen, but it is certainly suggestive of an interesting difference between these two very similar species.

The pupa of *O. bogotanus,* like that of other *Opsiphanes,* looks like a three-dimensional dead, dry, brown pendant

13

leaf. This is to say, it did not evolutionarily go the direction of *Dynastor darius* (#54), the pupa of which is a superb snake-head mimic (Aiello and Silberglied 1978). However, the pupa of *Opsiphanes* certainly seems to have the raw ingredients in its pattern to be evolutionarily molded into resembling a snake head by some future session of natural selection.

CATERPILLAR VOUCHER: 04-SRNP-41528; JCM
ADULT VOUCHER: 01-SRNP-9756; JCM

13. *XYLOPHANES GUIANENSIS* – SPHINGIDAE

Xylophanes guianensis is a *Xylophanes* gone wrong. To begin with, the adults simply do not go to lights hung in the forest or on the edge of the forest, even though the adults are nocturnal and are present. This gives the impression that the species is not there or is so rare that you just never got lucky. Additionally, they are so similar in appearance to the adults of *Xylophanes ceratomiodes* that when you finally find one, you suspect that you had been seeing them on the lights all along, but ignored them, thinking that they were *X. ceratomiodes.* Then you spend years peering intently at every suspect *X. ceratomiodes* at the lights, hoping that it will have slightly broader front wings and a slight saw-tooth aspect to the forewing outer margin. But it never appears. The first and only adults encountered in the wild in twenty years of looking for Costa Rican sphingids were two adults roosting in the daytime, in 1979, under the palm thatch roof of the main dormitory building at Sirena, in Corcovado National Park on the Osa Peninsula. They were there with several other species of sphingids, *Aleuron* and *Pachygonidia,* that only rarely come to lights. The usual conclusion emerged that these sphingids must be quite rare members of the deep rain forest, which is why they have never been seen in thousands of hours of light trapping in Costa Rica. But that conclusion couldn't be more incorrect.

In 1998, at the opposite end of the country and on the interface of dry forest and rain forest on the northern lower foothills of Volcan Orosi, the *gusaneros* found a very strange and almost black last-instar caterpillar with an irregular cream fungus patch on each shoulder. Now, more than seventy-five rearing records later, it is clear that *X. guianensis*'s usual food plant is the very widespread lowland to mid-elevation rubiaceous treelet *Palicourea guianensis* (there are also a few records from a species of *Psychotria,* many species of which are fed on by many species of *Xylophanes*). When Janzen saw the first one, he took an entire roll of film of this caterpillar, being quite unable to guess to what genus it belonged (and this, after having reared some fourteen species of *Xylophanes*). A month later he was visiting the Estacion Los Almendros rearing barn, and he asked the *gusaneros* if it had pupated, and if it had, to please find the rearing bag so that he could photograph the pupa. When they brought him a bag with an obvious *Xylophanes* pupa in it, he thought initially that they had mixed up the bag numbers. He asked them to search the bags with numbers with which it could have been confused. They insisted that there was no error. He did not believe them. A month later he took a newly eclosed but frozen (stored) moth out of its envelope and there was *X. guianensis* with its original and properly marked voucher code.

Six years later at the Estacion Caribe rearing barn, in a rearing bag hanging in line among a set of *Xylophanes porcus* found feeding on *Palicorea guianensis,* Janzen found a bag containing a slim, green third-instar sphingid with a medium-broad, yellow, lateral racing stripe from the tail end to, and including, the head. He spent another full roll of film on this weird caterpillar that he concluded must be one of the few yet-to-be-reared small species of ACG sphingids. But two months later he came to the startling conclusion that it was a third-instar *X. guianensis*. While the adult and pupa conform to the unmistakable morphology of *Xylophanes,* selection has driven the caterpillar into being a mimic of a yellow leaf vein in its early instars. The later instars are like a rotten dead branch with a moldy spot. This could well have been driven by a bird or mammal predator of caterpillars when the species existed as some small restricted population, a predator that otherwise was not at all bothered by the scare tactics of the thoracic false eyespots of classical *Xylophanes* caterpillars.

CATERPILLAR VOUCHER: 04-SRNP-33450; JCM
ADULT VOUCHER: 01-SRNP-24026; JCM

14. *EACLES IMPERIALIS* – SATURNIIDAE

As currently perceived (Lemaire 1988), *Eacles imperialis* is the New World saturniid with the largest geographic range among all species in the family, ranging from Ontario, Canada, to Argentina. In this sense, it groups with humans, coyotes, peccaries, and ospreys as appearing to be an extreme habitat generalist and food-plant generalist. It has a close relative in the southwestern United States, *Eacles oslaris,* and many tropical relatives. In Costa Rica it is found throughout all lowland habitats, from the very driest to the very wettest. Although it is the

14

only species of *Eacles* in dry forest, it is accompanied by *E. masoni, E. penelope,* and *E. ormondei* in rain forest and lower cloud forest.

Things are not always as they seem to be, however. When we DNA-barcoded *E. imperialis* in the ACG, we found that the rain-forest specimens have one set of mitochondrial DNA sequences while the dry-forest specimens have another. Are they one species, or two? Only larger samples on the one hand, and samples from where the dry and rain forest come together on the north slopes of Volcan Orosi on the other hand, will give definitive answers. Yet it does appear as though this seemingly widespread species might be a complex of species, whether separated by geography or ecosystem or both.

Caterpillars of *E. imperialis* in the dry forest, the only place where we have a substantial number of wild-caught caterpillar rearing records, are serious generalists. It appears that the females lay eggs on at least thirty-five species of plants in sixteen families. There are many hundreds of species of plants on which we have not yet found the caterpillars, so we want to avoid the impression that it eats any and all species. It definitely has the ability to avoid the defensive chemicals of a wide array of plant species, however. Given the ease with which impregnated females can be obtained from light traps in the dry forest at the beginning of the rainy season, this moth would be an ideal animal to test against the entire array of ACG dry-forest species, to see what it actually can eat (probably many species) in comparison to what it is actually found to be feeding on. Such feeding trials using caterpillars and a wide variety of potential food plants are simple to set up and produce standardized, easy-to-compare data. Examples of these types of studies have been conducted using gypsy moth caterpillars fed leaves of a variety of plants, including angiosperms (Miller and Hanson 1989a,b) and gymnosperms (Miller et al. 1991).

Most wild-caught *E. imperialis* caterpillars are green, with the occasional yellowish, pink, or dark chocolate morph (as is ours seen here). But when raised in bulk in large nets over a tree (to protect them from birds), the nongreen morphs are much more frequent. This is probably because inside the protective nets, they frequently encounter each other, and this in turn triggers a response in some, but not all, to turn to a nongreen morph. The result in nature is that if there are several *E. imperialis* caterpillars on a single individual plant, they have a high chance of being different colors. As a consequence, visually orienting predators are less likely to get both of them since the predator forms a search image based on the first caterpillar encountered. This pattern of color dimorphism is commonplace in ACG caterpillars that occasionally occur in high density. For example, the large caterpillars of *Aellopos titan* (Sphingidae) on *Randia monantha* and *R. aculeata* (Rubiaceae) are either green or black-purple when they defoliate their food plants (Janzen 1985b) and become a very visible target for foraging birds and monkeys. Distinct light and dark color morphs also occur in *Xylophanes juanita* (#5).

CATERPILLAR VOUCHER: 04-SRNP-ACGLAB; JCM
ADULT VOUCHER: 00-SRNP-4217; JCM

15. *OTHORENE PURPURASCENS* – SATURNIIDAE

The ecotourist virtually never encounters *Othorene purpurascens* caterpillars because their typical microhabitat is the crown of sapotaceous trees twenty to forty meters tall from extreme dry forest to rain forest and even in cloud forest. In the latter two habitats they appear to be extremely rare but obviously present across Costa Rica. The usual method of sighting *O. purpurascens* adults is with a light trap at ground level, and they simply do not fly much at ground level. In the ACG dry forest, they can be moderately abundant at a light trap, though this may well be biased by the fact that the particular light trap at "ground level" is on the top of a cliff, with the view looking directly out into the crowns of several tall adult *Manilkara chicle* trees, the caterpillar's food plant.

15

The *M. chicle* tree is well known to the general public without actually knowing it. It is the original source of chewing gum. If you cut through the bark into the cambium, the living layer just underneath the dead bark, you are cutting through the network of latex vessels that lace through all of the above-ground tissues. The white latex that flows out and was collected by the *chicleros*, or chicle-tappers, is the original World War II chewing gum—just add sugar. As the caterpillar of *O. purpurascens* starts to eat a *M. chicle* leaf, it cuts the leaf halfway through at its base, and sometimes in other points on the midrib, precisely to avoid getting a face full of white latex with each bite. With the leaf's latex-vessel network cut off from that of the remainder of the tree, the defensive latex, crude liquid rubber, is just another bit of potential food in the leafy sandwich being snipped into pieces and swallowed. Other saturniids conduct this type of surgery on their food plants as well, including *Copiopteryx semiramis* [#41] caterpillars, which also feed on *M. chicle*.

Four species of sapotaceous trees occur in ACG dry forest, but it appears that *O. purpurascens* uses only *M. chicle*. Yet it can eat *Chryosphyllum brenesii* leaves when offered in the laboratory. This rare tree, which really has not been extensively searched yet for caterpillars, might be another natural host. Since *M. chicle* occurs only in dry forest, the *O. purpurascens* adults that come to lights in the cloud and rain forest of the ACG and the remainder of Costa Rica must have fed on other species of Sapotaceae when they were caterpillars. To date, however, only *Pouteria exfoliata* in the ACG cloud forest is known to be one of these rain-forest sapotaceous food plants for *O. purpurascens*. How do we know that it does not also eat other families of plants? We cannot with absolute certainty, but like all host plant records, the best we can do is infer a more inclusive hypothesis from the narrower set of data at hand.

Caterpillars of *O. purpurascens* belong to the ever-growing group of caterpillars united by the fact that they are attacked by only one or two species of specialist parasitoids. To date only

Thyreodon santarosae, a large, black, ichneumonid wasp parasite of ceratocampine caterpillars that resemble green sphingids (Gauld and Janzen 2004), and the tachinid fly, *Leptostylum* sp. 01, are known from *O. purpurascens*. In the ACG dry forest the tachinid performs the miraculous task of being an extremely low-density parasitoid of three subfamilies of saturniids: Ceratocampinae, Hemileucinae, and Saturniinae. There are also three rain-forest records of this fly attacking other families of caterpillars, raising the suspicion it is yet another species of *Leptostylum*.

CATERPILLAR VOUCHER: 83-SRNP-1347; DHJ
ADULT VOUCHER: 03-SRNP-13029; JCM

16. *SYSSPHINX QUADRILINEATA* – SATURNIIDAE

Caterpillars of *Syssphinx quadrilineata* are denizens of small, shrubby legumes such as *Mimosa, Calliandra,* and *Senna.* However, in striking contrast to their relative, *Syssphinx mexicana* (#67), which eats only ant-acacias (Janzen 1967), *S. quadrilineata* is not able to penetrate the ant defenses of ant-acacias, even though they can eat ant-free foliage in the laboratory. The food plant of *S. quadrilineata* remained an enigma for decades in the ACG dry forest. The caterpillars were not found until our focus was turned to the very common shrubs of *Mimosa xanti* (Fabaceae) in combination with searching at night. In the daytime, the *S. quadrilineata* caterpillars with their

16

green and silver dorsal (harmless) projections are extraordinarily hard to find when viewed against the finely compound leaves of *M. xanti,* unless you are looking right at them and close up. At night, however, their waxy cuticle and silvery coloration reflect brilliantly against the dull green compound leaves, which are partly closed up as well, offering less camouflage.

Throughout the New World, *Syssphinx* caterpillars have variously developed spiny projections, as does *S. quadrilineata*. But this is complex. When the same species is reared on a plant that has large broad leaflets, the caterpillar has a minimum number of spines, if any at all, sometimes being as spine-free as a *Syssphinx molina* caterpillar. When sibs are reared on plants with large numbers of highly divided leaflets, they tend to have more, longer silvery projections by the time they are a fifth instar. It is likely that the caterpillar is somehow detecting the level of light passing over it, or at least passing over its "eyes" or stemmata (Briscoe and White 2005), and adjusting its morphology to that environmental cue.

Adults, especially the distinctive males, are common at lights. The females are like small versions of *Syssphinx colla* and quite hard to distinguish from this congener.

Syssphinx quadrilineata is one of the seven ACG ceratocampine hosts of *Thyreodon santarosae* (Gauld and Janzen 2004). This large ichneumonid wasp is known only from the ACG, but probably occurs elsewhere in Costa Rican dry forest. It is black, as is usual with diurnally searching ichneumonids, and flies through the foliage, clambering from leaf to leaf, in search of caterpillars. Why a wasp like this does not also parasitize other large dry-forest caterpillars, even of the same saturniid subfamily, is unlikely to be due to its failure to search the right food plants. Its host caterpillars eat many species of food plants in very different genera, so it must search for the caterpillar itself, rather than for a food plant. The egg is deposited right through the caterpillar cuticle and the first-instar wasp lives hidden somewhere in the host body until the caterpillar, in its last instar, has finished feeding and made a chamber in which to pupate. Then the wasp larva begins to feed voraciously and in a few days has consumed the entire contents. Next it emerges through the caterpillar cuticle and spins an incredibly tough and desiccation-resistant silk and resin cocoon in the caterpillar pupation chamber at the surface of the soil-litter interface. The wasp emerges from the cocoon by chewing a round hole through one end one to twelve months later.

CATERPILLAR VOUCHER: 84-SRNP-123; DHJ
ADULT VOUCHER: 83-SRNP-290.1; JCM

17. *EUDOCIMA COLUBRA* – NOCTUIDAE

There is a reason why we illustrate so few Noctuidae caterpillars in this tome. A great number of the noctuids are cryptic, small, green or brown, and finely patterned to look like bark or foliage.

They feed largely at night, hiding during the day. They have been slow to accumulate records in the caterpillar inventory because they are hard to find and hard to identify in the field. But there are a very few that are aposematic or mimics of aposematic species. Most of these are some combination of red, orange, black, and white, such as *Heterochroma sarepta* (#79). Then there are a few species that have struck out on their own different evolutionary voyage regarding appearance. *Eudocima colubra* is one of these "different" species. It is in the same category as sphingid and saturniid caterpillars. That is to say, it is cryptic at a distance, quite as are many sphingids in the genus *Xylophanes,* but when viewed up close, the spectacular false eyespot on each side of the thorax is very evident, just as the thoracic eyespots are on *Xylophanes* caterpillars. In the earlier instars, the sharply marked white patterns are largely a cryptic case of looking like a dark twig with fungi on it. However, it is easy to visualize how, as the caterpillar becomes larger, there is more intense selection for the evolution of the lateral, circular fungal rings to become an ever more glaring eyespot. These false eyespots are of course independently evolved from those seen on sphingids, notodontids, hesperiids, and papilionids—also largely independently evolved—and reflect this independence in their different forms of symmetry and placement of central highlights. In other words, eyespots have many origins and occur in many lineages of caterpillars.

Adult *E. colubra* are one of the tropical "underwings," with a color pattern displayed by North American noctuids in the genus *Catocala*. Like *Catocala, E. colubra* are so-called bait moths. This means that instead of visiting flowers (or being nonfeeding as are saturniids, limacodids, and apatelodids), they feed on rotting and fermenting fruit and on yeast-filled fermenting wounds in tree trunks. Perched in the daytime on a tree trunk, they look like yet more tree bark. But when the moth is discovered or molested by, for example, one of the many species of wood creepers such as *Dendrocolaptes* that forage on tree trunks, it launches into a fast flight to another tree, easily traced by the bright yellow hind wings. But then it abruptly disappears, just about the time that the bird has a fix on that bright flag. It settles rapidly and hides the bright flag under the bark-colored forewings. This method of escape by adults is used not only by a scattered variety of other noctuids but also by many sphingids (e.g., *Erinnyis crameri,* #37), a few notodontids (e.g., *Rhuda dificilis,* #61), and some geometrids. Its efficacy depends strongly on whether the moth is able to launch rapidly into flight at daytime (warm) temperatures. Many observers have made the mistake of generalizing from the typical sluggish capacity to launch in cool or cold night temperatures for moths that come to lights and settle there. They conclude incorrectly that the postulated yellow-hind-wing escape mechanism won't work. When these moths are disturbed at elevated daytime warm temperatures, however, they are quite capable of rapid

18

flight without a long session of shivering their thoracic muscles to attain the temperature needed for take-off.

CATERPILLAR VOUCHER: 03-SRNP-23449; DHJ
ADULT VOUCHER: 00-SRNP-10690; JCM

18. *ARSENURA ARMIDA* – SATURNIIDAE

Arsenura armida has an unambiguously aposematic caterpillar. As noted in the introductory chapter, there is not just one individual but ten to fifty of these cigar-sized last instars clustered in a patch on a bare tree trunk. They are fully exposed to every passing vertebrate predator—monkeys, coatis, squirrels, and many tens of species of insectivorous birds—yet they are not preyed on by vertebrates. Not even the thousands of species of insects that prey on caterpillars attack them. Not one of thousands of large caterpillars brought to nestling trogons, *Trogon elegans* and *Trogon melanocephalus*, was an *A. armida*. The parent birds were foraging in the very forest heavily occupied by *A. armida* caterpillars in the second month of the Santa Rosa rainy season. We made the gruesome mistake of feeding some caterpillars of *A. armida* to three trogon nestlings. The birds were dead the next morning. The experiment was not and will not be repeated.

But despite their evident protection from some predators, their known and common ACG food plants are not defoliated: *Bombacopsis quinata* (Bombacaceae) and *Guazuma ulmifolia* (Sterculiaceae) from the dry forest, and *Rollinia membranacea*

(Annonaceae) and *Heliocarpus americanus* (Tiliaceae) from the rain forest. Something is causing high mortality. Perhaps predators, like the mouse *Liomys salvini,* eat the pupae in the soil. Predators also eat the bright and very gregarious young instars (Costa et al. 2004) sitting on the foliage. We suspect the vespid wasps, *Polistes instabilis* and *Polistes canadensis,* to be the likely killers. Vespid wasps are in fact major caterpillar predators in the ACG dry forest.

Parasitization is easier to document. *Winthemia subpicea,* a large tachinid fly, glues its eggs directly to the large last instar. This fly kills a high percentage of the caterpillars after they have pupated. The maggot continues its development in the pupa in the soil, eating out the insides before emerging to form its own puparium in the soil. There is also a rare ichneumonid wasp, *Barylypa broweri,* named in honor of Charles Brower (Gauld 2000). He was the lead lawyer for the government of Costa Rica in the infamous case of expropriation of the Santa Elena Peninsula to incorporate it into the ACG (Santa Elena is where Oliver North ordered an airstrip built during the Contra war). Females of *B. broweri* inject their eggs directly into *A. armida* caterpillars and the young wasp larva hides somewhere, inactive, until the moth pupa is well formed in the litter. Many months later it initiates development and eats the host tissues. Pupation occurs inside the host pupa and the adult wasp ecloses at the beginning of next year's rainy season, just in time to find the next generation of *A. armida* caterpillars.

The evident cluster of large *A. armida* caterpillars on the trunk of the food plant and the masses of brightly ringed younger instars in the foliage has led behaviorists to ask how the caterpillars follow each other around and maintain group cohe-sion. The beginning of the answer lies in their gregarious origin and the hundreds of sibling caterpillars that eclose from a single egg mass (see the introductory chapter). Later, they follow each other using trail pheromones originating from glands on the caterpillar cuticle (Costa et al. 2003). The physiology of these glands and their role in caterpillar behavior are not yet fully understood.

The large adults of *A. armida* occasionally come to lights placed in the forest. As expected, they are almost entirely males. They are among the last to appear in the succession of species of Saturniidae that emerge after the start of the rainy season (Janzen 1993a). What seems very strange about the few females that come to lights is that even though their wings are unworn, indicating that the moth is only a few days old, they have always already laid all of their eggs. This is in stark contrast to other species of saturniid females. This puzzle was resolved by discov-ering that when a female finds the larval food plant, normally on the first night after the night of eclosion and copulation, she either lays all her 300–400 eggs in one mass on one leaf, or splits them into two batches. Either way, she lays all her eggs in one night, but the now egg-expended body lives out the usual life span of five to eight days and sometimes even comes to a light hung in the forest.

CATERPILLAR VOUCHER: 03-SRNP-ACGLAB; JCM
ADULT VOUCHER: 01-SRNP-16756; JCM

19. *PERIGONIA ILUS* – SPHINGIDAE

Perigonia ilus is an annoying caterpillar. It cannot be distinguished from the caterpillar of *Perigonia lusca* in any reliable way except that in ACG dry-forest *P. ilus* caterpillars usually eat *Calycophyllum candidissimum* (393 records) and rarely *Guettarda macrosperma* (32 records), whereas *P. lusca* caterpillars are almost entirely found feeding on *G. macrosperma* (91 records) and rarely on *C. candidissumum* (7 records). Both species of food plants are large deciduous trees in the Rubiaceae, common in early successional forests and rare in old-growth forests. The adults are not much easier to distinguish and are often confused in

19

museum collections. However, *P. ilus* can be reliably identified by the presence of much more yellow on the hind wings and more blunt forewings than is the case with *P. lusca*. The literature equally has confused them, variously regarding *P. lusca* as "variable" (meaning that both species were lumped into one variable species called *P. lusca*) or *P. ilus* as a "subspecies" or "form" of *P. lusca* (e.g., D'Abrera 1986). The latter is unambiguously not the case since they co-occur and breed in the same ACG dry forest while maintaining their biological distinctiveness. Yet the genitalia of the adults are essentially identical, and the first sphingid taxonomist to see them said they were just a single variable species based on this trait. Janzen took his word for it but remained bothered by the slight differences in the adult wing shape, focusing on the slightly more pointed wings in *P. lusca* versus the more blunt wings in *P. ilus*. Then Jean-Marie Cadiou, a sphingid expert, looked at the reared specimens and declared that he had long suspected that there were indeed two species, and the observations of both of them in the same place at the same time reinforced this. At first Janzen did not notice the caterpillar food-plant dichotomy, but was startled to find that the migrants newly arriving in Santa Rosa at the beginning of the rainy season were larger than the offspring of the first generation to eclose two months later in July. While measuring the wing lengths to establish this, he discovered that *P. ilus* had significantly shorter front wings for a moth of given body weight than did *P. lusca*. When Ian Kitching and Cadiou completed their definitive checklist for the sphingids of the world (Kitching and Cadiou 2000), they reinforced this further by agreeing with Haxaire (1996) that the moths are two species. Now, after sequencing their DNA, it can be said that they are indeed two species, albeit closely related.

Although we cannot easily distinguish the caterpillars of these two species, a large parasitic ichneumonid wasp, *Thyreodon maculipennis,* is extremely good at doing so. Although there remains the slight doubt that these caterpillars were misidentified (as *P. ilus* when they were in fact *P. lusca*), it appears that this wasp only attacks caterpillars of *P. ilus* (Gauld and Janzen 2004). Such extreme host specificity is commonplace among ACG parasitoid wasps, but it is still amazing that this wasp apparently discriminates among such very similar caterpillars in the same forest.

CATERPILLAR VOUCHER: 84-SRNP-1391; DHJ
ADULT VOUCHER: 90-SRNP-726; JCM

20. *EUHAPIGIODES HALLWACHSAE* – NOTODONTIDAE

We scooped the adults of this large notodontid off the black-light sheet in moderate numbers in the early 1980s, never dreaming that something so easy to find with a light trap and so large could be an undescribed species. Then we took our blossoming moth collection to Cornell University for identifications by Jack Franclemont, the taxonomic godfather to many moth taxonomists, and John Rawlins, who was just finishing his Ph.D. thesis research on *Bertholdia,* an arctiid we rear from time to time in the ACG. We spread the insect boxes out onto tables in Winifred Hallwachs's apartment. Dr. Franclemont zeroed in on the box containing what would become known as *Euhapigiodes hallwachsae*—the first new species of big notodontid he had seen from Central America. As we slogged through drawers and museums over the following years, the expectation was that we would encounter it eventually, but it never appeared. Shortly before Franclemont's death, Jim Miller

20

teamed up with him to describe it in a new genus, while describing another common ACG dry-forest notodontid, *Hapigiodes sigifredomarini* (Miller et al. 1997).

There is no sign of *E. hallwachsae* in the wetter parts of the ACG. It appears to be a true dry-forest endemic, despite the existence of several ACG rain-forest species of *Lonchocarpus,* its food plant. The pupae can certainly pass the long dry season dormant in dry soil, as can *H. sigifredomarini*. Nearly all the wild-caught specimens of *E. hallwachsae* in the INBio national biodiversity inventory are from the ACG, except for a few from the Nicoya Peninsula dry forest and one from Carara, on the boundary between dry forest and rain forest in central Pacific Costa Rica.

It was strange, however, that while the adults were common at the lights, no caterpillar of *E. hallwachsae* had been encountered by the ACG inventory. Then on 15 January 1990, long before the moth was scientifically baptized, Hallwachs shouted to Janzen from the laundry area (distinguished by the presence of an oversized bucket just outside the house) that there was a gorgeous, large female clinging to a leaf, which implied fertile eggs and eventually a hatching. Since we had no notion of what food plants would be suitable, newly eclosed first instars were placed on the foliage of eleven species of common dry-forest trees, including two species of *Lonchocarpus*. They fed only on the two species of *Lonchocarpus*. From those eggs we obtained the first caterpillar, and a good hint about where to look for more caterpillars, which we later found. In a happy marriage of data, we found that the large "mystery" notodontid caterpillars brought to *Trogon elegans* nestlings, noted four years earlier, were in fact caterpillars of *E. hallwachsae*. The caterpillar of *E. hallwachsae* is dorso-ventrally counter-shaded in hues of green, as are the large green caterpillars of the other large ACG notodontids *Hapigia, Hapigiodes, Rhapigia,* and *Antaea*. The color combination is a light leaf green dorsally and a dark green ventrally, along with a white to thin red lateral line dividing the two colors. The caterpillars are amazingly difficult to see when perched on twigs, midrib, or a cut part of the leaf (see 83-SRNP-1179 in the inventory database on the ACG Web site). Speaking of cut leaves, many Notodontidae, *E. hallwachsae* included, are inclined to eat away a major portion of one side of a leaf while perched in the gap in the leaf blade that is created by their feeding.

CATERPILLAR VOUCHER: 93-SRNP-6598; DHJ
ADULT VOUCHER: 99-SRNP-8554; JCM

21. *TALIDES* BURNS01 – HESPERIIDAE

Imagine you have found a *Heliconia* plant (Heliconiaceae, the Neotropical version of wild banana) with a portion of a leaf blade folded over and lightly tied with silk to the blade below. Inside this nest of folded leaves is a large, translucent, greenish caterpillar, with such a clear cuticle that the internal network of trachea branching out from the lateral spiracles is quite visible. Trachea are the tubes that carry air to the inner workings (muscles and other tissues) and exchange carbon dioxide, a very

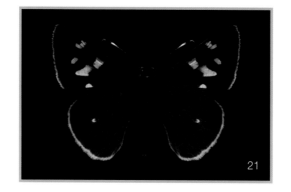

different way of breathing than is done by vertebrates. Equally, you can see the dorsal heart, pulsating along the length of the body from rear to front, pumping haemolymph, insect blood, to bathe the brain.

Why can we see the trachea so clearly in this particular caterpillar? Trachea are present in all caterpillars but generally hidden behind the heavily pigmented cuticle. The trachea are visible because *Talides* BURNS01 is a species that lives its life largely in a wet, folded leaf nest, a very protected world where the loss of a desiccation-resistant, thicker, and more colorful cuticle is not detrimental. In fact, if there has been any selection for appearance other than the head colors of this caterpillar, it has probably been to look like a rotting, fungus-filled piece of slimy leaf fragment. Now who would want to eat that? Many other hesperiids, however, have retained a thicker and more colorful cuticle.

Taxonomy, as illustrated by the ACG species of *Talides*, is a dynamic field of study. If the head is bright reddish orange in the last instar, with a dark black triangle in the middle of the "face" ("clypeus" and "frons" to the entomologist), the caterpillar is *Talides sinois*, a large, common, and widespread Neotropical species. If the face is pure orange, without the black, then the caterpillar staring you in the face is *Talides sergestus*. It all seems so simple. But John Burns, the skipper taxonomist for the ACG caterpillar inventory, kept warning us that *T. sinois* would turn out to be several species and sorting them would be a nightmare. Well, when DNA barcoding came on the scene, we associated nucleic acid patterns with morphology and applied it to the perceived realm of *T. sinois*. A sequence of events followed: 1) We barcoded a few individuals at random and found a suggestion of several DNA groups, or to be more formal, several DNA haplotypes; 2) John sorted them by the morphological traits he found useful; 3) We barcoded numerous additional individuals; 4) John studied further and more intensively the morphology of the species groups as indicated by barcoding; 5) We superimposed information on the food plants and the ecosystems within which they occurred, and anguished and ranted and raved about patterns; and 6) Finally, we now know that in the ACG, *T. sinois* is at least three species, and that perhaps none of them are true *T. sinois*. One species is what we are calling *T.* BURNS01, or something very similar to it, our image. The other two suspect taxa are in the queue for John to match them with a type specimen, waiting patiently in a museum somewhere. Either this will show that one of them is a described species, such as *T. sinois*, or, alternatively, he will describe them as new.

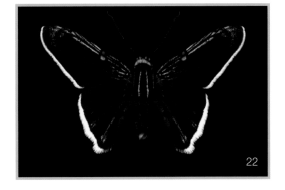

22

But what of that distinctive caterpillar face? This is only the tip of the iceberg. While there is no clue as to what is selecting for that distinctive color pattern, something clearly is. Two species of as-yet-unidentified ACG *Saliana* (Hesperiidae) caterpillars feeding on Marantaceae and *Costus* (Costaceae, the new-world gingers), respectively, have that facial pattern. Also, there is *Cynea anthracinus* (Hesperiidae), feeding on yet another genus of ginger, *Renealmia,* that has this caterpillar facial pattern. Making things even more complex, it is just the last instar that has this pattern. The earlier instars have black heads, rendering them

almost impossible to distinguish from many other skipper caterpillars that feed on this group of broad-leafed monocots.

CATERPILLAR VOUCHER: 03-SRNP-3939; JCM
ADULT VOUCHER: 00-SRNP-22077; JCM

22. *PHOCIDES LILEA* – HESPERIIDAE

Caterpillars of tropical skipper butterflies (Hesperiidae) are famous for fierce false faces. There are over 100 species in the ACG that display them. Many of these faces are of the kind brandished here by *Phocides lilea,* bright yellow, red, or white unicolored eyespots against a dark head capsule. But in some cases, for instance *Chioides catillus* (#34), the pattern is reversed, with jet-black eyes against a yellow or orange head capsule. False eyespots usually first appear vaguely in the second instar and become larger and more apparent as the caterpillar passes through successive instars. True caterpillar eyes are just a few tiny, light-gathering stemmata almost out of sight at the lower lateral corners of the head.

In contrast to the fairly complex eyespots displayed on the thorax and other body parts of other caterpillars (see *Xylophanes, Eumorpha,* and *Nystalea*), skipper caterpillar facial spots are directed forward rather than laterally or dorsally. Why? The most likely answer is that skipper caterpillars spend most of their daylight hours hidden away in leaf and silk shelters, and their encounters with vertebrate predators, surely the selective agent for these facial patterns, occur when the monkey or bird tears open a shelter to peer inside. It is greeted by a vertebrate face staring up from the dark depths of the nest. The would-be predator flees from the potential threat driven by an embedded (hard-wired) genetic program to flee and not become prey itself (see the species account for *Xylophanes chiron*, #51). Go ahead, stare at that face and convince yourself that those are just random color patterns and not really a face with glaring eyes that are focused directly on you, wanting to make lunch out of you. In the same vein, the very striking false eyes on skipper pupae are also at the front end, "looking" forward, the very end that is first encountered when tearing into a nest.

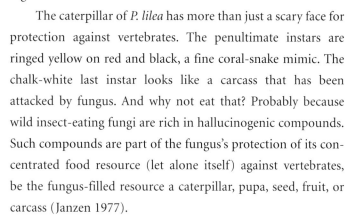

23

The caterpillar of *P. lilea* has more than just a scary face for protection against vertebrates. The penultimate instars are ringed yellow on red and black, a fine coral-snake mimic. The chalk-white last instar looks like a carcass that has been attacked by fungus. And why not eat that? Probably because wild insect-eating fungi are rich in hallucinogenic compounds. Such compounds are part of the fungus's protection of its concentrated food resource (let alone itself) against vertebrates, be the fungus-filled resource a caterpillar, pupa, seed, fruit, or carcass (Janzen 1977).

CATERPILLAR VOUCHER: 03-SRNP-395; JCM
ADULT VOUCHER: 82-SRNP-683; JCM

23. *ROTHSCHILDIA TRILOBA* – SATURNIIDAE

While caterpillars of the slightly smaller *Rothschildia lebeau* can be found with relative ease by searching their handful of dry-forest food plants in the second month of the ACG rainy season (but hardly at all at other times of the year), the large, green countershaded caterpillars of *Rothschildia triloba* are much harder to find in their rain-forest and dry-forest ecosystems. This is because they feed on a much longer species list of lower-density food plants, and because they themselves occur at a much lower density throughout the year (though you would hardly know it by looking at records of adults collected at lights). *Rothschildia lebeau* also occurs in the ACG rain forest, as well as the other lowland rain forests of Costa Rica, but at an even lower density. The existence of these huge moths at very low density brings to mind the power of sociality through pheromones. Like snakes and *Morpho* butterflies, if *R. triloba* were the size of an ordinary small moth, we would hardly know of their existence. The density of adults is probably less than one per square kilometer. Imagine finding cryptic members of the opposite sex at that population density and in the black darkness of the night. With pheromones it is a breeze to follow a trail of wafting perfume; with visual methods it seems nearly impossible.

Rothschildia triloba caterpillars, just as those of the other two ACG *Rothschildia*, spin a dense, bag-like, pendant silk cocoon with a complex exit constructed at the top and a long silk extension firmly binding the cocoon to the twig. Cocoons of *R. triloba* are the sloppiest of the three congenerics, appearing to be dead, brown, and twisted leaves hanging off a stem. Their cocoons, as are those of the other two species, are spun down low in the relatively monkey-safe and large bird–safe zone of one or two meters above the ground, even if the caterpillar did its feeding tens of meters above in the canopy, which is where *R. triloba* caterpillars are normally found.

Adults of *Rothschildia* are often the first saturniid that the tourist really notices on the wall below the light facing the forest on their visit to a Costa Rican "jungle." The salad plate–sized wing expanse and the curious large, scale-free transparent "windows" in all four wings often draw a gasp and a search for the camera. Such images are often sent to the ACG staff as an e-mail attachment, with many questions. The clear areas in the wings give rise to the Costa Rican name of *cuatro ventanas* or *cuatro espejos*.

24

What are they? When you meet this moth hanging on the forest foliage in the daytime, their function becomes obvious. Light shining through them breaks up the characteristic (and very large) wing profile that is a certain "food" indicator to monkeys and birds. Viewed in direct sunlight, the wings add strongly to the adult's mimicry of a dry, fungus-filled rotting leaf. The great majority of moth species are small, and as such their various cryptic patterns disappear into the collage of leaves, twigs, bark, shadows, and sun flecks. Huge moths are conspicuous. Their survival depends on their mimicry of large, dead leaves, since crypsis is the mechanism that they employ to survive the daytime resting period.

CATERPILLAR VOUCHER: 04-SRNP-33568; JCM
ADULT VOUCHER: 00-SRNP-863; JCM

24. *LEPIDODES GALLOPAVO* – NOCTUIDAE

Lepidodes gallopavo is an exceptional caterpillar for inclusion in our gallery. It is a cryptic noctuid among an ocean of gaudy sphingids, saturniids, hesperiids, notodontids, and nymphalids, and a few gaudy noctuids. No false eyespots, no urticating spines, no bright warning colors. This caterpillar's goal in life is simply not to be seen during the long daylight hours when vertebrate predators are on the lookout. Once seen, it becomes lunch. Its cryptic defense is reflected not only in its colors but in its behavior. When handled, it does its best to behave like a piece of rotten wood. In the early instars, it is patterned green, clinging to the underside of a piece of leaf like a malignant lump of distorted and diseased plant tissue. In the older and hence larger instars, it walks onto the green leaf to feed only at night, perching during the day tightly pressed to a brown or multi-colored stem like a stray bit of rotten stem stuck there by fungal hyphae.

This resting site stands in striking contrast to its dry-forest congener, *Lepidodes limbulata,* which feeds on Malpighiaceae as well, but is colored in a suit of bright new-leaf green in all instars. All instars stay firmly perched on the undersides of the leaf blade whose color they match so well.

The caterpillar of *L. gallopavo* is a medium-large, dicot-eating beast of the rain forest. Hundreds of species in the ACG fit this description, each with a cryptic larva and the behavior to match. There are an amazingly large number of ways for evolution to create a caterpillar that looks like a dead leaf, a green leaf, a rotten twig, a diseased leaf, a petiole, or a twig fragment. The ACG inventory has been slow to find them. They often feed only at night and hide off the green leaf in the daytime, occur at very low density, and feed only on low-density new shoots. They grow very fast and may spend their entire caterpillar life in the crown of a tree. On top of it all, they may pupate in a thin, cryptic cocoon spun on a brown twig high in the canopy.

In contrast to an ephemeral caterpillar phase, the fruit-, sap-, flower-, carrion-, and fungus-feeding adults may live for many months while courting, migrating, and searching (or waiting) for a food plant in just the right developmental stage upon which to lay their eggs.

Both species of *Lepidodes* (known in earlier literature as *Baecula*) are parasitized by the same species of tachinid fly, *Leschenaultia* sp. 13. This fly parasitizes only these two species of caterpillars of the many thousands of similar-sized caterpillar species available, even though they live in entirely different climates. *Lepidodes gallopavo* is a rain-forest species, and *L. limbulata* a dry-forest species, with the two being sympatric at the rain-forest/dry-forest interface. The parasitoid fly unambiguously ranges from the driest dry forest to deep into the rain forest and even up to the lower limits of the cloud forest on Volcan Cacao. The fly finds a *Lepidodes* caterpillar and glues a few of its tiny "microtype" eggs firmly to the leaf blades near the caterpillar. As the caterpillar continues to feed, it swallows an egg whole, which then hatches in the caterpillar gut. The tiny, first-instar fly maggot then hides somewhere in the caterpillar where the caterpillar defenses cannot get to it (see Ichiki and Shima 2003). When the caterpillar is full-sized and prepupal, about the time it is beginning to spin its tough silk cocoon, the fly maggot then turns on its development and rapidly consumes the muscle, fat, and other nutrient-rich goodies in the caterpillar. The maggot next pokes through the cuticular body wall of the host cadaver to emerge. Finally, it drops to the soil below where it makes its own fragile pupa inside a tough puparium made of its old larval cuticle.

CATERPILLAR VOUCHER: 04-SRNP-35619; JCM
ADULT VOUCHER: 04-SRNP-35563; JCM

25. *EUSELASIA EUBULE* – RIODINIDAE

This is one of the so-called head-to-toe caterpillars. *Euselasia eubule* does everything but pupate as a group. The eggs, laid in a cluster, hatch on the same day (about six days after oviposition) and the caterpillars then feed side by side throughout their five instars. In the two cases of our rearing *E. ebule,* this group formation occurred on *Eugenia valerii* (Myrtaceae). When caterpillars move to a new leaf or hiding place, they march off in tight formation, with each individual placing its head tightly nestled against the rear of the caterpillar ahead. If you mischievously tease them apart, they quickly re-form into their tight formation and move ahead. When they reach a resting place, they make a tight circular patch of side-by-side caterpillars. Of course, accidents happen, and while they may start out as a group of as many as thirty siblings in one place, through the trauma of wind, predator attacks, and perhaps even willfulness of individual caterpillars, it is commonplace for the initial large group to get fractured into smaller groups of five to ten caterpillars. When it comes time to pupate, each caterpillar will go off onto nearby leaves to spin its own silk pad and anchor the naked pupa to it. The adult ecloses nine to ten days later.

The males emerge one day after the females in most species of Riodinidae. This suggests an internal physiological calendar that counts days (actually degree-days, a physiological clock based on temperature above a developmental threshold). Such a calendar is presumably a mechanism to minimize the chance that the males will mate with one of their sisters who emerges just a few centimeters away. The two clutches of *E. ebule* that we have reared, however, suggest that the males and females of this species eclose on the same day. Perhaps, because *E. ebule* is a rare species of riodinid, it just might be that in such a very low-density species, mating with someone, even your sibling, is better than having no mate at all.

The gregarious behavior of the caterpillars of many species (if not all) of *Euselasia* and a number of other species of riodinids begs the question of why caterpillars live in a group. Many gregarious caterpillars are highly aposematic, leading to the suggestion that by staying together, they make a larger, therefore more visible, warning signal with higher impact. This might be especially true for young instars, which are quite small and may attract a visually orienting predator just by their movement. However, *E. ebule* and various other species of gregarious ACG riodinids are not particularly aposematic. Then again, they do resemble the strongly urticating/stinging caterpillars of hemileucine saturniids. Many of these—*Hylesia, Lonomia, Paradirphia, Pseudodirphia, Dirphia*—are gregarious in their first three instars (and sometimes in later instars) and have the same movement and feeding behaviors as do *E. ebule*. Curiously, the hemileucines have subtle aposematic warnings, not the extreme reds and yellows that often flag aposematic insects. At a distance they appear to be cryptic, avoiding being found by squirrel cuckoos, trogons, and other birds that readily prey on urticating caterpillars, but when seen up close they signal to the other predators that they are painful. The somewhat cryptic gregarious *E. ebule* caterpillars seem to be mimicking the early instars of these gregarious hemileucines.

CATERPILLAR VOUCHER: 03-SRNP-3933; DHJ
ADULT VOUCHER: 03-SRNP-3935; JCM

26. *HYLESIA LINEATA* – SATURNIIDAE

The highly urticating and gregarious caterpillars of *Hylesia lineata* are the champion food-plant generalists of the ACG dry forest (Janzen 2003), though with additional decades of rearing records to come it might be found that *Hypercompe icasia* and *Hypercompe albescens* (Arctiidae) will run a close second. We began the caterpillar inventory in 1978, and in 1979 there was an enormous population outbreak of *H. lineata* caterpillars (Janzen 1984b). It has not happened again. They have been omnipresent at moderately low density ever since. We have no concrete explanations for what led to the peak numbers, but it was probably a fortuitous joining of just the right kind of weather (the beginning of the rainy season) combined with a moderately high density of egg-laying females at the end of the previous rainy season. But it was clear what stopped it. The last half of the 1979 rainy season began with last-instar *H. lineata* on practically every woody plant, defoliating hundreds of trees of many dozens of species. It ended with virus-killed larvae hanging everywhere from the foliage at densities that must have averaged at least one per square meter. In other words, in the space of one generation, the population went from extraordinarily high density to being almost eliminated, not from defoliating many food plants and not from predators and parasitoids, but from a lowly virus that has never been identified. The disease was probably caused by a

26

species of nuclear polyhedrosis virus that persists in the population at a very low density.

A unique feature in the life cycle of *H. lineata* is that it is the only ACG dry-forest butterfly or moth that is known to pass the long dry season as a cluster of dormant eggs, rather than as a dormant pupa or prepupa, sexually dormant adult, or a migrant out of the dry forest. The latter three strategies are used by essentially all other species. In nonoutbreak years the female lays all her eggs (in a single mass glued to a twig) on one of about ten species of trees. Favorites are *Annona purpurea* (Annonaceae) and *Casearia nitida* (Flacourtiaceae). As the ball of eggs takes form, she wipes her abdomen over it in such a way that the abdomen hairs come off and form a tight, beige felt cover that is riddled with short, barbed hairs. These needles are covered with a highly irritating yet unstudied chemical, which undoubtedly protects the quite visible and very evident egg mass from being eaten by birds, monkeys, and rodents. When the first rains and hence the first cool days of the rainy season arrive, the eggs hatch, and for a few days the first instars forage together feeding on a leaf and then returning to the felt-covered mass. The caterpillars then begin to stay on the leaves full time, individuals feeding side by side. Within a few weeks of exposed feeding, the group begins to silk together several leaves into a nest that it occupies in the daytime and leaves at night to forage. When they have defoliated their plant, they march off in procession in search of another food plant.

In the image we show here, they were marching in a circle around the tire on a car, a loop from which they eventually managed to escape. At the moment of the photo, they were disturbed by Janzen's voice, some tonality of which probably resembled a close-flying parasitoid tachinid fly. They are heavily parasitized by several species of tachinids, and one of their defenses, upon hearing the fly, is to rear up and thrash at the air. From the viewpoint of the individual caterpillar, this

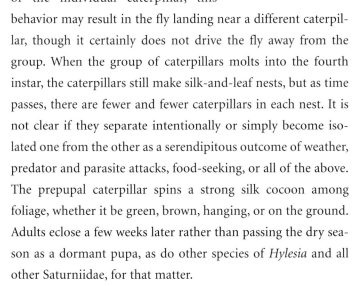

behavior may result in the fly landing near a different caterpillar, though it certainly does not drive the fly away from the group. When the group of caterpillars molts into the fourth instar, the caterpillars still make silk-and-leaf nests, but as time passes, there are fewer and fewer caterpillars in each nest. It is not clear if they separate intentionally or simply become isolated one from the other as a serendipitous outcome of weather, predator and parasite attacks, food-seeking, or all of the above. The prepupal caterpillar spins a strong silk cocoon among foliage, whether it be green, brown, hanging, or on the ground. Adults eclose a few weeks later rather than passing the dry season as a dormant pupa, as do other species of *Hylesia* and all other Saturniidae, for that matter.

CATERPILLAR VOUCHER: 85-SRNP-312; DHJ
ADULT VOUCHER: 84-SRNP-1506; JCM

27. *PHOBETRON HIPPARCHIA* – LIMACODIDAE

The caterpillar of *Phobetron hipparchia* does not look like anything to be wary of, much less a caterpillar, especially an urticating limacodid caterpillar. Perched on the upper surface of a leaf, its usual habit and habitat, it resembles a piece of trash—irregular, bumpy, torn, dead. It comes in about every color you expect from death—black, gray, beige, brown, rust, split pea, and grungy yellow—all the colors of fungus-rotted leaves. Sometimes it is all one color, sometimes a mix. The gait, if you can dignify crawling with hardly more than bumps as feet as having a gait, flows with almost imperceptible motion, "millimetering" forward. It eschews jerky actions, bumps, stride, or pace, and offers nothing to suggest that it is alive. Some patterns seen in this caterpillar can also be thought to look like a newly molted "skin" of a large insect or spider, or a crumpled mushroom. But if you pick it up, you quickly feel a sharp stinging sensation from the urticating spines that cover the entire dorsum of the body and project in all directions. In this sense *P. hipparchia* employs the tactic of nondescript camouflage for the sake of being a generalist feeder to what may be its physiological limit. Out of 136 rearing records, we have documented sixty-five species of plants it consumes, in about fifty families. This level of polyphagy ranks it alongside *Hypercompe icasia* and *Hypercompe albescens* (Arctiidae), *Hylesia lineata* (#26) and *Automeris zugana* (#3)

(Saturniidae), and *Spodoptera latifascia* (Noctuidae) as the all-time champions of generalist feeders. Even at this extreme, however, *P. hipparchia* is a caterpillar of woody broadleaf plants—no grasses, no herbs.

The eggs are laid in batches of many tens, tightly packed together in lines. The early instars quickly wander off onto different species of plants. Throughout its slow growth, a single individual may feed on many species of plant. However, if confined to just one food-plant species in a rearing bag, it completes its development quite normally. Not surprisingly, in view of its extreme polyphagy, it extends from the driest and most seasonal parts of the ACG to the deepest rain forest, from strongly insolated early secondary succession on the edges of fields and roads to the shady and stable trees of old-growth canopy and understory. But, as is the case with many species of lowland Limacodidae, it does not extend up into the cold, wet climate of the cloud forest.

Phobetron hipparchia seems to have no specialist parasitoids. It is parasitized by *Systrophus* bombyliid flies and *Austrophorocera* tachinid flies, species that utilize other hosts as well.

CATERPILLAR VOUCHER: 04-SRNP-15367; JCM
ADULT VOUCHER: 04-SRNP-6486; JCM

28. *MIMOIDES BRANCHUS* – PAPILIONIDAE

Mimoides branchus is one of those caterpillars that you definitely remember once you meet it, if you ever do. They are very rare, yet almost everywhere, from lower cloud-forest margins into Santa Rosa dry forest and very wet rain forest on the Caribbean side. Always sitting on the top side of a broad Annonaceae leaf (*Annona reticulata*, *A. holosericea*, and *A. purpurea* in the dry forest, and at least *Rollinia membranacea* in the rain forest), its appearance is very similar to that of *Parides* or *Battus* (Papilionidae). They are all purplish black with a white saddle and light tubercles. They are models and mimics to a foraging bird as well. This is more than coincidence. *Parides* and *Battus* are believed to be stuffed with highly toxic aristolochic acid from their *Aristolochia* food plants, and all reasoning leads to the conclusion that *M. branchus* is doing exactly what its generic name suggests. Whether it resembles a toxic caterpillar species but is benign (Batesian mimic), or is itself one of several look-alike species of toxic caterpillars (Mullerian mimic), is moot. It is quite striking that the *Protographium* papilionid caterpillars, which also feed on the upper sides of these same species of *Annona* in ACG dry forest, appear as expected—green with light black and yellow markings to nearly black ostentatious patterns, an appearance that signals it too should not be picked off by foliage-gleaning birds. This suggests that the caterpillars have acquired some noxious material from their food plant, and if *Protographium* can do this, then *M. branchus* may as well. This kind of puzzle—allelochemical protection—can only be verified with careful, laborious, and rather brutal feeding experiments with hand-reared adults and nestling birds.

Whatever the case with the caterpillar's toxicity, the generic name, *Mimoides,* is actually based on the appearance of the adults. *Mimoides branchus* used to be placed in the genus *Eurytides* along with its close ACG relatives *Protographium epidaus* and *P. philolaus,* which, with their long tails and black and white stripes, do not look the slightest bit like *M. branchus.* Adult *M. branchus* are exact mimics of adult *Parides* and even fly as they do.

When *M. branchus* was split out of *Eurytides, Mimoides euryleon,* which inhabits the rain forest to lower cloud forest, was also moved. Caterpillars of *M. euryleon* also eat *Rollinia membranacea* leaves and are suitable subjects for the same questions about toxicity, exhibiting a brilliant yellow-and-blue-striped caterpillar perched on the top of the leaves.

Mimoides branchus produces a striking, green, fat pupa (chrysalis) that, like its former congeners from the genus *Eurytides,* characteristically becomes dormant for many months to nearly a year. This caterpillar is parasitized only by tachinid flies in the genus *Lespesia.* All but two tachinid records are a highly host-specific undescribed species of fly that occurs in dry forest, rain forest, and up to the lower edge of cloud forest. The *Lespesia* is a host specialist, attacking only *M. branchus.* It has been reared from caterpillars on all of the cater-

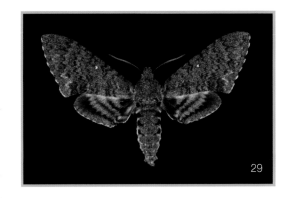

29

pillar's food plants, so it likely searches using caterpillar cues rather than any specific food-plant cues. The fly maggots display the outstanding behavior of remaining dormant as very young instars in the dormant pupa until the last few weeks of pupal development. They then quickly mobilize their development and eat the pupa. The parasitoid larvae break out of the host and drop to the ground to pupate. Adult flies eclose a few weeks later at exactly the correct time to begin the process of laying eggs on the next generation of *M. branchus* caterpillars.

CATERPILLAR VOUCHER: 04-SRNP-ACGFIELD; JCM
ADULT VOUCHER: 03-SRNP-15177; JCM

29. *MANDUCA MUSCOSA* – SPHINGIDAE

Among the fifteen species of ACG *Manduca, Manduca muscosa* is perhaps the strangest, though not the rarest. Whereas most species usually feed on the leaves of perennial vines, shrubs, saplings, and trees, *M. muscosa* has clearly gone to ground level and into the trashy world of herbaceous composites (Asteraceae, the dandelion family, which used to be called Compositae) and onto a single introduced species of Verbenaceae, *Lantana camara.* This means that as succession pushes the ACG dry forest back into tall old-growth status, it is one of the species that will become rare. It will then be surviving on the few ruderal Asteraceae and *Lantana* growing on permanently disturbed sites such as large ravines and river banks, landslide-prone habitats, and (very rarely) in a gap left by falling trees. Today, its food plants occur by the millions along roadsides, field edges, regenerating trashy pastures, gardens, and other insolated microhabitats created by humanity. During the first four months of the rainy season, it is almost guaranteed that a *M. muscosa* caterpillar can be found at any time on the weedy perennial *Verbesina gigantea*, which grows one to three meters tall along the roadsides and around house sites of the ACG's administrative area.

The very bumpy and whitish surface of the cuticle serves well to render *M. muscosa* caterpillars cryptic against the rugose, hairy, bumpy, sandpapery—anything but slick plastic green—leaves and twigs of their asteraceous hosts. In fact, it is close to a waste of time to search for them in the daytime. It is much more efficient to search the low roadside vegetation with a strong flashlight at night. The waxy cuticle covering the caterpillar, common to all caterpillars, reflects the beam of the flashlight much more brilliantly than does the foliage, making the caterpillar stand out like a green-white bicycle reflector among the less-reflective leaves. In fact, easily 90 percent of the *M. muscosa* caterpillars in the inventory database were found by searching at night. Night searching also tends to yield *Manduca rustica* (#30).

Manduca muscosa appears to be an exclusively dry-forest sphingid in Costa Rica, yet the pupae in captivity have not as yet demonstrated proclivity for prolonged dormancy. Ninety-five days has been the longest duration for pupal development. There are as many as three generations in a rainy season, but we are forced to conclude that in the late rainy season, the pupae must become dormant in their underground chamber and wait out the six-month dry season. Adults emerge with the first rains. It is also possible that the adults migrate to the moist foothills of the volcanoes and pass through dry-season generations there before flying back into the core dry forest of the ACG in mid- to late May with the first rains.

There exists an adult look-alike, *Manduca opima,* but this is a moth of the rain-forested uplands of central Costa Rica. It has never been found in the ACG, and its caterpillar is unknown.

CATERPILLAR VOUCHER: 81-SRNP-163.2; DHJ
ADULT VOUCHER: 81-SRNP-163.1; JCM

30. *MANDUCA RUSTICA* – SPHINGIDAE

The widest food-plant range of any species of sphingid in the ACG (and probably, for that matter, in Costa Rica if not all of Central America) is exhibited by *Manduca rustica* caterpillars. Or, more accurately, the female of this species oviposits on more plant species belonging to the greatest number of families than does any other sphingid. The caterpillars simply stay home, feeding on the foliage their mother selected, rather than "wandering" as do some instars of Saturniidae and Arctiidae that have long food-plant lists (Janzen 2003). The food-plant list for *M. rustica,* though long, is still restricted to just a small proportion of the many hundreds that are available—some thirty-five species to date among the dry-forest Bignoniaceae, Verbenaceae, Sterculiaceae, Lamiaceae, Tiliaceae, and even a single Rubiaceae *(Genipa americana).* The latter case is clearly a "lost" caterpillar or a consequence of confused oviposition, since of the many thousands of sphingids found on *G. americana,* this was the only individual of any species of *Manduca.* Nonetheless, it did feed well, pupated, and an adult eclosed.

Caterpillars of *M. rustica* are the largest and heaviest of all

ACG *Manduca,* and frankly, that is sometimes the easiest way to tell them from some of the look-alike but smaller morphs of *Manduca dilucida* (which may also feed on *Tabebuia ochracea,* a bignoniaceous tree used by *M. rustica*). As is the case with many other ACG dry-forest sphingid cater- pillars, *M. rustica* has a striking poly- morphism. The morph that we show is green with white and maroon lateral slashes, but there is a deep black and maroon morph also displayed by *M. dilucida, M. lanuginosa, M. lefeburii,* and *M. occulta,* but not by *M. florestan, M. sexta, M. barnesi, M. pellenia,* and *M. albiplaga.* For the human caterpillar

30

hunter, this polymorphism is extremely effective, unless con- sciously alerted to it. The hunter tends to discover one or the other of the two color morphs perched on a given individual vine, but not both. In this context, among the thirty-eight last- instar *M. rustica* brought to the nestlings by free-foraging *Trogon melanocephalus* and *Trogon elegans* (Trogonidae) over the years in the ACG dry forest, thirty-seven have been the green morph. We have no independent estimates of the relative abundance of the two caterpillar color morphs in nature, however. As is the case with other sphingids, searching at night is a very effective way of finding *M. rustica* when it is feeding on a variety of plants.

Adults of *M. rustica* migrate out of the ACG dry forest into rain forest (and even the lower margins of the cloud forest) at the end of the first generation of the rainy season (late July, early August). This migration is why they are common at lights placed in passes through the central Costa Rican mountains that sepa- rate the Pacific (often dry) side from the Atlantic (rain forest) side. Only a very few individuals stay behind and lay eggs, their caterpillars then being found in the second half of the rainy season, from September to December. But the migrating adults clearly fly much far- ther than just the other side of Costa Rica. *Manduca rustica* is the only species of sphingid to have made it to the Galápagos Islands, where the sub- species *M. rustica galapagensis* is endemic. Also, *M. rustica* occurs throughout the Caribbean islands, probably as both island- hopping adults and resident populations. The species occasion- ally occurs in the United States and may even pass through a generation in Florida and Texas, ranging to the south as far as Argentina.

CATERPILLAR VOUCHER: 85-SRNP-342; DHJ
ADULT VOUCHER: 90-SRNP-2050; JCM

31. *COLAX APULUS* – NOTODONTIDAE

This is the largest notodontid in the ACG dry forest. *Colax apu- lus* was a mystery for a long time. Only the occasional adult appeared at the lights. This engagement was sufficiently rare that it seemed possible that it was a wanderer from wetter forests on the volcanoes at the eastern margin of the lowland dry forest. Fifteen years after beginning the ACG inventory, in 1993, the *gusaneros* carefully inspected the only known surviving large tree of *Pterocarpus michelianus* (Fabaceae) in the ACG lowlands. It stands over the dry, rocky ford where the lowland road crosses the Rio Calera, just a few hundred meters inland from the coastal mangroves. The first caterpillar of *C. apulus* that they found was parasitized by a small ichneumonid that attacks a respectable list of Notodontidae and Noctuidae. Fortunately, other caterpillars from this lone tree of *P. michelianus* produced adult moths and the mystery of their whereabouts was solved. It appears that *P. michelianus* is the sole food plant of *C. apulus* in the ACG dry forest. This tree was nearly extinguished from the ACG dry forest by settlers and ranchers. The question remains unanswered as to why they sought it out to cut it down, as it apparently grows well only in the vicinity of ravines and streams (waterless drainages in the dry season). This is a classic case of a rare tree feeding a rare moth. We have found only eleven caterpillars to date. The trees have bright yellow flowers in the middle of the dry season, providing a beacon for the *gusaneros* to locate previously undetected trees and collect more caterpillars of this species during the rainy season, the time when caterpillars are present.

Caterpillars of *C. apulus,* with their distinctively black dotted heads and sparse black stubble, are usually an ordinary leaf green with a slender white-yellow lateral line and red highlights, presumably an up-close mimic of *Automeris* and *Periphoba*

31

warning colors. As such, they are ordinary large notodontid caterpillars. A few of them, however, are the bright yellow-orange to almost red morph that we show. As with many other species of caterpillars, it is generally believed that the presence of two or three morphs of this nature, a green one and a yellow one being the most common, with the third being some kind of pink-orange, red, or purple, are selected for by the tendency of predators to form search images based on what they find first. Thus, natural selection favors the color morph not found initially. The expression of a cryptic and noncryptic color polymorphism occurs in the ACG among various primarily cryptic Noctuidae, Sphingidae, Saturniidae, Notodontidae, and Geometridae. Predictably, the polymorphism is absent from what appear to be truly aposematic caterpillars, presumably for the obvious reason that they avoid predators in a quite different manner—via their warning colors.

CATERPILLAR VOUCHER: 93-SRNP-4155; DHJ
ADULT VOUCHER: 00-SRNP-19038; JCM

32. *CRINODES BESCKEI* – NOTODONTIDAE

Crinodes besckei has to be ranked at the top of the list in the category of "most common big caterpillar in early secondary succession ACG dry forest." In many years these large green, brown, pink, or some combination thereof, and highly patterned caterpillars festoon their common food-plant vine, *Gouania polygama* (Rhamnaceae), to such a degree that there are almost no leaves left. About the middle of June, three or four weeks after the rains begin, it seems like every tourist brings one in to identify. Although it is easy to label these variable- and leafy-colored large caterpillars as "cryptic" in a photograph, in nature they are really very obvious because their food-plant vine bears a relatively small number of leaves quite far apart and because when not feeding, the caterpillar perches on a naked vine stem, curled back into a "C." One presumes that this may look like a torn or partly eaten leaf, but in fact it is quite evident, at least to the human searcher. When the vine is touched, these large caterpillars literally let go and drop off, which is presumably a viable escape method from monkeys and birds. If one falls onto open ground from a height of more than about three meters, however, it lands with a burst much like a water balloon (see the species account for *Schausiella santarosensis* [#40] for a more favorable outcome to the "plopping" technique).

In early succession along field edges and roadsides, where *G. polygama* grows in profusion, almost all the ACG dry-forest *Crinodes* encountered are *C. besckei*. They are notable for their diagnostic white lateral line over the first three abdominal prolegs. Scattered in among the *C. besckei* will be a few *Crinodes ritsemae*. They are the same size but lack the white lateral line. These are usually a dark, rotten-leaf color, presumably being more cryptic in the more shaded, heavily forested

32

habitats where they often constitute almost the entire array of *Crinodes* caterpillars. The adults of these two species are easily distinguished, since *C. ritsemae* has a false eyespot (or fungal spot mimic, if you like) in the middle of the forewing. This trait is lacking in *C. besckei*. They both also occur, but very rarely, in ACG rain forest, where they feed on *Gouania polygama* and another rain-forest *Gouania,* along with the much larger *Crinodes striolata,* whose caterpillar resembles a gigantic *C. ritsemae.* Typically, *C. striolata* has several lateral white spots on the first several abdominal segments, rather than just one. It occurs at very low density, perhaps as few as one per hectare.

The nearly epizootic abundance of *C. besckei* caterpillars in many years in much early successional vegetation of the ACG dry forest is a puzzle. Many species of birds as well as the white-faced capuchin monkeys, *Cebus capucinus,* do not eat them, but squirrel cuckoos, *Piaya cayana,* do bring them to their nestlings. Thus, *C. besckei* is not entirely free of predation by vertebrates. However, out of over 3,000 large caterpillars brought to *Trogon* nestlings, only eight were *Crinodes.* This suggests that trogons are not willing to forage in low, brushy, secondary successional vegetation, or that they do not like to eat *Crinodes,* or both.

At the end of the first generation, after the rains begin, there are an enormous number of *Crinodes* pupae in the litter. Adults eclose from these pupa about the period of peak rainfall in the second rainy season in September, presumably to have a second generation. This second generation is, however, trivial in terms of numbers of caterpillars on the *G. polygama* plants. One can only conclude that it is the combination of occasional acts of predation on caterpillars and pupae, and perhaps pupae not very resistant to the rigors of the long dry season, that result in *Crinodes* being so terribly abundant in the early rainy season yet not completely defoliating their food plants throughout the remainder of the year.

There is only one known species of specialist parasitoid, *Winthemia* sp. 23, but this tachinid fly occurs at a very low frequency. There are only six rearing records out of over 600 for the two species of dry-forest *Crinodes* combined. They are susceptible to a generalist tachinid, *Patelloa xanthura*, with seven rearing records.

CATERPILLAR VOUCHER: 04-SRNP-ACGFIELD; JCM
ADULT VOUCHER: 81-SRNP-35; JCM

33. *DYSCOPHELLUS* BURNS01 – HESPERIIDAE

Caterpillars of *Dyscophellus* BURNS01 are the most widespread of the ACG *Dyscophellus*, which are all rain-forest caterpillars. The larvae are one of two species that are the easiest to find, the other species being the also abundant look-alike, *Dyscophellus phraxanor*. The food-plant list for *D.* BURNS01 caterpillars consists of four ACG species of *Croton* (Euphorbiaceae): *C. shiedeanus* (448 records), *C. megistocarpus* (53 records), *C. bill-*

bergianus (one record), and *C.* "unknown-15002" (three records). There is no problem with confusing *D.* BURNS01 with its caterpillar look-alike, *D. phraxanor,* since *D. phraxanor* feeds only on Myristicaceae: *Virola guatemalensis, V. koschnyi, V. sebifera,* and *Otoba novograntensis.*

An extreme look-alike to *D.* BURNS01, both as an adult and a caterpillar, is *Dyscophellus porcius.* The latter species has been encountered only one time in the ACG, in deep rain forest, and interestingly enough it was feeding on *Croton* 15002. There is no photograph of the *D. porcius* caterpillar, but it was described as looking like *D.* BURNS01. The identity of the *D. porcius* caterpillar will remain unknown until we find where it really lives, probably in yet lower-elevation rain forest than generally covers the ACG. Whereas *D.* BURNS01 appears to be only known from the ACG, it is possible that there are other specimens in other collections, likely hiding under the name *D. porcius,* and ranging from Costa Rica to northern South America. The capitalized name is an interim nonscientific name, used as a place-holder until it has been described.

In addition to being common and relatively easy to find, *D.* BURNS01 is exceptional among large rain-forest hesperiid caterpillars in being attacked by a frequently reared, host-specific species of ichneumonid wasp, *Hyposoter* PRO-3. This small wasp has never been reared from any other species of caterpillar (out of over 230,000 caterpillars collected and reared). The wasp oviposits in the second and third instars (and maybe the first) and the single wasp larva then mummifies the second (usually) or third (more rarely) host instar. The wasp spins its cocoon inside the mummy. The adult wasp emerges six to twelve days later. About 20 percent of all *D.* BURNS01 caterpillars found in the wild are attacked by this parasitoid. The percent killed in nature is yet higher since 20 percent of the wild-caught caterpillars were penultimate or last instars, and therefore could not have contained the wasp. If we eliminate these older caterpillars from the sample, the age-class specific percent mortality due to this wasp rises to 26 percent, which is close to, if not actually, establishing an ACG-wide record high regarding the percentage of attacks by an ichneumonid wasp.

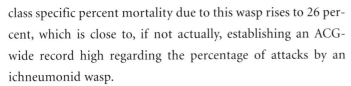

34

CATERPILLAR VOUCHER: 04-SRNP-3017; JCM
ADULT VOUCHER: 02-SRNP-33865; JCM

34. *CHIOIDES CATILLUS* – HESPERIIDAE

For years, the face-on view of *Chioides catillus* has been the screen saver on Janzen's slide-show talk to explain the ACG at fundraiser events. Audience members can stare at it for many long minutes and never be able to convince themselves that it really is not a face and those are really not eyes. Close up it looks like something an eleventh-century warrior would paint on his face mask before going into battle. The real eyes are nothing more than a few light-gathering stemmata low down on the sides of the head, just above the base of the mandibles. False eyes as portrayed here are very abundant among the many ACG species of medium- to large-sized pyrgine hesperiid caterpillars.

However, these eyes are usually a white, yellow, red, or orange against a dark background, and seem to glow at the viewer out of the dark inner recesses of the rolled leaf in which the caterpillar is hidden. The dark head disappears against the dark background, leaving only the eyes as the point of attention. In what is basically a reverse of colors, *C. catillus* has obviously evolved its eyespots independently of the other pyrgines, going for black against a light background. It is tempting to conclude that this says something about the sunlight conditions surrounding the leaf nests of *C. catillus*, which certainly are bright and sunny, because it feeds on *Rhynchosia* and other fabaceous vines that sprawl over early successional vegetation in full sun. In this context, though, it is very striking that *Urbanus, Epargyreus,* and *Proteides,* all being skippers closely related to *Chioides* and living in the same sunny habitat, have dark heads with light-colored false eyes, as does *Chioides zilpa,* a close relative.

The adult of *C. catillus* is the longest-tailed of the long-tailed ACG skippers, along with its look-alike *C. zilpa,* which has a slightly different white pattern on the underside of the hind wings. What is the real function of these long, trailing extensions of the hind wings? The commonplace arm-waving reply, which has long been among the myths of entomology, is that they are "deflectors" of striking birds, working on the basis that they attract the attention of the predator and, in essence, become sacrificial body parts. We are not convinced that this is a viable hypothesis, but it is all we have at the moment. These tails are apparently independently evolved in a number of groups of pyrgine Hesperiidae (e.g., *Polythrix, Typhedanus, Urbanus*), and have not evolved in either Pyrrhopyginae or Hesperiinae, though there are several species of large Hesperiinae with nubbins on the hind wings that would not take much natural selection to become long tails. Such tails are also an entirely New World phenomenon, not having evolved in any Old World hesperiid.

CATERPILLAR VOUCHER: 04-SRNP-55350; JCM
ADULT VOUCHER: 04-SRNP-35177; JCM

35. *NAROPE* JANZEN01 – NYMPHALIDAE

Narope JANZEN01, and in fact the other species of Costa Rican *Narope,* if indeed there are two, is arguably among the very rarest of Costa Rican nymphalid butterflies, at least in collections. It is also about the most nondescript brown adult among all the butterflies and moths. The males and females are very different in appearance, and we have not yet achieved rearing a male, which is why we show an image of a female and why we cannot yet offer a scientific name for the caterpillar in the image. We have encountered only a single free-flying male, perched

35

during the day on the ceiling of a restaurant. They apparently do not come to bait traps, and certainly not to flowers. Flying at dusk or even in the dark, they are extremely difficult to encounter even in places where you know they occur.

However, diligent search of ACG dry-forest bamboos has located the caterpillars. They are so cryptic that one wonders if a bird ever will achieve the same. The highly ornate head and general body shape certainly suggests that they are correctly placed in the Brassolinae. It is evident that there was extreme selection at some time to strongly resemble slender brown stems of the very small shrubby dry-forest bamboos no more than two or three meters tall, such as *Guadua paniculata,* the only known ACG food plant. The short, stubby pupa looks very much like a brown curved leaf off a bamboo stem. The bottom line is that we do not have much more information about this truly poorly known group of butterflies. We don't even have a species name for this reared bunch of caterpillars as they occur in Central America. At least the complex taxonomy of *Narope* has been addressed for South America (Casagrande 2002).

CATERPILLAR VOUCHER: 03-SRNP-14859; DHJ
ADULT VOUCHER: 03-SRNP-25161; JCM

36. *ARCHAEOPREPONA MEANDER* – NYMPHALIDAE

The caterpillar of *Archaeoprepona meander* is the *Archaeoprepona* that extends from the cold cloud forest on the top of the volcanoes (common) down into the lowest lowland rain forest (very rare), and even over to the edge of the dry forest on the lower slopes of Volcan Orosi (common) at Estacion Los Almendros. Strangely, though, it does not extend out into dry forest, largely the home of the common *Archaeoprepona demophoon* (#69), which feeds on a single species of Lauraceae, *Ocotea veraguensis*. This plant is, however, not used by *A. meander* as a food plant on Volcan Cacao or anywhere else, based on rearing 430 wild-caught caterpillars found feeding on *Licaria, Cinnamomum,* and others.

Archaeoprepona meander is one of the four species of *Archaeoprepona* that thoroughly occupy the ACG. They all start out in the same way, a single egg laid on the upper surface of one of their lauraceous food plants, except that *Archaeoprepona demophon* feeds on a small botanical garden of non-Lauraceae. The first-instar *A. meander* goes to the tip of a leaf and eats a bit of blade on both sides of the tip of the midrib. It perches on the bare midrib tip, looking like a bit of leaf trash. As the days go by and more and more of the leaf blade is consumed, the caterpillar ties tiny leaf fragments to the midrib with silk so that the small first and second instar is mingled among bits of dead and drying leaf trash colored just like it. Experienced collectors of butterfly caterpillars learn to watch for this signature damage of charaxine nymphalid caterpillars, and it would not be surprising to find that certain birds and even par-

36

asitoids learn this configuration as well. By the third instar, the caterpillar is large enough to look like an actual portion of dead leaf, as depicted by our image. The fourth and fifth instars leave their perch on top of the leaf and drape themselves along a twig or stem, looking like a dead, rolled leaf that has happened to lodge onto the twig. On closer inspection, however, striking false eyespots, one on each side of the upper shoulder of the thorax, become very obvious. The caterpillar, disturbed perhaps by a hunting bird or monkey, expands its thorax and pulls in its head to make its front end appear even more snakelike.

The undersides (ventral side) of the wings of *A. meander*, which is shown in our adult image because the blue and black upper sides of the species of *Archaeoprepona* are essentially identical, are notably different from the burnished silvery gray of the other three species. The ventral sides of *A. meander* wings are a combination of beige and brown that matches the beiges and browns of rain-forest tree bark better than the more silvery dry bark of many dry-forest trees in the dry season. This color match is particularly relevant because all of the adult *Archaeoprepona* are inveterate feeders on sap flows, often rich in fermentation microbes, in cracks in large tree trunks and broken branches high in the canopy. In contrast, the dorsal surface of the wings of the ACG *Archaeoprepona* presents an intense iridescent blue stripe on a black background, which says to the bird, "Don't bother." It may also say to any bird that does bother,

"Look at me," upon which the butterfly disappears abruptly when it lands on tree bark with its wings held shut over its back.

CATERPILLAR VOUCHER: 96-SRNP-6880; DHJ
ADULT VOUCHER: 98-SRNP-2857; JCM

37. *ERINNYIS CRAMERI* – SPHINGIDAE

If you found this *Erinnyis crameri* caterpillar in the ACG dry forest in the daytime, it was not eating leaves and it was not perched on the green parts of the plant. No doubt it was hugging a brown stem of *Stemmadenia obovata* (Apocynaceae), making it look like the stem was a little fatter than it should be. Often, it even manages to find the outer curve of a forked branch and insert itself exactly in that shallow angle (the armpit of the fork), becoming invisible for all practical purposes. In its first three instars, it perched on leaves in the daytime, but the fourth

37

and fifth instars are the caterpillars that become swellings on the brown bark of the food plant. At night, *E. crameri* caterpillars venture out into the green foliage and consume copious amounts of the soft watery leaves. It shares these leaves with *Callionima falcifera* sphingid caterpillars which, in ACG dry forest, eat primarily this plant and match the green color of the leaves in all instars.

When a last-instar *E. crameri* is molested, its *Erinnyis* nature becomes immediately evident. It pulls in its head and expands the thorax upward, displaying a single, huge red eye with a black center in the middle of its back, a glaring cyclops. When the molester disappears, the caterpillar relaxes and the folds of skin close the eye, once again turning the caterpillar into a swelling on the branch. An interesting strategic question is how long the caterpillar should hold the eye in place when molested. It should pop open when the potential predator encounters the caterpillar, but should it remain open, giving the predator an opportunity to examine the offending object from a safe distance, or should it snap shut, as though expecting that the predator has turned its attention to other things? In contrast to *Xylophanes* caterpillars hidden in the mottled dark and light of leafy *Psychotria* crowns, *E. crameri* caterpillars are fully exposed on the stem well below the large *Stemmadenia* leaves, easily examined at a distance of several meters.

Even if the visual defenses fail, most likely *E. crameri* is well protected from vertebrate consumers. Although it is a large package of meat and fat, theoretically desirable to any carnivore, it is feeding on foliage liberally laced with the cardiac glycosides for which Apocynaceae are justly famous. These small, secondary compounds are vertebrate heart-stoppers, and are one of the active ingredients in emetics fed in gentle doses to mist-netted birds to get them to vomit up their most recent meal. This is, as someone commented, a powerful incentive to learn to not get caught in a mist net. Just because a caterpillar eats food rich in cardiac glycosides, it is not a given that it sequesters them. As a case in point, 112 of the 4,515 big insects brought by trogons to their nestlings were last-instar *Erinnyis: E. crameri, E. oenotrus, E. ello,* and *E. alope;* all feeding on extremely toxic plants. Yes, trogons are famous for eating what are believed to be quite toxic insects, and their dietary insects may well be toxic to some laboratory test animal, but it also may be that *Erinnyis* does not sequester the nasty chemicals that are in the plants it eats. Furthermore, the cardiac glycosides may not be nasty to it, given its lack of a vertebrate heart. Once the adult trogon has bashed the caterpillar enough to have knocked out most of its gut contents, the cigarette within the caterpillar, it may be hardly more than a mildly contaminated piece of meat and fat.

CATERPILLAR VOUCHER: 03-SRNP-13307; JCM

ADULT VOUCHER: 86-SRNP-209; JCM

38. *NYCERYX TACITA* – SPHINGIDAE

The caterpillar of *Nyceryx tacita* is highly cryptic and crawls in glaring contrast to its gaudy congener, *Nyceryx magna.* Both species feed on the same food plant, *Pentagonia donell-smithii* (Rubiaceae), in the same ACG rain-forest understory, and sometimes even on the same leaf. But whereas *N. magna* caterpillars have so far been found feeding only on *P. donell-smithii, N. tacita* also heavily uses two other species of rain-forest understory Rubiaceae: *Chimarrhis parvifolia* and an unidentified species of *Chimarrhis.*

The striking difference in appear-

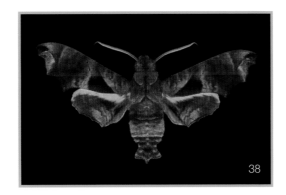

38

ance of these two very closely related caterpillars living in the same microhabitat provides a good platform to mention at least briefly "ecological fitting" (Janzen 1985a). It is commonplace to think of species with tight species-specific interspecific relationships, such as a caterpillar and its food plant, to have evolved or even coevolved into that juxtaposition. The fact is that these species probably evolved into separate species millions of years ago and under circumstances that could have been quite different from what is encountered today. Their color pattern and their oviposition behavior likely evolved long ago as well. They then spread into their respective species ranges, covering tens of degrees of latitude in the lowland tropics, ate what suited them (what their mother's senses say to lay eggs on), and endured the fitness consequences. As natural selection will have it, if they survive, then they survive by ecologically fitting into any given habitat at whatever density ensues and in the context of whatever else happens to be there. Then, if together long enough, the caterpillar and its food plants, as well as other compatriots, may coevolve, but it is not mandatory or even expected. It certainly is not to be expected that these two caterpillars are grossly different in appearance because each is today subject to a quite different yet sympatric selective regime for their particular color pattern.

Adults of *N. tacita* (and *N. magna*) essentially never come to lights, even when those lights are hung in the forest in which the caterpillars are common. There are almost no adults in collections, except those very few collected when visiting flowers. The moth is very poorly understood and might well occur throughout Costa Rican lowland rain forest, a silent, unseen member of the great community of visitors to, and pollinators of, white fragrant flowers that open at night both in the understory and the canopy of the forest. There is, however, no suggestion that either of these species occurs in ACG dry forest, or any Costa Rican dry forest, for that matter.

Just to emphasize the ecological similarity of these two species, both are parasitized at almost the same frequency by the small ichneumonid *Cryptophion espinozai*, a wasp found throughout the ACG lowlands. This wasp parasitizes the third instar of a select small subset of Sphingidae. Based on 380 rearings, it is the only species of parasitoid that either species of caterpillar experiences.

CATERPILLAR VOUCHER: 03-SRNP-6431; JCM
ADULT VOUCHER: 02-SRNP-19224; JCM

39. *ADELONEIVAIA JASON* – SATURNIIDAE

This is one of those very startling and beautiful caterpillars. You are staring somewhat blankly at the green wall of small leaflets on an *Inga* tree in the rain forest. Nothing particular catches your attention. Then your eyes focus on this big green package festooned with spikes down its back and you recognize the pattern of garish, broad white side-slashes. Totally harmless, this

very cryptic (until you see it) caterpillar manages to look ever so ferocious when discovered.

The big yellow eggs of *Adeloneivaia jason*, a medium- to large-sized moth, are laid singly on rain-forest *Inga* leaves and hatch in about six days. The first instar has the usual array of spiky scoli and hairs, a mimic of urticating hemileucine saturniid caterpillars and the appearance of all young ceratocampine caterpillars. With progressive molts it begins to take on the last-instar appearance by the third instar. After having grown for about six weeks, the very robust last instar takes on a pinkish cast, voids the bulk of its gut contents in a greasy, black, sticky mass, lets go, falls to the ground, walks a bit on the litter, burrows in, and pupates in the litter-soil interface. The adult ecloses a month later. The bright orange-yellow (yet quite cryptic) moth then lives about six to ten days, without feeding.

Adeloneivaia jason is omnipresent in ACG and Costa Rican rain forests, extending up to the lower cloud line on the volcanos as well. It never occurs at high population densities but it is steadily present (though in all fairness, this impression may well be due to the *gusaneros*' regular search of the many species of *Inga* for all species of caterpillars). There is an enigmatic, presumably isolated population of *A. jason* in the gorge of the Rio Pozo Salada in Sector Santa Rosa dry forest. The assumption is that it is feeding on *Inga vera*. This is the only dry-forest *Inga* in the ACG and occurs throughout the network of creeks, gullies, and seasonal rivers, as well as along the ever-flowing rivers coming down from the volcanos in the ACG dry forest, including the deep valleys of the Santa Elena Peninsula. Oddly, however, there is no trace of the *A. jason* population following the *I. vera* population throughout its dry-forest distribution, except in the river valley of the Rio Pozo Salada. Because of this, *A. jason* is not considered to be an ACG dry-forest moth, even though it does indeed occur in one place in the dry forest. The truth is that the population in the gorge of the Rio Pozo Salada was found by putting a light trap on the *Mirador* (lookout) at the end of the trail bordering the Quebrada Costa Rica (currently termed the "Los Patos Trail," though why is not clear, since there are no ducks in the area). The *Mirador* is about where the Quebrada Costa Rica plunges down into the upper canyon of the Rio Poza Salada. No caterpillars have been found in this area, but about

ten males came to that light. Because light trapping in some parts of the ACG dry forest has been very intense, but almost nonexistent in others, *A. jason* may indeed be found to have a true "dry-forest" distribution someday, albeit restricted to dry and wet watercourse margins where *I. vera* is common. Additionally, large trees of *I. vera* do occur in upland ACG old-growth dry forest, so the plant may once again have a broad, general dry-forest distribution and bring *A. jason* along with it.

CATERPILLAR VOUCHER: 03-SRNP-4766; JCM
ADULT VOUCHER: 97-SRNP-6255; JCM

40. *SCHAUSIELLA SANTAROSENSIS* – SATURNIIDAE

Schausiella santarosensis is a medium- to large-sized saturniid and stands out as the only largish moth that is endemic to the ACG dry forest. On a broader scale it is one of about a dozen species of Saturniidae that are endemic to Costa Rica. This very restricted distribution is particularly strange because its caterpillar's food plants, leaves in the crowns of *Hymenaea courbaril* trees twenty to thirty meters tall, range from southern Mexico well down into South America (or at least did before the Mesoamerican dry forest was devastated by cutting or burning during the past four centuries of clearing by European colonists). The pupa lies just one or two centimeters below the leaf litter. The moth ecloses in the last half of May, stimulated into development by the cool temperatures at the beginning of the rainy season. The moth does not feed and lives just five to eight days, during which time females glue their golden eggs singly to *H. courbaril* mature leaves in the evergreen canopy, ten to thirty meters above the ground.

Hymenaea courbaril is the sole food plant, though if there were other species of *Hymenaea* in the ACG, it might use them as well, since other members of *Schausiella* eat *Hymenaea* in South America (Lemaire 1988). The early instars are brick red with long thoracic scoli and transform to bright leaf green in the last two instars. About a month later, the full-sized caterpillar (ten to fifteen grams) voids its gut contents and simply lets go, falling with a plop on the forest floor ten to thirty meters below. A few minutes later it recovers its composure and marches off across the forest floor for a few meters and burrows below the leaves and upper soil horizon to pupate. Most of the pupae remain dormant for eleven months—through the remainder of the rainy season and through the six-month dry season. The cycle is repeated with the onset of the next year's rains. However, a few moths eclose after only one or two months of pupal dormancy and initiate a second generation within the long rainy season. This species ranges in abundance from simply present in some years to extremely common in others, such as in late June 2004 when it defoliated some of its huge host trees. It has no parasitoids, if we can assume that the rearing of many hundreds of wild-caught caterpillars represents a sufficient sample.

The name, *S. santarosensis,* was assigned to this species in 1982 in honor of the original Parque Nacional Santa Rosa (today, Sector Santa Rosa of the ACG) by the Frenchman Claude Lemaire, a recently deceased Saturniidae expert (see the foreword in Lemaire 2002). There are two other members of *Schausiella* in Costa Rica and eight in South America (Lemaire 1988). The genus was named in 1930 for William Schaus, a Neotropical moth taxonomist who collected extensively in Costa Rica shortly before World War I, and who described many hundreds of species of Costa Rican moths. Despite its large size and ease of capture by rearing or by light trapping at the beginning

of the rainy season, *S. santarosensis* escaped his collecting by living only in Costa Rica's northwest. At that time this area was only arduously and distantly accessible from the cultural, political, and scientific nexus of San Jose, the center of the country, and Schaus did not visit it.

CATERPILLAR VOUCHER: 04-SRNP-11679; JCM
ADULT VOUCHER: 02-SRNP-11397; JCM

41. *COPIOPTERYX SEMIRAMIS* – SATURNIIDAE

We did not find the caterpillar of *Copiopteryx semiramis* until quite late in our inventory of the saturniids of the ACG dry forest. The beautiful and exaggerated adults appeared occasionally at the lights, but no caterpillars were encountered through "normal" searching. Then one day at the end of the rainy season in 1983, after the water had stopped flowing in the seasonal river of the Quebrada Guapote, Janzen was walking over the bare rocks in the riverbed and noticed a cluster of large fecal pellets on the ground. They were directly below a healthy, young *Manilkara chicle* about seven meters tall, but he knew of no large caterpillar at that time that ate *M. chicle* leaves. (The chewing-gum brand Chiclets derives its name from the indigenous name for this tree in Guatemala—in Costa Rica it is called *nispero*.) So he asked Roberto Espinoza, today the resident botanist of the ACG, to shinny up the tree and see if he could find it. Roberto proceeded to perch on a convenient fork in the lower crown and search each and every branch. He found not a trace of the caterpillar, which was puzzling given the evidence on the ground. Befuddled, Janzen then shinnied (much more laboriously than Roberto had) up behind him. As he approached the fork where Roberto was sitting, there, a few centimeters from being squished, he saw a big green-and-white caterpillar happily munching on *nispero* leaves attached to a tiny twig. Roberto had climbed right over it. We now knew the food plant of *C. semiramis*. It was only a matter of time before females collected from the lights gave us eggs to grow the beautiful younger instars with their very different pattern. The third instar, which we show here, presumably looks like a defective and fungus-damaged leaf fragment.

The adults of *C. semiramis* are by far the smallest and lightest of the ACG arsenurine saturniids. This gives a clue as to the function of the long tails. When the moth is in flight, the tails do not simply trail behind, but rather spin in large, circular arcs. Certainly this makes the moth look huge, as large as a "normal" arsenurine, and is therefore exaggerated on an insectivorous bat's radar screen. It is possible, of course, that bats prey on moths as large as arsenurines, but it is possible they are not taken in full free flight as are smaller moths. In short, if there is natural selection to make a smaller arsenurine flying machine—less food eaten means you can develop on a lower-quality food, or

42

faster, or both—one way to do it without losing the protective advantage of being large is to have long, thin (energetically cheap) extensions on the wings, extensions that make you appear large. The wings themselves, as with all arsenurines, are simply large, dead-leaf mimics as the moth hangs in the forest canopy during the day, hiding from a foraging monkey or bird.

We have found only about ten wild *C. semiramis* caterpillars in the field, so their parasitoids are not understood. However, it is clear that this species, with its huge range from Mexico to South America, lives in both rain-forest and dry-forest ecosystems. It probably feeds on *Manilkara* and other Sapotaceae throughout its distribution.

CATERPILLAR VOUCHER: 04-SRNP-ACGFIELD; JCM
ADULT VOUCHER: 03-SRNP-12763; JCM

42. *ARSENURA BATESII* – SATURNIIDAE

The caterpillar of *Arsenura batesii* plays the "look-at-me" game in a totally different way from the brightly colored, ostentatious, and highly gregarious *Arsenura armida* (see species account #18). We show the antepenultimate (third) instar, equipped with long tentacles. These are lost at the molt into the final instar. The huge caterpillar of a last instar does its very best to look like a large, dead tweedy brown stick perched solitarily in the daytime on a small-diameter brown tree trunk one to three meters above the ground. At night it walks out into the foliage to eat various entire *Guazuma ulmifolia* (Sterculiaceae) leaves in a single sitting. Then, just before dawn, the caterpillar returns to perch on the main trunk of the small tree. The same perch each day? No one has ever looked. If molested in its daytime resting and hiding site, it pulls its head back into its thorax, presumably to make the head harder to grab. This gives the appearance of an even more blunt, brown mottled stick about the diameter of a finger. It does not flee, nor does it let go and drop to the ground (often the escape tactic of small cryptic caterpillars).

The huge eggs, 2.5 millimeters in diameter, are glued singly to the top of the leaf of one of thirteen species of Malvales: Bombacaceae, Tilliaceae, and Sterculiaceae. They hatch about twelve days later. The first and second instars, like many solitary Arsenurinae, are irregular combinations of maroon and black, with greenish-white, long, flexible scoli. They look like a discolored and twisted portion of a torn, dead leaf hanging below a living leaf. How many foliage-gleaning birds are fooled by this appearance is anyone's guess. Molting to the fourth and fifth instars, it takes on the appearance of a rotten twig, greenish brown and mottled with greenish-white patches of fungi on the sides and a fungal extension serving as the remnant of the tail horn.

The ACG *Arsenura* have quite distinctive yet sympatric to parapatric microgeographic ranges. *Arsenura armida* occurs everywhere, extending up to about 1,100 meters in the secondary succession of old fields on the sides of Volcan Cacao, though probably not to as high an elevation in old-growth forest. *Arsenura batesii* rings the rain-forested lower slopes, its last instar being almost identical to that of the much larger *Arsenura sylla*, which, however, feeds on *Hirtella racemosa* (Chrysobalanaceae) and seems to be restricted to the wetter parts of the lower slopes. Then the wettest and coldest upper half of the volcano (higher on the dry Pacific sides and lower on the even wetter Atlantic sides) is occupied by *Arsenura drucei,* whose last instar is again almost identical to that of *A. batesii* and *A. sylla* and also feeds on Malvales.

All three non-*armida* species of *Arsenura* are conspicuous in having failed (so far) to generate any parasitoids in the ACG inventory. This observation stems from 182 wild-caught caterpillars. In contrast, the highly gregarious *Arsenura armida* has two host-specific tachinids and one host-specific wasp. Although the lack of parasitoids seems rather improbable for a slow-growing, large caterpillar, the non-*armida* species' solitary behavior may be part of the secret of escape.

CATERPILLAR VOUCHER: 04-SRNP-22929; JCM
ADULT VOUCHER: 99-SRNP-1584; JCM

43. *ADELPHA CELERIO* – NYMPHALIDAE

The caterpillar of this butterfly is one of two somewhat generalist nymphalids among the *Adelpha* of the ACG, the other being *Adelpha melanthe*. Although the great majority of the over seventy-five wild-caught *Adelpha celerio* caterpillars were feeding on the weedy shrub *Conostegia xalapensis* (Melastomataceae), a species that dots trashy, unkept rain-forest pastures, its caterpillars have also been found on two other species of Melastomataceae and on *Heliocarpus americanus* and

Heliocarpus appendiculatus (Tiliaceae), *Triumfetta lappula* (Sterculiaceae), and *Myriocarpa longipes* (Urticaceae). In general terms, caterpillars that can feed on a variety of plants often exhibit a style of crypsis that does not depend on a direct match with the color and texture of the food-plant leaf. This is certainly the case with *A. celerio,* which takes on the form and color of a piece of moss or other lower plant, which in turn could be perched anywhere. The pupa ("chrysalis" in butterfly terminology)

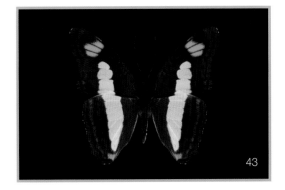

43

likewise escapes from the match-the-leaf-color problem by being brilliant polished silver with a few dark markings, vacillating in appearance between a hole through a leaf to a brilliant sky beyond or as a glistening, large water drop. No matter how it functions, the pupa reminds one of a polished piece of medieval body armor for a very elegant prince. In comparison, the many other species of *Adelpha* in the ACG, other than *A. melanthe,* are all proving to be extremely host specific to a family, genus, or species of plant. However, all of them have some variant on the body morphology displayed by *A. celerio,* that is, lots of projections, a spiny head, and a tendency toward gray, green, and pastel mottled colors.

In striking contrast to the caterpillars, the adults are very obvious. They all bear brilliant white and orange patterns, like that of *A. celerio,* though sometimes lacking the white. They are unambiguous mimics of each other and are also mimicked by

Riodinidae and other Nymphalidae, neither Batesian nor Mullerian. Rather, their brilliant contrasting patterns say, "Don't bother to try and catch me, because if you do, you won't get me." Regardless of whether this adult butterfly defense is based on the predator's hard-wired genetic coding or is learned, it seems to work very well. *Adelpha* with bird-bill marks on their wings from failed attempts are essentially nonexistent, yet the butterflies may be met in large numbers about anywhere in the ACG.

Even the cloud forest has two common species of *Adelpha,* though it is noteworthy that their color patterns have deviated very far from the standard *Adelpha* pattern. Instead, they each display browns and black-and-white. The very similar species of adults of *Adelpha* have fortunately been thoroughly scrutinized by Keith Willmott (2003; his taxonomic monograph includes photographs of many tens of species looking very much like *A. celerio*).

Aside from the occasional attack by one of the generalist tachinid flies, such as *Patelloa xanthura* or *Chetogena scutellaris,* and two records of attacks by an undescribed ichneumonid wasp, the genus *Adelpha* in the ACG is noteworthy for being attacked moderately strongly by specialist parasitoids. There has been a 2 percent rate of parasitism within a sample of 1,570 wild-caught caterpillars, all by the action of a single species of distinctive tachinid, *Zizyphomyia arguta.* This fly has been reared from six of the fifteen species of ACG *Adelpha,* mostly from *Adelpha basiloides.* The distribution of the fly ranges from Mexico to Argentina (Monty Wood, pers. comm.), coincident with the range for the species of *Adelpha.*

CATERPILLAR VOUCHER: 89-SRNP-855; DHJ
ADULT VOUCHER: 94-SRNP-9852; JCM

44. *ACHARIA HYPEROCHE* – LIMACODIDAE

The caterpillars of three species of *Acharia*—*A. hyperoche, A. sarans,* and *A. apicalis*—are very similar in their general color pattern and commonly termed "saddleback caterpillars." However, *A. hyperoche* is the only one in the ACG with two greenish-yellow dots, like false eyes, on the tail-end and no spot in the same position on the thorax. There is no doubt that the violently gaudy color of the caterpillar, in combination with being diurnally active and often resting on the dorsal surface of the leaf, is aposematic. The spines decorating the body and tubercles are extremely painful to the touch. Speaking of spines, the last instar in our image is indeed eating its newly molted cuticle, spines and all, as caterpillars generally do. This species, like many but certainly not all limacodids, is polyphagous. So far, the 270 caterpillars reared to date have been found feeding on the mature leaves of species in seventeen plant families. The caterpillars rear well on the foliage of the plant on which they are found resting or feeding, but in nature a given caterpillar probably wanders far and wide volun-

44

tarily, and therefore eats a quite varied diet as it grows very slowly through its larval life. Slow growth is the operative phrase. Any species of *Acharia* may use up to two months or more to reach the prepupal stage because its gut system extracts very few of the nutrients contained in the food that it eats.

Acharia hyperoche is the most frequently encountered ACG deep rain-forest *Acharia* caterpillar; none have been found in dry forest. Adults are rare in collections and rarely encountered at lights. *Acharia nesea* is the most common congener in the dry-forest/rain-forest interface on the north slopes of Volcan Cacao. None of the three *Acharia* species found in ACG dry forest are common.

The orange eggs are glued tightly in single-file and somewhat hair-covered rows on a leaf and hatch as many as twenty days later, which is very long for a moth egg. The early instars of *A. hyperoche* (and *A. nesea*) feed together, side by side at first, but quickly split up and by the penultimate and ultimate instars are quite solitary. In contrast, the caterpillars of *A. ophelians* and *A. horrida* often remain as a group through the penultimate instar. The adults of all *Acharia* are nearly pattern free, dark mahogany brown, but *A. hyperoche* commonly bears one or two somewhat circular white dots on the forewing, allowing confirmation of the larval identification once an adult has eclosed.

Although this slow-moving and slow-growing caterpillar is nearly free from parasitoids, it is attacked at very low density by two undescribed host-specific species of ichneumonid wasps and two undescribed species of tachinid flies (*Uramya* spp.) that are restricted to parasitizing species of *Acharia*. Only eight out of 1,532 field-collected *Acharia* have been parasitized by a braconid. Such a low frequency may be because they are most often collected in the penultimate or ultimate instars, and the subfamily of braconids that attack them, the Rogadinae, usually parasitize and mummify the earlier instars of their host species. In other words, the parasitized larvae are not reared because early-instar caterpillars are difficult to find.

CATERPILLAR VOUCHER: 02-SRNP-18466; DHJ
ADULT VOUCHER: 01-SRNP-1467; JCM

45. *ANUROCAMPA MINGENS* – NOTODONTIDAE

One fine day Janzen was walking up the trail in the lower cloud forest of Volcan Cacao. Under the forty-meter-high canopy and right on the rain-cleansed surface of mud were dozens of pea-sized caterpillar droppings stuck in a tight clump over a circular area of about one square meter. How can an object as small as a pellet of caterpillar excrement fall out of the canopy and land in such a tight dispersion in a target area that small? After staring wildly up into the distant canopy, he then focused more closely. Only four meters above the ground were two turquoise lumps the size of his thumb. The magnificent caterpillars of *Anurocampa mingens* had wan-

45

dered into science. The six- to ten-gram caterpillars are unambiguously the largest (heaviest) notodontid caterpillars in the ACG cloud forest, and even in Costa Rica, if not all of Central America. In the dry forest, this honor goes to *Naprepa houla* (#46), which weighs in just a bit smaller. The brilliant turquoise, blue, white, yellow, and red *A. mingens* caterpillars defy all explanation in terms of crypsis. They are nicely counter-shaded, with light green on the back and dark green below, so they probably are mimics. The white-and-red side stripe suggests the markings of some urticating hemileucine caterpillars, such as *Periphoba arcaei* (#88).

The forty-five recorded caterpillars of *A. mingens* have been found feeding only on *Eugenia valerii* (Myrtaceae), though the other tree-type species of Myrtaceae on Volcan Cacao have not been exhaustively searched (yet). They eat whole leaves one at a time, and since a given caterpillar may stay in one place for many days, it can produce a heavily defoliated branch on which it is quite conspicuous. This may not be such an awful strategy for a mimic of the highly urticating hemileucines. Since they are not in the high upper canopy, these gaudy caterpillars are probably not encountered by the insectivorous monkey *Cebus capucinus*. This leaves foliage- and branch-gleaning birds as the major threat. It is likely that their major avian predators are the orange-bellied trogon, *Trogon aurantiiventris;* squirrel cuckoos, *Piaya cayana;* and the aracari,

Pteroglossus torquatus. These upper rain-forest and lower-margin cloud-forest birds do prey on urticating hemileucines.

When *A. mingens* caterpillars reach the prepupal phase of the last instar, they turn a dull green and descend to the litter (it is unclear whether they walk down or drop, but they probably drop). The tough silk cocoon is strongly glued to a framework of dead leaves. The prepupal caterpillar remains in its cocoon for as many as ten to thirteen months before molting to a pupa. The adult emerges a few weeks later. The passing of an inimical season (inimical from the insect's viewpoint) as a prepupal caterpillar is commonplace in large Notodontidae (e.g., *Lirimiris, Hapigia, Naprepa, Colax*). Yet it is not really obvious why being a dormant, albeit shrunken, semimobile caterpillar in a cocoon is better than being a more desiccation-resistant pupa. Many univoltine lowland species of small moth caterpillars, such as Pyralioidea, Limacodidae, and Megalopygidae, use the same behavior to pass much of the remainder of the rainy season and the long dry season. The seasonality of adult eclosion by *A. mingens* is quite mysterious, showing two patterns. Cocoons held in captivity tend to produce an adult either 1) in late April to early May, which is the beginning of the rains, or 2) in late September to early October, which is the peak of the most intense rain, often after a somewhat warmer and drier veranillo in August. These patterns suggest there are both univoltine and bivoltine genera-

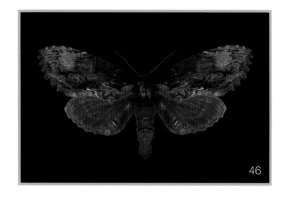

46

tions running simultaneously in the Volcan Cacao cloud-forest habitat.

CATERPILLAR VOUCHER: 04-SRNP-35555; JCM
ADULT VOUCHER: 00-SRNP-9927; JCM

46. *NAPREPA HOULA* – NOTODONTIDAE

The last instars of *Naprepa houla*, weighing between five and seven grams apiece, are the largest (heaviest) notodontid caterpillars in the ACG dry forest, though *Colax apulus* (#31) is a close runner-up. This caterpillar is one of the easiest to find by searching saplings of *Miconia argentea* (Melastomataceae) in late June (first generation), August (second generation), and October-November (third generation). The brilliant colors of the caterpillar are especially visible against the light beige underside of the large *M. argentea* leaves, where it perches when not feeding. This ostentatious behavior strongly suggests that it is rejected by birds. It is probably indicative of this rejection that more than 3,000 *Trogon* caterpillar prey items captured within a few hundred meters of where *N. houla* is common have never included this species. The striking false face at the tail end of the caterpillar suggests that at least at some time in the evolutionary history of *N. houla*, there were and perhaps still are predaceous vertebrates who would eat it if not deceived into thinking that it is a snake or other predator. Its cloud-forest relative in the ACG, *Naprepa pulcheria*, also has the rear-looking false face, as does its rain-forest relative,

Naprepa cyllota. In both of these, the striking body spots are more ordinary colors of white to green, however. As a prepupa, and still walking in search of a cocoon-spinning site, *N. houla* turns intense, shiny dark blue with orange dots, looking very much like a piece of decorative porcelain. Again, this pattern is presumably aposematic or mimetic of a very inedible object. Having nonfeeding and nonmigrating adults, it passes the long dry season, late December through mid-May, as a dormant prepupa in a strong silk cocoon, which is generally spun against a leaf in the litter. Dormancy as a prepupa, rather than a pupa, is a common trait in large, dry-forest Notodontidae. Shortly before the rains, the prepupa molts to a pupa. It is probably responding to either the hottest temperatures or the abrupt drop in temperatures when the first rains occur.

Although the large caterpillars of *N. houla* have been studied mostly in the ACG dry forest, they also occur in ACG rain forest, feeding on several species of woody, sun-loving Melastomataceae. In the ACG dry forest there is only one species of big, woody Melastomataceae. Given its apparent restriction to this family, it can only be monophagous. Its food plants are those of secondary succession, and presumably were originally low-density denizens of natural disturbance sites. It is therefore impossible to know if *N. houla* is truly a dry-forest species that has followed human disturbance, with its attendant drying, insolation, and heating, into the rain-forest side of Costa

47

Rica (as have many other Lepidoptera), or is a species equally native to both major ecosystems.

Parasitism of *N. houla* is very rare and entirely due to two species of Tachinidae. *Winthemia* sp. 11 is a parasitoid of at least seven other species of medium to large Notodontidae in the ACG dry forest, whereas *Winthemia* sp. 09 appears to be a parasitoid of hairy Arctiidae caterpillars but recorded from *N. houla* caterpillars on two occasions.

CATERPILLAR VOUCHER: 03-SRNP-ACGFIELD; JCM
ADULT VOUCHER: 04-SRNP-40324; JCM

47. *SOSXETRA GRATA* – NOCTUIDAE

Sosxetra grata, known to us as "sorpresa Santa Rosa," and given a truly odd spelling of its generic name, is a most improbable noctuid caterpillar. For many years it was the only species of extremely hairy noctuid caterpillar that had been reared in ACG dry forest. It is undoubtedly a mimic within the mimicry complex of white and hairy Apatelodidae, Riodinidae, Megalopygidae, and Arctiidae caterpillars found throughout the ACG and the remainder of the tropics. It should be emphasized that nearly all noctuid caterpillars have some short hairs, setae to be entomologically correct, scattered over their green to brown and quite cryptic bodies. But when noctuids are aposematic (warningly colored) or mimics of other caterpillars, it is usually in the form of bright colors and false eyespots, rather than looking like the hairy (and presumably stinging or digestively toxic) families of caterpillars mentioned above. This caterpillar is not found except by searching species of Meliaceae. We have found only sixty individuals in twenty-five years, and fifty-two of those were on the mature foliage of *Guarea excelsa,* a large, evergreen dry-forest tree that is quite scarce in secondary succession. We have no way of knowing if this tree was common in the ACG old-growth dry forest, since there is so little of this forest remaining. The other eight caterpillars we have seen were scattered among three species of *Trichilia.* It is commonplace for Noctuidae that feed on broad-leafed woody plants to be very host-specific, so this family-level specificity is not surprising.

The adult is painted in cryptic colors that match bark, dead leaves, and twigs, as are nearly all adult noctuids. The adult of *S. grata* does particularly well at looking like a rotten and fungus-ridden fragment of a dead leaf, no matter where it is perched during the day. Adults turn up at the lights in the lowland rain forests of Costa Rica, not because they breed in the dry forest and migrate to the other areas, as is the case with sphingids and many other large noctuids, but rather because they also occur in the rain forest where their caterpillars very likely feed on Meliaceae. We suspect them to be nonmigratory because they are not caught at light traps in mountain passes between the two major ecosystems.

The adult of *Ceroctena pictipennis,* a rain-forest medium-sized noctuid, has much in common with the *S. grata* form of crypsis. *Ceroctena pictipennis* is dark green with a white rim to the wings, with abundant "fungus" hairs sticking out from the margins. When resting on a leaf, it looks like a fungus-ridden hole through a leaf, with the dark green being the forest under-story showing through the leaf. Although we have yet to photo-graph the caterpillar of *C. pictipennis,* the *gusaneros* have reared it three times, all from ACG rain forest and eating *Guarea glabra* and another *Guarea.* In all three cases it was thought to be a lasiocampid based on its extremely hairy body. It is very tempt-ing to think of *S. grata* as the dry-forest version and *C. pictipen-nis* as the rain-forest version of a hairy, mimetic noctuid cater-pillar with an adult that looks like a hairy, rotten leaf.

CATERPILLAR VOUCHER: 84-SRNP-2044; DHJ
ADULT VOUCHER: 95-SRNP-7604; JCM

48. *YANGUNA COSYRA* – HESPERIIDAE

Yanguna cosyra, formerly named *Pyrrhopyge cosyra* (see Mielke 2002), is one of the reliably collectible pyrrhopygine Hesperiidae caterpillars (Burns and Janzen 2001). It is the largest ACG pyrrhopygine caterpillar and the easiest to locate. We have reared more than 800 wild-caught *Y. cosyra* caterpillars from the cloud forest to the lowest-elevation rain-forest areas of the ACG. The *gusaneros* have stopped collecting them unless they are in the last instar. Not only do we have a very large number of rear-ing records, but also the caterpillars seem to feed forever. Actually, they typically feed for only a few weeks to a few months, but in doing so they put a high demand on the *gusaneros'* time, time that could be better spent on rearing scarcer species. Wherever there are *Chrysochlamys glauca, C. psy-chotrifolia,* and *Clusia spp.* (Clusiaceae, or the family Guttiferae of old) in rain or cloud forest, there are *Y. cosyra* caterpillars. To find one at a particular moment, however, it may be necessary to inspect a number of plants. On rare occasions they are also found feeding on the common understory shrub *Symphonia globulifera* (Clusiaceae), but the scarcity of these caterpillar records implies that the females only very rarely oviposit on this species of plant (since it has been searched thoroughly). There are also three enigmatic records of *Y. cosyra* caterpillars feeding on *Ardisia crassiramea* (Myrsinaceae), a cloud-forest treelet with thick *Chrysochlamys*-like leaves. This plant is

48

not taxonomically related to Clusiaceae. Despite high *Y. cosyra* abundance, we have never met a *Y. cosyra* adult in the field. They are probably tree-top skipper butterflies, darting down for a moment to lay an egg and then returning to their elevated habitat. We will find out some day, probably at some tall, flowering tree.

The caterpillars of *Y. cosyra* are adroit at copiously and strongly silking several of the thick and tough clusiaceous leaves together into a strong nest that is actually fairly easy to find once you learn to look for it. The *Chrysochlamys* and *Clusia* leaves, except for the large leaves of *Clusia minor,* are just the right size to be silked one on top of the other into a silk-leaf-caterpillar sandwich. If this nest is abruptly ripped open and a large last instar is the occupant, its response is not to flee, but rather to exude a clear-green drop of what appears to be blood (haemolymph) from a pore on each side of each segment. This fluid is probably bitter or otherwise obnoxious,

because of the way it is produced and because it is accompanied by the pattern of a very black caterpillar with orange vertical slashes—aposematic coloration. Like all other ACG pyrrhopygines, *Y. cosyra* caterpillars have their faces heavily covered with long, dense white hairs rather than displaying the fierce false face commonplace on medium to large species of pyrgine hesperiid caterpillars. Interestingly in this context, pyrrhopygine pupae (Burns and Janzen 2001) also lack the false faces commonplace on pupae of other pyrgines.

The adults of Pyrrhopyginae are known by the lack of a small, needle-like projection on the end of their spindle-clubbed antennae. This projection occurs on the ends of the club of other Hesperiidae antennae.

Parasitism of *Y. cosyra* caterpillars is exceptional among the Pyrrhopyginae because it is relatively high—at about 5 percent—and due to three strongly host-specific species of ichneumonid wasps. *Casinaria* CAS-07, RR-sp. 6, and Genus M-sp. 1 also rarely are found parasitizing a few other species of large pyrgine Hesperiidae caterpillars, mostly in the Volcan Cacao cloud forest. There is one species of tachinid fly, *Chlorohystricia* sp. 01, that likewise almost entirely attacks only *Y. cosyra* caterpillars. As is usually the case among caterpillars of all species, generalist tachinid flies also attack *Y. cosyra*.

CATERPILLAR VOUCHER: 04-SRNP-41190; JCM
ADULT VOUCHER: 99-SRNP-17126; JCM

49. *PHOEBIS SENNAE* – PIERIDAE

We feature only one species of Pieridae, which is the family of the sulphur butterflies and whites, so prominent on any landscape, tropical or extra-tropical. This is largely because whereas the classical pierid adults are so very visible, flying in bright reflection across open, sunny places, males puddling at mud for sodium, the (usually) green cryptic caterpillars are not easily found. *Phoebis sennae,* the coliadine pierid we show, is no exception. The caterpillars of *P. sennae* come in two color morphs—the common green morph feeding on green foliage, and a bright yellow-orange morph (our image) that feeds on the large, bright yellow-orange flowers of its food plant, perches on them, and looks for all intents and purposes like a part of the flower. It is not clear whether the yellow morph is always yellow (unlikely) or whether it changes to this color morph when it has flowers to eat. Furthermore, it is unknown whether the change, if any, occurs when it molts or while it is feeding. The yellow morph found eating

49

a flower can eat and grow on green foliage when confined in a rearing container. Much exploratory work remains to be done with these color morphs. The green morph, with slight black, yellow, and blue markings here and there, is largely invisible among the small-leafed foliage of its *Senna pallida* (Fabaceae) food plant. When approached, the caterpillar remains motionless, relying on the fact that you have not seen it, and often you have not. There can be ten individuals in the top of a *S. pallida*

shrub, and you may find only two, despite intensive search. Incidentally, this food plant was long known to Costa Rican field biologists as *Cassia biflora*. In the early 1990s, however, it was discovered that this name should apply to a Venezuelan plant, thereby elevating *S. pallida* to the name we use. At the same time, the huge genus *Cassia* was broken up into smaller units, one of them being *Senna*.

This butterfly is among the famous migrating pierids. Huge numbers of adults can be encountered flying across the open sea of the Caribbean, or simply flying down roads in the ACG. When the rains arrive in the middle of May, moderate numbers of adults fly into the ACG dry forest from the rain-forest side of Costa Rica (their precise origin is unknown). They have one very large generation followed by a feeble, partial second generation on the plentiful *Senna pallida* and occasionally may be found feeding on five other species of *Senna* and even *Cassia emarginata*. Most of the newly eclosed adults then disperse and head back to the rain forest. In the wetter parts of Costa Rica, they develop through multiple generations on a year-round basis while feeding on the same herbaceous and shrubby genera of plants. The population dynamics, food plants, and migration behavior encountered today are probably grossly altered from the circumstances under which this butterfly evolved—their food plants are now very common as ruderal species in pastures, along roadsides, and associated with other kinds of anthropogenic semi-permanent disturbances. One needs to visualize this butterfly in a world covered mostly with old-growth forest. In this scenario, their food plants would be both rare and widely scattered in natural and isolated disturbance sites such as landslides, riverbanks, marsh edges, cliffs, and so on. This situation, incidentally, applies to the great majority of the species of plants and animals encountered and viewed by the casual visitor to the tropics (or in fact, just about anywhere on Earth's surface). People are where people want to stay, and where people stay, the floral and faunal communities and ecosystem dynamics have been grossly altered in recent times. Yet the wild animal still acts, based on its genetic program, as if it is in a wilderness.

CATERPILLAR VOUCHER: 00-SRNP-433; DHJ
ADULT VOUCHER: 01-SRNP-79; JCM

50. *LYCOREA CLEOBAEA* – NYMPHALIDAE

When the black- and yellow-ringed caterpillar of *Lycorea cleobaea* is first encountered, it feels natural to associate it with the caterpillar of the monarch butterfly, *Danaus plexippus*. But when you see the adult of *L. cleobaea*, fluttering like one of the tiger-striped species of heliconiines or ithomiines, it never crosses your mind that it is a monarch relative.

Caterpillars of *L. cleobaea* feed with impunity on the upper side (most often) or lower side of the large leaves of: figs, *Ficus*

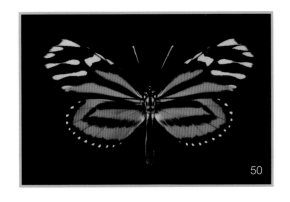

50

spp. (Moraceae); papaya, *Carica papaya,* and *Jacaratia dolichaula* (Caricaceae); *Sebastiana pavoniana* (Euphorbiaceae); milkweed vines, *Macroscepis* (Asclepiadaceae); and *Prestonia allenii* and *Forsteronia spicata* (Apocynaceae). What trait do all these food plants share? The common denominator is their copious white latex. All danaids seem to have the ability to thwart the defense mechanism of the latex plant by biting off the latex-laden vessels in the leaf in the pattern of a semi-circle around the area where they are going to eat. In this manner they do not get a face full of what amounts to a poisonous version of white glue every time they take a bite. The Asclepiadaceae are famous for having nasty cardiac glycosides and perhaps other small, toxic molecules in the white latex. As with monarch caterpillars, the *L. cleobaea* caterpillar presumably sequesters these toxic molecules to become part of its defenses, and then the adult's defense as well. Yet because they also feed on Moraceae and Caricaceae, there is an intriguing contradiction to aposematism. The latex of these two plants does not contain small, toxic molecules that can be easily transported and stored by the insect. Rather, the latex is rich in large, protective molecules such as the digestive enzymes ficin and papain. These digestion inhibitors are large protein molecules that do their damage by interfering with the gut digestion process. Because they do not pass through the gut wall of the consumer, they are unlikely to be taken up by the caterpillar for defense. Furthermore, a digestion inhibitor is not a potent defense against a carnivore that might eat hundreds of other caterpillars along with a single caterpillar so defended. This means the *L. cleobaea* caterpillars that feed on these plants may well be defenseless, and thus are Batesian mimics of their sibs reared on cardiac glycoside–bearing plants and of some of the other brightly ringed caterpillars in the habitat. Examples of the latter are the three species of *Danaus* feeding on *Asclepias* and the two species of *Tithorea* on both Asclepiadaceae and Apocynaceae. It is striking that, at least in the ACG, we have far more records of *L. cleobaea* from *Ficus* and *Carica* (introduced garden varieties) than from the families of food plants rich in small, toxic molecules. One wonders if *L. cleobaea* might be a danaid that has evolutionarily left behind the defenses to be obtained from plants and either makes its own defensive compounds or has none as a caterpillar or adult.

The phenomenon of mimicry is a tangled web. In the present case, *L. cleobaea* caterpillars are unambiguously part of a large complex of species possessing Batesian and Mullerian mimic caterpillars. As indicated above, however, it will take some chemical analysis and probably some feeding trials with unfortunate birds to correctly place them in this framework. Then there is an additional complexity. Irrespective of which kind of mimicry it may be, the entire situation may be moot for many carnivores and caterpillars. It may well be that many of the birds, for example, are simply genetically programmed to avoid

51

capturing brightly ringed caterpillars. Evolutionarily, this would be due to their similarity to lethal prey such as coral snakes, *Micrurus* spp. It may also be due to the presence of small molecules that are toxic enough to have selected for many species of birds to avoid even taking a taste of anything resembling brightly ringed tubes. Whichever is the case, mimicry theory has long stagnated in a world of thinkers lacking the field experience and attention to studies such as those of Susan Smith (1975). Both theory and field experience should have led long ago to the introduction of genetically programmed avoidance into the algebra of what happens in nature.

CATERPILLAR VOUCHER: 04-SRNP-60500; JCM
ADULT VOUCHER: 90-SRNP-536; JCM

51. *XYLOPHANES CHIRON* – SPHINGIDAE

Xylophanes chiron offers a double dose of the prominent false eyespots that adorn the thorax. Compare these to the single, bulging eyespots of *Xylophanes germen* (#52). But the champion of multiple body-wall eyespots is *Xylophanes tersa*, which has big to little false eyes on each segment. It is easy to imagine how the pair of eyes on *X. chiron*, developmentally produced by duplication of a single eye, could be evolutionarily pushed into being a "lateral," complete face. This would be a full face on each side of the caterpillar, rather than just a single-faced, double-eyed mimic of a predator when viewed from the front. This caterpillar has, like many species of *Xylophanes*, two very different last-instar color morphs, each displaying the distinctive double false eyes. The more common, which we portray here, is bright apple-green, almost blue-green on occasion. The other is dark brown (see *Xylophanes juanita*, #5; also see 82-SRNP-537 at http://janzen.sas.upenn.edu), and the eyespots are less conspicuous in this morph. We do know that the green morph rests on the undersides of green leaves. What we do not know is if the brown morph rests on brown stems.

In the ACG, the caterpillars of *X. chiron* have been found feeding on no less than fifty species of Rubiaceae in dry forest and rain forest, giving the impression that it is a Rubiaceae specialist. But it has never been found feeding on the numerous species of the more tree-like Rubiaceae in the same habitats, such as *Calycophyllum candidissimum, Guettarda macrospermum,* and *Genipa americana,* which are host plants for other Sphingidae, but not *Xylophanes.* These latter tree species have been thoroughly searched. Even more striking are three records of *X. chiron* from the new shoots of sapling *Vochysia ferruginea* and *Vochysia guatemalensis* (Vochysiaceae), two large rain-forest trees. What properties these Vochysiaceae have in common with understory rubiaceous shrubs remains to be discovered.

Adult *X. chiron* range from southern Florida and Texas to Argentina, and even occur on the Caribbean islands. They seem to be found in all kinds of ACG habitat. They are highly migratory, however, tracking the seasons across their geographical homeland. In the ACG, they breed in the first half of the rainy season in the dry forest. They then migrate to the rain forest and lower cloud forest for several generations before returning to the dry forest at the beginning of the next year's rainy season. When migrating, they often fly through upper-elevation passes. These passes are favorite sites for entomologists to hang their light traps. The moths' presence at the lights leads to the illusion that they are residents at these upper elevations, but really the adult *X. chiron* are just passing through. This is also reflected in the nearly equal sex ratio of the adults at lights (the moths at lights in the breeding grounds are nearly all males).

CATERPILLAR VOUCHER: 84-SRNP-778; DHJ
ADULT VOUCHER: 03-SRNP-15879; JCM

52

52. *XYLOPHANES GERMEN* – SPHINGIDAE

The *Xylophanes germen* caterpillar illustrates the epitome of the false-eyes warning tactic. Imagine you are a ten-gram bird, searching among the shadows and leaves of montane rain-forest understory shrubs for insects in the dim light of the usual cloudy day. A vertebrate eye abruptly appears in your largely monocular field of vision as you slip around a leaf. If you wait one millisecond to evaluate, you could be lunch. You will not live the ten- to twenty-year life span for which small tropical forest birds are famous. So, you are programmed to leave, fast, and not go back to see if that just might have been a large, edible caterpillar. Chalk one up for *X. germen* with its bulging red thoracic false eyespots. Stare at them. See how hard it is for you, a tall, intelligent thinker, to convince yourself that they are not eyes, and that they are not looking at you. These caterpillar traits go back to the evolutionary dawn of visually operative predators and their prey.

Adults of *X. germen,* like the other twenty-odd species of *Xylophanes* in the ACG dry forest, cloud forest, and rain forest, are cryptic, drab, olive-colored adults. They rest motionless during the day on the foliage and bark, avoiding an encounter with a searching, insectivorous vertebrate. In this regard, they resemble many thousands of other species of moths that, like *Xylophanes,* have some other kind of adult escape trick (for instance, see *Archaeoprepona meander,* #36). The ancestral *Xylophanes,* the first species with a xylophanoid caterpillar, must have evolved quite impressive false eyespots on its caterpillar's thorax. Since the genus is undoubtedly many tens of millions of years old, one presumes that this was a defense against some rather early member(s) of both our ancestors (primates) and birds. As the genus has speciated across millions of years, the thoracic eyes have evolved to appear as bulged (*X. germen, X. crotonis,* and *X. titana*), multiplied (*X. chiron* [#51] and *X. tersa*), divided (*X. juanita* [#35] and *X. adalia*), and even shrunk to hardly more than dots and irregular patches (*X. guia-*

53

nensis [#13], *X. porcus,* and *X. godmani*). Interestingly, none of these eyespots have engineered the ability to wink at you, as do the false eyes on the dorsal rear of some other sphingids, such as *Eumorpha labruscae* (#83), or to hide the eye and display it only when annoyed as in *Erinnyis ello* (#63), *Erinnyis alope, Erinnyis crameri* (#37), *Erinnyis oenotrus, Eumorpha labruscae* (#83), *Madoryx oiclus, Madoryx plutonius, Madoryx bubastus, Hemeroplanes triptolemus* (#53), and *Hemeroplanes ornatus.*

However, all the *Xylophanes* with "good" false eyes tend to pump up the thorax and pull in the head, thereby displaying the false eyespots all the more prominently and threateningly, creating a profile of a snake's head. When handled frequently, such as in changing food while rearing them in plastic bags, they gradually stop pumping up the thorax. It thus requires an ever more vigorous disturbance for them to display as they normally would do in a millisecond when first approached or touched in the wild. They need the ability to habituate, as indeed they must also do in the wild, so as to avoid constantly reacting to every wind-driven foliage vibration.

CATERPILLAR VOUCHER: 03-SRNP-4508; JCM
ADULT VOUCHER: 02-SRNP-24452; JCM

53. *HEMEROPLANES TRIPTOLEMUS* – SPHINGIDAE

Hemeroplanes triptolemus is the caterpillar that all hard-core nature photographers want to see. Even when they do see it, they can hardly believe their eyes. Janzen first met this caterpillar forty-two years ago in a brushy pasture in Veracruz, Mexico, and he could just as well have encountered it in Brazil or Ecuador. Its broad range is characteristic of hundreds of species of lowland tropical sphingids. Feeding on the leaves of apocynaceous vines, it is never common, but with months of searching you can find it about anywhere in the ACG lowlands. In the rain forest it has an adult look-alike, *Hemeroplanes ornatus,* and we suspect that the yet-to-be-seen caterpillar will be very similar to that of *H. triptolemus.* In fact, it is entirely possible that some of the rain-forest *Hemeroplanes* caterpillars found within the ACG have been misidentified by confusing these two species.

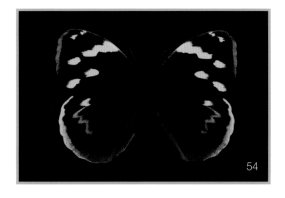

54

When the caterpillar is undisturbed, it looks very much like a beige-gray and black mottled dead stick or a dirty yellow stick, depending on the color morph. When threatened by a prodding snout, beak, or finger, it twists the anterior half of the body 180 degrees, folds its thoracic legs tightly against the ventral side of the thorax (which is now "dorsal") and pulls its head in somewhat. This contortion expands the thorax into a morphological configuration that is an excellent facsimile of a viper, and just the right size to look like *Bothriechis schelgelii* (Viperidae) as the model. The snake is better known by its older name, *Bothrops schlegelii.* The caterpillar is not just a snake morph. The coloration perfectly fits that of a multi-colored snake, including eyes, scales, and nostrils. There is absolutely no doubt what this caterpillar is mimicking. After five to fifteen minutes of holding this pose, the last instar gradually returns to its cryptic position. If poked at this point, however, it quickly reassumes the snake-like pose and even strikes at the offending hand—though there is no mouth to open. It is extremely difficult to convince your reflexes that it is harmless, and not to jerk your hand away at the moment of attack. The first through third instars are more ordinary-looking classic green sphingid caterpillars with slight markings, quite hard to see among the foliage of their vine and adjacent plants.

Hemeroplanes triptolemus is one of the sphingids whose caterpillars apparently never become common, even when its apocynaceous food plants, *Mesechites* in the dry forest and *Mandevilla* and *Fischeria* in the rain forest, are quite abundant along roadsides and ravines. Equally, the adults are only very rarely encountered at lights, making this species a legitimate candidate for a species that is truly low density.

CATERPILLAR VOUCHER: 03-SRNP-11366; DHJ
ADULT VOUCHER: 87-SRNP-1156; JCM

54. *DYNASTOR DARIUS* – NYMPHALIDAE

Dynastor darius, a brassoline nymphalid (Aiello and Silbergleid 1978), takes the prize for the pupa that best mimics a snake head. The caterpillar snake-head prize goes to *Hemeroplanes triptolemus* (#53), a dry-forest and rain-forest sphingid. Viewed face on and mentally blurring out the background attachment to the leaf, it is very hard to convince oneself that the *D. darius* pupa is not a snake head, complete with scales, eyes, and mouth line. This protection is made all the more dramatic by realizing that all the other large, solitary brassolids—*Morpho, Caligo, Opsiphanes, Antirrhea, Catablepia*—have equally large pupae, but they are all either leaf-green or brown dead-leaf mimics. The gregarious *Brassolis isthmia* has a pupa much like a highly colored monstrous riodinid pupa, presumably mimicking something quite other than a snake. It is not hard, however, to see how, with a few adaptive moves of emphasizing and de-emphasizing, a cryptic brown *Caligo* or *Opsiphanes* pupa can evolutionarily morph into a *D. darius* snake-head pupa.

The large green *D. darius* caterpillar depends entirely on crypsis as its mechanism for predator avoidance. Feeding on the very elongate, dark green, and finely lined leaves of the terrestrial bromeliads in ACG dry forest, namely, *Bromelia pinguin* and *B. plumieri* (formerly called *B. keratas*), *D. darius* caterpillars are likewise colored, with the exception of a brown dorsal oval spot, presumably selected to look like a small, brown-edged wound in the leaf. The caterpillar feeds at night on the end of the leaf, thus rendering the leaf to look as if someone had whacked off the end with a machete. In the daytime it retreats down into the axil of the leaf. Its brown and black face, peering upward, resembles some blob of dead plant tissue that has fallen into the dark abyss. In the rain forest *D. darius* is rare and feeds on *Aechmea*, the terrestrial rain-forest analogue to *Bromelia*. Occasionally it feeds on large, epiphytic bromeliads. The cater-

pillar also rarely feeds on the leaves of commercial pineapple, *Anas comosus* (Bromeliaceae). The eggs are laid one per *Bromelia* and normally there is just one caterpillar per plant, except when there is an exceptional peak in density. On these occasions there can be several caterpillars per plant and almost every leaf has its end eaten off.

In the ACG dry forest, *D. darius* caterpillars range from very rare to extremely common in different years. When abundant, the large dark and white-barred adults fly from plant to plant at dusk, checking to see where to glue a single egg. There is much testing from plant to plant, and it is likely that it is checking to determine whether the plant is already occupied, although how they determine this is a mystery. *Dynastor darius* overlaps food-plant use with the furry pale-green, beige, and white caterpillar of *Voltinia umbra*, a riodinid known formerly as *Napea umbra* that eats distinctive rectangular windows out of the upper and lower sides of the leaves. The plant stem is also mined by the large caterpillars of two species of *Zegara* (Castniidae), but all that has been seen to date is the female *Zegara* dropping her orange eggs into the axils of the leaf.

Caterpillars of *D. darius* are only parasitized by an undescribed and host-specific species of *Winthemia* (Tachinidae). The fly glues tens of its white ovoid eggs directly to the thorax of the caterpillar. The maggots do not begin to mature and consume the caterpillar until it has pupated. They then quickly consume the contents of the pupa, burrow out through the pupal skin, and form their puparia in the soil below.

CATERPILLAR VOUCHER: 03-SRNP-29373; DHJ
ADULT VOUCHER: 00-SRNP-4480; JCM

55. *COCYTIUS LUCIFER* – SPHINGIDAE

If you find a caterpillar in the ACG that is really big, green, and not finely hairy, and it eats Annonaceae, it is likely a last instar of one of three well-documented species of *Cocytius*—*lucifer, duponchel,* or *antaeus*. To date, a fourth species, *C. beelzebuth,* has not been observed in the ACG. The easiest to identify is *C. antaeus,* with its sharp-margined, white lateral stripe, obliquely slashed, on its posterior segments. Next, *C. duponchel* has a similar stripe, but the posterior margin of the slash blurs into a bluish shadow instead of being a sharp margin. Finally, *C. lucifer* often has almost no stripe at all, just a faint suggestion of one and a large blurry area. Sometimes if there is a stronger slash, then there is a dark border along the forward/upward edge. There may even be, as in our image, traces of dark slashes along the sides of the entire abdomen. The latter are particularly evident in the penultimate instar. *Cocytius beelzebuth* is a rare rain-forest moth whose caterpillar is unknown. One other species of sphingid fits into this suite of *Cocytius*. The huge last instar of *Neococytius cluentius,* unambiguously closely related to *Cocytius,* has a fine pile of very short hairs scattered over the body and generally has numerous white slash marks overlaying the green.

Like the other two ACG *Cocytius* and *N. cluentius, C. lucifer* migrates into the ACG dry forest with the first rains in May. The single, very large green eggs are laid on the leaves of *Annona reticulata* and *Annona purpurea* (usually the latter), and a two-month generation occurs. The newly eclosed adults then leave the dry forest, presumably migrating back over to the rain forest from which they came. A few remain to have a second generation in October–November and these adults then flee the coming dry season. Throughout these cycles, the very long-tongued *Cocytius* are presumably active visitors to, and pollinators of, the various species of ACG plants with long, white corollas, flowers that open at night. On the rain-forest side of the ACG, *Cocytius* have additional generations on rain-forest Annonaceae such as *Desmopsis schipii, Xylopia frutescens,* and *Rollinia membranacea.* Curiously, there is no indication of oviposition on the dry-forest species of *Desmopsis,* and *Sapranthus palanga* has only been found to be used once, despite being a very common plant.

In the ACG dry forest in Santa Rosa, all three species of *Cocytius* are heavily parasitized by *Leschenaultia* sp. 12, which also rarely attacks six other species of very large Sphingidae. It is not at all clear how this tachinid manages to attack only large caterpillar sphingids, since the species with small caterpillars eat the same foliage as do the species of *Cocytius.* This fly lays its eggs on the foliage and they are swallowed by a feeding caterpillar. The mature maggots exit the large last-instar caterpillar or

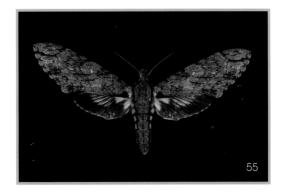

55

pupa and make their puparia in the soil. A single *C. lucifer* caterpillar may produce as many as twenty-five of the large black flies.

CATERPILLAR VOUCHER: 03-SRNP-6520; JCM
ADULT VOUCHER: 04-SRNP-31296; JCM

56. *MANDUCA PELLENIA* – SPHINGIDAE

The caterpillar of *M. pellenia* is unmistakably a *Manduca*. It has a large tail horn, dorsally rounded head (all the *Cocytius; Adhemarius* and *Protambulyx* have pointed tops to their heads), somewhat bumpy cuticle, and a gentle and blurry pattern of white stripes based on extended and angled side slashes. The white stripes on the last instar are quite conspicuous when the caterpillar is exhibited like a Ming vase against a black background as we have done here, but when the caterpillar is perched on the underside of a leaf among the mottled shadows, various

56

greens, shafts of sunlight, and many irregular shapes of foliage, it disappears, except at night. As with other large caterpillars patterned green and white, *M. pellenia* practically glow like bicycle reflectors when they are caught in the beam of a headlamp at night. The waxy layer that adorns the outermost surface of all insect cuticle is clear in the daytime and allows the various colors underneath to be seen through it. The caterpillar simply appears to be green and white. But at night, for reasons not at all obvious, the wax reflects the light somewhat in the way that a

clear plastic bag does. This renders the caterpillar a quite different "color," if one at all, than the green leaf next to it. Leaves also have a waxy cuticle on their surfaces, but they do not reflect light the way a caterpillar does and appear to be a much more normal green in the beam of the flashlight.

Although easy to see at night, identification of the caterpillar is not a simple matter. *Manduca pellenia* is one of those annoying rain-forest caterpillars for which you need to know the family of the food plant to know what species of *Manduca* is at hand. The caterpillars of *M. pellenia* and some morphs of *Manduca florestan* (#96) are essentially identical. However, based on eighty-three caterpillar food-plant records, *M. pellenia* is a Solanaceae specialist known to eat some twenty-four species in more than four genera: *Solanum, Lycianthes, Cestrium, Cuatresia,* and various unidentified genera. On the other hand, there are no confirmed records of *M. florestan* eating Solanaceae. It is specialized on some fifty species of Bignoniaceae, Verbenaceae, and Boraginaceae, plus one record from Olacaceae. In the ACG dry forest, the caterpillar is easily recognized as that of *M. florestan* because *M. pellenia* is a rain-forest moth. But in the rain forest it could be either, because the caterpillars of both species can be found a few meters apart. It is a microgeographic puzzle as to why *M. pellenia* does not extend its population just a few meters to kilometers to the west and become part of the dry-forest fauna, especially during the rainy season. The dry forest contains an ample salad of Solanaceae. Furthermore, at night the dry forest and rain forest are yet even more similar climatologically.

Differentiating adults has its problems as well. In South America and north into Panama, there exist *M. pellenia* and several other species of *Manduca* look-alikes with unknown caterpillars. Fortunately, the sphingid expert Jean-Marie Cadiou feels that, at least to date, all the ACG-reared moths identified as *M. pellenia* as well as the wild-caught individuals from Costa Rica are truly *M. pellenia.*

CATERPILLAR VOUCHER: 01-SRNP-2411; DHJ
ADULT VOUCHER: 02-SRNP-2300; JCM

57. *PHIDITIA LUCERNARIA* – APATELODIDAE

There is a dark-green, nearly evergreen bignoniaceous vine (the *Catalpa* tree family), *Cydista aequinoctialis,* that is scattered through early successional ACG dry forest. Just about every large vine seems to have a *Phiditia lucernaria* caterpillar, or even many of them, feeding on it during the first half of the rainy season. The nonfeeding adult female *P. lucernaria,* very much in the family Apatelodidae but acting as if it were a small hemileucine saturniid, lays almost all of her eggs in large clusters on this species of vine. The bright orange, black, and white caterpillars start out feeding as a group but rather quickly split up, as individuals within the group are preyed upon, knocked about by the

57

weather, or just simply not inclined to remain together. This stands in contrast to the rain-forest *Phiditia cuprea* and *Sorocaba* JANZEN01 (#76), two close relatives that have caterpillars remaining as tight groups as long as externalities allow it. *Phiditia lucernaria* prefer the very new foliage as food, and a growing evergreen vine tends to have the new foliage widely scattered at the tips of the many different vine ends rather than a huge number of new leaves together in the same place. Thus, the growth form of the plant results in the aggregation breaking up as the caterpillars scatter in search of this highly dispersed food.

During the second half of the rainy season and all of the long dry season, *P. lucernaria* remain as naked, dormant, and very hard pupae in the soil just below the litter. In captivity, the newly eclosed pupal shells are quite distinctive. They appear to have been broken open in the middle, almost like breaking an egg, rather than more precisely fractured along sutures of the wing and antennal impressions, as is the case with many pupal cuticles that are not so tough. The pupa, like that of most other Apatelodidae, appears designed for very long survival as a naked (no cocoon) pupa in the predator- and decomposer-rich litter-soil interface.

The adults of *P. lucernaria,* as is commonplace with dry-forest cryptic Lepidoptera, range from a mottled pale honey-beige to almost gray-black in overall color. The light-colored moth morphs are those that eclosed from pupae in relatively warmer circumstances, presumably indicating to the insect that it is still in dry season conditions with dry, pale foliage. The darker moth morphs, generally, are those that eclosed during the cooler rainy season when background colors are darker. Associated with long dormancies and a proclivity for becoming dormant rather than emerging a few weeks after pupation, a given brood of *P. lucernaria* may well emerge throughout the wet months of the calendar. The dark morphs of *P. lucernaria* are obnoxiously similar to the dark rain-forest *Phiditia cuprea,* and it is easy to imagine *P. lucernaria* being a dry-forest evolutionary spin-off from *P. cuprea,* or *P. cuprea* being a rain-forest spin-off from *P. lucernaria.* The two species co-occur on the northern flanks of Volcan Orosi, where the Guanacaste dry forest wraps around into the Atlantic rain

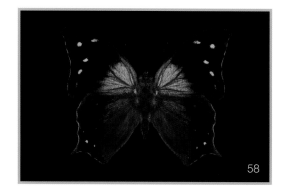

58

forest in the eastern ACG. The intergrade zone between dry forest and rain forest is the home to many such pairs of "sister species."

CATERPILLAR VOUCHER: 96-SRNP-8342; DHJ
ADULT VOUCHER: 96-SRNP-7543; JCM

58. *MEMPHIS PITHYUSA* – NYMPHALIDAE

Two groups of medium-sized butterfly caterpillars have independently evolved the behavior of rolling up a leaf, or using silk to tie several leaves together, and living inside. Hesperiidae are one, and the trait is almost universal among them from the first instar to the last. The other group is a subset of Nymphalidae, at least the genera *Memphis, Anaea, Fountainea,* and *Consul.* In the first through third instars, *Memphis pithyusa* caterpillars perch on the defoliated tip of the leaf with a few bits of leaf silked next to them for yet more camouflage (just as described in the species account for *Archaeoprepona meander,* #36). In the last two instars, the caterpillar leaves this ruse behind and rolls a *Croton* leaf (Euphorbiaceae) in which to spend the day, with its mildly spiny head blocking the entrance. The inner wall of the roll is thoroughly lined with a layer of strong silk applied by the caterpillar's spinneret, located on the labium (part of its mouthparts). At night, the caterpillar ventures outside the leaf roll to eat neighboring leaves. It does not cut off leaf parts and bring them back to the roll to eat in private, and it does not eat the inner leaf material of the roll (as do the leaf-rolling and webbing Pyraloidea moth caterpillars).

Caterpillars of *M. pithyusa* are found on at least five species of *Croton* in dry forest, rain forest, their intergrades, and even up to the lower edges of cloud forest. Yet *M. pithyusa* does seem to be far more abundant in rain forest than in dry forest. It may even be that it really is a rain-forest species that creeps out into dry forest if there is an adjacent rain forest. It may well not be able to sustain a population in the dry forest, however. Working out the distribution of *M. pithyusa* in the ACG has been maddeningly frustrating because the caterpillars are extremely similar to those of *Memphis forrerri, Memphis artacaena,* and *Memphis niedhoeferi,* though they are easily distinguished from the black-with-white dotted *Memphis aulica* and the green-mottled-with-brown *Fountainea eurypyle.* All of these species feed on *Croton* and all may be found together at any rain-forest site.

Although this defensive action has not actually been observed, *M. pithyusa* (and its other look-alike *Memphis* species) has a most endearing face on its rear end (but it is probably frightening to a small bird). The rear projects out of the back end of the leaf roll if some animal attempts to tear into the front of the leaf roll. Viewed from the rear, the tail end bears the appearance of a large snout with somewhat smallish black eyes on each side, highlighted behind with white. This projects an image easily perceived as snake-like. What we lack are empirical tests of the effects of this face on small birds, which is no easy task. Also, we have not peered down the inside of the nest often enough to have an opinion as to whether the mid-caterpillar dorsal white spots might also serve to create the illusion of eyes within the illusion of a face. These color patterns require more empirical examination. In the context of fore and aft and miscellaneous behavioral adaptations, *Memphis* leaf nests have the back door open. The pellet-shaped excrement falls out this opening as it is produced. Hesperiid caterpillars, on the other

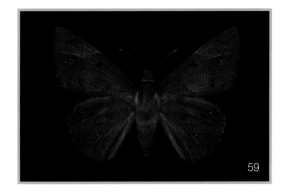

59

hand, generally have just the front of the nest open and defecate out the front door.

CATERPILLAR VOUCHER: 92-SRNP-3186; DHJ
ADULT VOUCHER: 85-SRNP-367; JCM

59. *DYSCOPHELLUS* BURNS02 – HESPERIIDAE

The caterpillar of *Dyscophellus* BURNS02 is among the most gaudy of the large and nocturnal ACG skippers in a group of closely related genera: *Bungalotis, Dyscophellus, Salatis, Ocyba,* and *Porphyrogenes.* Once one realizes what to look for, it is easy to distinguish its caterpillar from the look-alike sister species *Dyscophellus ramon* by markings on the top of the head. *Dyscophellus* BURNS02 has two bright lemon-yellow spots there (barely visible from the side in our image), whereas the top of the head in *Dyscophellus ramon* is immaculate and uniformly chocolate colored. Caterpillars of *D. ramon* are relatively common on mature foliage of insolated saplings of several species of rain-forest Lauraceae, especially at ACG forest edges. The adults are never seen flying in the daytime and rarely appear at lights, the source of nearly all *Dyscophellus* specimens in collections. Earlier efforts in the identification of these two skippers did not distinguish the species because, by a quirk of sampling, the first caterpillar found and photographed looked like the common *D. ramon* and was labeled as such. However, it actually was the much rarer *D.* BURNS02, and that caterpillar died. It thus failed to provide an adult for an accurate label on the photograph. Because the differences in color patterns of the head were not noticed, subsequent collections and rearings of caterpillars were assigned to the species name *D. ramon,* which was incorrectly attributed to the original photograph. This went on for several years. Then, several *D.* BURNS02 were encountered feeding on Annonaceae, a plant on which they are found even more rarely. These were reared through to adulthood, and once it was realized that there was a second, similar species in the habitat, the legacy of the earlier caterpillar photographs was correctly set into the record books.

Caterpillars of *D.* BURNS02 display an example of what occurs occasionally with highly host-specific species of skippers. They have a "usual" food plant, in this case various species of Lauraceae, and then, occasionally a single individual is found feeding and developing nicely on a species in an unrelated family of plants, in this case two species of Annonaceae. Given the sedentary nature of hesperiid caterpillars and the actual locations of the few Annonaceae records, it is clear that this is not due to the caterpillar wandering to these two species of Annonaceae. Rather, they were deliberately put there through their mother's choice of oviposition site. The implication of discovering two very different food plants is that we are seeing the raw ingredients for an evolutionary food-plant switch. All it would take is for a *D.* BURNS02 population to be isolated in some valley or on some mountain (or island) lacking Lauraceae but having Annonaceae. These would be the right conditions for intense selection for the traits required for obligatory oviposition on some species of Annonaceae. This could be followed by the newly endowed population getting onto the "mainland" with large numbers of Annonaceae to support a population and spread about. Hypothetically, we then have three species of look-alike *Dyscophellus* in the same place, one eating only Lauraceae (*D. ramon*), one eating both (*D.* BURNS02), and one eating only Annonaceae (the putative new species spun off from *D.* BURNS02). If there is a mating barrier of any sort between the new and the parent population, species richness has just gone up by one. If there is no barrier, then the new species may well genetically blur right back into its parent population. It also could, at least hypothetically, alter the behavior of the Lauraceae specialist (*D. ramon*) via introgression of genes that provide the programming code for feeding on Annonaceae. If these species were abundant enough to have any impact on each other, there might also be competitive exclusion dynamics at play. Both species of *Dyscophellus* are so rare, however, and their food plants so abundant, that this seems unlikely. Finally, if they had a host-specific parasite that might be favored by the appearance of yet more prey, there could be yet another dynamic, but records to date show that both species of *Dyscophellus* are almost untouched by generalist parasitoids, and neither have a specialist parasitoid.

CATERPILLAR VOUCHER: 04-SRNP-2748; JCM
ADULT VOUCHER: 02-SRNP-7471; JCM

60. *VENADA DANEVA* – HESPERIIDAE

The very first skipper caterpillar found in the cloud forest on Volcan Cacao was that of *Venada nevada,* feeding on a relative of avocado (Lauraceae) in the misty, cold, and wet forest understory. Gradually, we came to understand that this was the most abundant of the four ACG species of *Venada*. It feeds on several tens of species of understory Lauraceae from the cloud forest down into mid-elevation rain forest on the Atlantic side of the ACG. However, no *Venada* follows the only dry-forest Lauraceae, *Ocotea veraguensis*, into the Pacific lowlands. Two other cloud-forest species of ACG *Venada* have been found, each being substantially scarcer than *V. nevada*. Then the *gusaneros* found a

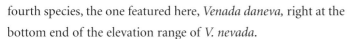

60

fourth species, the one featured here, *Venada daneva*, right at the bottom end of the elevation range of *V. nevada*.

These four species of *Venada* are essentially sympatric or parapatric and were undescribed when the ACG inventory began. Specimens of this genus are very scarce in museum collections. The reason is evident. Even in forests where the caterpillars are common, the adults are almost never seen, and when they are seen, they are just a brown blur zipping by at rocket speeds. John Burns at the Smithsonian Institution National Museum of Natural History has worked out their species-level taxonomy and formally published their descriptions (Burns and Janzen 2005). Somewhat ironically, it is not clear whether the original type species for the genus, *Venada advena*, even occurs in Costa Rica, or whether it might be the same as one of our four new species.

Although the adults are superficially very similar, and certainly indistinguishable while in flight, they are easily separated by their DNA barcode. Somewhat more arduously, they may be accurately identified through careful examination of the fine details in the shades of brown and orange on the wings, patterns, and wing shape. The caterpillars are, however, very easily distinguished by their distinctive pattern of lateral bars or discs, and basic colors (Burns and Janzen 2005). *Venada nevada*, with its lateral yellow bars, one to a segment, appears to be the "primitive" state. This trait is perhaps derived from the motif of complete body rings, a common pattern in many Hesperiidae caterpillars. The other three species have evolutionarily reduced these bars to four yellow-orange discoid spots, as displayed in our image of *Venada daneva*.

CATERPILLAR VOUCHER: 03-SRNP-6535; JCM
ADULT VOUCHER: 04-SRNP-2090; JCM

61. *RHUDA DIFICILIS* – NOTODONTIDAE

Our image of the caterpillar of *Rhuda dificilis* is one of just a few of our portraits that is shown as viewed from directly above. At this angle the many-colored, complex patterns—bright yellow, red, blue, and green—actually look like a portion of a rotted yellowing leaf. The unique projection from the center of the dorsum of the second abdominal segment, which is not well developed in earlier instars, adds a three-dimensional perspective to the look of a rotting, torn leaf.

There are two species of *Rhuda* in Costa Rica, *R. dificilis* and *R. tuisa*. The former is the rain-forest species and the latter is the dry-forest species. What is so peculiar about the name "*tuisa*" is that Tuis is a town on the Caribbean side of Costa Rica in the classic rain forest. It was a primary collecting locality of William Schaus in the early 1900s, and thousands of specimens of moths in the world's large collections bear the locality label "Tuis." One would expect that *R. tuisa* was named after the town where it was first collected, but no modern specimen of *R. tuisa* has ever been collected near Tuis or in the rain forest of Caribbean Costa Rica. The dry forest occupied by *R. tuisa* is several hundred kilometers from Tuis. There is undoubtedly a place somewhere in Costa Rica where both species may be caught at the same black-light, however, and the most obvious prediction would be in the forests on the north lower slope of Volcan Orosi, where the Pacific dry forest and the Caribbean (Atlantic) forests blend into each other.

Our records to date reveal 242 caterpillars of *R. tuisa* found only on *Mouriri myrtilloides* (Melastomataceae). It is a peculiar dry-forest tree with small and polished sclerophyllous leaves and no obvious parallel secondary venation, the signature venation of Melastomataceae. We have eighty-six records of *R. dificilis* caterpillars from eleven species of Melastomataceae on the rain-forest side of the ACG. Not surprisingly, there are thirteen rain-forest records from two species of *Vochysia*, a large tree in the Vochysiaceae and not at all related to Melastomataceae. Why not surprising? Because *Vochysia*, like *Dichapetalum*

61

(Dichapetalaceae), appears to be one of those peculiar plant species that is occasionally fed on by species of otherwise very host-specific caterpillars. Perhaps the most spectacular and unexpected case is the three records of *Xylophanes chiron* (#51) from this *Vochysia* in the ACG rain forest, when *X. chiron* is typically an inveterate consumer of Rubiaceae.

CATERPILLAR VOUCHER: 03-SRNP-10802; DHJ
ADULT VOUCHER: 02-SRNP-5308; JCM

62. *MARPESIA PETREUS* – NYMPHALIDAE

Marpesia petreus caterpillars are favorites of the ecotourist, sometimes being the very first caterpillar that the visiting dry-forest bird-watcher brings to us for identification. During a 2003 caterpillar workshop held at Santa Rosa, it took less than thirty seconds for a busload of camera-happy entomologists to be clustered around a fig tree at the Casona, sighting and photographing their first *M. petreus* caterpillar. The image we show was captured during part of that mob scene. For centuries, Costa Rican ranchers planted the introduced (from Venezuela) evergreen fig, *Ficus goldmanii* (Moraceae), around their houses and corrals for shade for themselves and the cattle. The first Costa Rican range cattle were not those white cebu dotting the sunny countryside, loving the blazing-hot dry-season sun, but red shorthorns of many kinds, all of which were quite fond of shade during the long dry season. Newly arrived female *M. petreus*, migrating in from the rain-forest side of Costa Rica, readily oviposit on the five native species of ACG dry-forest figs in May to early June. However, they are equally or perhaps even more attracted to the large new leaves of *F. goldmanii.*

The bright, multi-colored caterpillars—steel blue, red, and yellow—perch with seeming impunity on the top sides of leaves, as diurnal butterfly caterpillars are wont to do. They are ever so visible to nature seekers and birds. To many birds they might well look like a torn leaf edge, somewhat damaged by fungus, especially in the mottled darkness among the smaller leaves of native figs. On the large, shiny, light-green plates of *F. goldmanii* new leaves, they are more visible. The mother butterfly has no idea what the caterpillar's background will look like. All she can do is lay an egg if the plant smells like a fig, feels like a fig, and perhaps tastes like a fig. The large crowns of *F. goldmanii* do

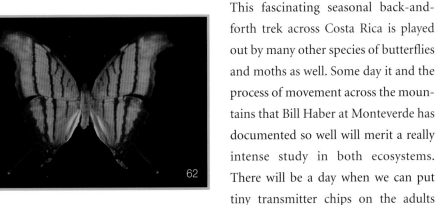

62

have another characteristic that discourages predators. They are right in the middle of human habitations. These, of course, are frequented by certain birds such as the magpie jays and house wrens, but the former are often focused on the garbage from the kitchen rather than searching patiently for single caterpillars, and the latter tend to forage at ground level rather than two to ten meters up in the tree crown.

First-generation adults of *M. petreus* eclose in June, about the time of the end of the first four to six weeks of the rainy season. These are the adults that have survived the numerous para-sitoids of both caterpillars and pupae. Nearly all of the adults leave the ACG dry forest, flying upwind through the passes over to the Costa Rican rain forest many tens of kilometers to the east. They do have very low-density populations (multiple generations, too) "over there" for the rest of the year. Then, some fraction of these great-great-grandchildren return to the ACG dry forest in May with the beginning of the rains to have their next "big" generation. A very few individuals remain to attempt a second or even third rainy season generation in the dry forest.

This fascinating seasonal back-and-forth trek across Costa Rica is played out by many other species of butterflies and moths as well. Some day it and the process of movement across the mountains that Bill Haber at Monteverde has documented so well will merit a really intense study in both ecosystems. There will be a day when we can put tiny transmitter chips on the adults and track them individually by satellite, just as has occurred with various fish, land mammals, sea turtles, and oceanic birds.

CATERPILLAR VOUCHER: 03-SRNP-ACGFIELD; JCM
ADULT VOUCHER: 88-SRNP-168; JCM

63. *ERINNYIS ELLO* – SPHINGIDAE

Caterpillars of *Erinnyis ello,* like many sphingids, exhibit a number of color morphs of green, gray, mottled brown, yellow, pink, and patterns of black, red, and white. The variety in the color patterns increases as the density of the caterpillars in an outbreak population increases. The trait of changing color, usually in the molt from the third to fourth or fourth to the fifth instar, seems to be induced by meeting other conspecifics. Selection for color shifts in caterpillars is driven by the formation of search images by visually orienting predators. There is therefore a selective advantage to being a different color pattern from that of your sibling, the one you just bumped into.

The easiest way to find an *E. ello* caterpillar is to examine the leaves of cassava plants growing by houses on small farms intermingled with secondary successional forest in the first few months of the rainy season. They are there later in the rainy season as well, though more sporadically. As a migrant moth, it comes and goes with the weather rather than remaining resident and passing the dry season as a dormant pupa (as do *Manduca lanuginosa* [#72], *M. dilucida, Xylophanes turbata,* and *X. juanita* [#5]). There is a caterpillar look-alike, *Erinnyis alope,* which also feeds on cassava, however, and it is very difficult to describe how to tell them from each other. *Erinnyis alope* almost always conform to the green and yellow pattern similar to the *E. ello* shown here. The adults are easy to distinguish by the large red area in the hind wing of *E. ello,* an area that is yellow on *E. alope.*

Whereas *E. ello* caterpillars are common on cassava, they can be equally common on wild dry-forest Euphorbiaceae, such as *Sebastiana pavoniana* and *Euphorbia schlectendalii,* as well as

63

another set of ten species now and then. The ACG inventory has also found *E. ello* caterpillars on three genera of Sapotaceae: *Chrysophyllum, Manilkara,* and *Sideroxylon;* one Caricaceae: *Carica,* the commercial and the wild papaya; and even seven times on the vines of *Forsteronia spicata,* Apocynaceae. This vine is often alongside caterpillars of *Erinnyis crameri* (#37) and *Pachylioides resumens.* All of these food plants have milky latex as a trait in common. The latex is an anti-herbivore defense, but there is more to it than that. There are many white-latex species (e.g., six species of *Ficus*) that definitely are not used by *E. ello,* and there is one feeding record on *Licania arborea* (Chrysobalanaceae), which does not have white latex as a defense. These food-plant records suggest we may be dealing with a caterpillar that can eat substantially more food plants than those chosen by the mother for oviposition.

Erinnyis ello is arguably the best-known Neotropical sphingid adult. This is not only because it is distinctive with its black-and white-banded abdomen and dimorphic sexes, but because it readily comes to lights. When migrating hundreds to thousands of kilometers, it frequently comes to lights at restaurants and in mountain passes. Additionally, the caterpillar is considered a major agricultural pest because it defoliates cassava plants, otherwise known as yuca or tapioca (*Manihot esculenta,* Euphorbiaceae). One pest-management technique used to combat this destruction employs a virus that is distributed in small packets from Colombia. Mixed with water and sprayed on plants, the contents of the package act as a kind of biological control. But virus-contaminated moths of *E. ello* may then fly into adjacent wild areas and may well become the source of a virus epizootic among *E. ello* and perhaps populations of other sphingids.

CATERPILLAR VOUCHER: 04-SRNP-12137; JCM
ADULT VOUCHER: 01-SRNP-9731; JCM

64. *UNZELA JAPIX* – SPHINGIDAE

The caterpillar of *Unzela japix* has a near look-alike twin species, the much scarcer *Unzela pronoe*. There is no reliable way to tell the two species from one another, other than to say that *U. japix* is slightly smaller and *U. pronoe* is slightly larger and always (so far) the dark morph. They eat the same food plants throughout the ACG. A second complication of *U. japix* caterpillar identification is that it has a green morph very similar to that of *Aleuron iphis,* but lacks the diamond pattern that *A. iphis* has on its back. In addition, because it ranges in color from green to pink-beige to brown, it is quite difficult to form a reliable search image for this caterpillar. The caterpillar spends the day perched on the midrib on the underside of the leaf. As it feeds, it cuts the end off the leaf, and then moves on to another leaf, leaving the previous leaf looking as if a pair of scissors had cut off its terminal third.

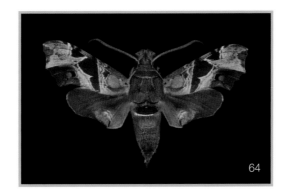

64

Caterpillars of *U. japix* have been found feeding on mature leaves of nine species of dilleniaceous woody vines, including *Davilla, Doliocarpus, Tetracera,* and *Curatella americana,* a dilleniaceous tree that grows in insolated dry habitats. These plants as a whole are distributed from the driest parts of the ACG to the wettest, but always below about 700 meters elevation. The caterpillars occur at relatively low density within the ACG, but generally one can be found by tenaciously searching many leaves on the low sprawling vines. It is quite notable that for the first several months of the rainy season in ACG dry forest, there are few or no *U. japix,* but their perennial and nearly evergreen food-plant vines, *Tetracera volubilis,* have large numbers of *Enyo ocypete* (Sphingidae) feeding on them. As the rainy season progresses, the *E. ocypete* density falls to nearly zero and the density of *U. japix* and *A. iphis* gradually rises until the end of the rainy season. At this time, however, they disappear entirely, presumably retreating to the rain-forest side of the ACG where there are year-round generations of *U. japix.*

This caterpillar is one of the most abundant of the small and truly nocturnal sphingids in the ACG, as evidenced by 892 rearing records through 2004. It was tempting to call a halt to its rearing, thinking that we had all the species of parasitoids fairly well documented. Just when we thought we had the full story, however, a few more caterpillars were brought in from yet another distinctive portion of the ACG ecosystems, and yet another species of parasitoid came to light. For example, after rearing more than 500 *U. japix* from the ACG dry forest, we obtained a series of caterpillars from the north slope of Volcan Cacao and reared our first *Drino alacris* (Tachinidae) flies, which have now been reared from twenty-four *U. japix*. All are from areas with more rainfall than the Santa Rosa dry forest gets. *Unzela japix* shares a different parasitoid, *Drino piceiventris,* with about twenty other species of Sphingidae (in strong contrast to the apparently host-specific *D. alacris*) in ACG dry forest and with a few other sphingids in rain forest. There are only two records of a

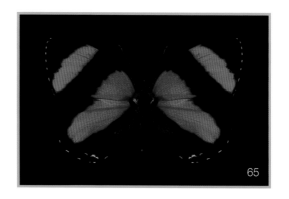

65

braconid (*Glyptapanteles,* Microgastrinae) attacking *U. japix*, and what appears to be the same species is normally a parasitoid of *E. ocypete* on the same food plant. There is also one doubtful record of an ichneumonid, which, again, is of a species that usually attacks a different species of sphingid.

CATERPILLAR VOUCHER: 04-SRNP-41546; JCM
ADULT VOUCHER: 00-SRNP-4460; JCM

65. *CALLICORE PITHEAS* – NYMPHALIDAE

The spiny, gray-green caterpillar perches on the upper surface of the leaf, with the fancy head ornament held forward and flush with the leaf surface. The purpose of the head ornamentation remains hidden deep in the realm of adaptation and some explanation of functional morphology. All of the species related to *C. pitheas* possess these head ornaments and all feed on sapinda-

ceous vines. Among all of these species, none have provided an answer to the question of the purpose of these structures. If all other nymphalid caterpillars were full of parasitoids, but *Callicore* and its relatives were not, then one might think that they are wasp or fly swatters of some kind. Indeed, it is the case that all of these nymphalids and their relatives have almost no parasitoids.

The last of these vivid red nymphalid butterflies that were encountered in October 2004 had decided that the laundry room in Santa Rosa had something absolutely fascinating in it. Each time it was approached for a photograph, the butterfly decided the person or the camera was too threatening and flew off. A few minutes later it was back again to perch on the screen door, looking as though it was convinced that there had to be some way through that screen. These strange butterflies are the one bit of extremely bright color that can be flushed from the environs while walking down a dry streambed in full dry season. The adults pass that time of year, when there are no leaves on which to oviposit, perched on a tree trunk in the cooler shade along dry streambeds through the forest. These microhabitats usually have a higher frequency of evergreens and semi-deciduous trees than do the surrounding uplands. The butterflies are not reproductive at that time, but may well be visiting sap fluxes and fermenting fruit. They do not visit flowers. They are pursuing the same dry-season strategy as do the skippers (Hesperiidae) that can be flushed out of dark crannies in the banks of the dry streambeds. The bright-red colors draw the eye, but then they abruptly disappear when the butterfly lands, to match its light pink and patterned underside with the irregular and light-colored patterns of dry-season tree trunks.

As soon as the rains come, *C. pitheas* adults disappear from the habitat. For decades we thought they might perhaps immigrate to some other area to breed, but they are never seen anywhere but in dry forest. Now we know that the few to survive the dry season mate after the rains begin. Why risk mating earlier—with someone incapable of making it through the dry season—before the true test of stamina? Soon after mating, they lay their eggs on the mature but not too old leaves of *Serjania atrolineata* (Sapindaceae) vines and then die. What a shame to trash such gorgeous wings. Two to three generations later, toward the end of the rainy season, the last adults eclose.

66

CATERPILLAR VOUCHER: 90-SRNP-2681; DHJ
ADULT VOUCHER: 91-SRNP-983; JCM

66. *CALYDNA STURNULA* – RIODINIDAE

This gorgeous but tiny green riodinid caterpillar—a really big one is fifteen millimeters long—with the magnificent hairdo was unknown to science until just recently (Hall et al. 2004). The "balloon setae," a fancy way to describe hairs modified into having a swollen distal end, and their chemicals are part of the caterpillar's defense against ants and other small predators. The diminutive caterpillars of *Calydna sturnula* feed only on *Schoepfia schreberi* (Olacaceae), a hemi-parasitic, small, shrubby, and very slow-growing tree in the ACG dry forest. The food plant is widely distributed from Mexico to Argentina, as is *C. sturnula*. They share this food plant with a second, more generalist species of riodinid butterfly, *Theope virgilius*, but this generalist caterpillar is, in contrast, deliberately tended by ants, which are its defense against certain natural enemies.

The strikingly black adult male of *C. sturnula* is dressed very differently from the finely mottled and tweed-patterned female. Whatever could have selected for this very striking difference is lost in the dim pages of millions of years of evolution. Male and female Riodinidae commonly differ only slightly in their color patterns. The sexes of Riodinidae can always be distinguished by the biologist with a magnifying lens, however. The males' front pair of legs are rather brush-like, densely covered with conspicuous long and fine hairs, whereas the front legs of females appear to be diminutive editions of the other four legs.

CATERPILLAR VOUCHER: 01-SRNP-15851; DHJ
ADULT VOUCHER: 95-SRNP-6705; JCM

67. *SYSSPHINX MEXICANA* – SATURNIIDAE

Although gaudy against its black background, the caterpillar of *Syssphinx mexicana* is almost invisible against the foliage of the ant acacia, *Acacia collinsii*, its food plant in the ACG. With sun and sky glinting through the finely divided acacia leaves, the silvery spines cause the body contour to disappear and the red stripe to become part of the reddish brown twigs. Here there may be an anachronism staring us in the face. Many *Syssphinx* and related genera, such as *Ptiloscola* and *Adeloneivaia,* bear this same general pattern of green and harmless spines. They are cryptic at a distance and a Batesian mimic of urticating hemileucine saturniids when viewed up close. But *S. mexicana* lives its entire caterpillar life within the crown of an ant-acacia tree and therefore within a colony of fiercely stinging ants that are adept at defending the tree against invaders (Janzen 1967). In the rainy season, these trees are free of vertebrates searching for prey, though sometimes in the dry season, when food is really scarce, white-face monkeys, *Cebus capucinus,* enter to break open the thorns and eat the ants. At this time of the year, however, *S. mexicanus* is safely below in the litter as a pupa. Caterpillars of *S. mexicana* could probably be just about any color and survive, thanks to the ant's aggressive behavior. Then again, one cannot avoid the thought that if it were bright yellow or pink, a squirrel cuckoo, *Piaya cayana,* or other smart and dedicated caterpillar hunter might well see it from a distance and tolerate the ants long enough to rush in and out of the canopy. Certainly the caterpillar-hunting rufous-naped wren, *Campylorhyncha rufinucha,* and banded wren, *Thryothorus pleurostictus,* know how to nest in these trees (Janzen 1969, Joyce

67

1993). In so doing they gain substantial protection against vertebrate predators, thereby serving as avian analogues of *S. mexicana,* and they would probably catch these caterpillars if they saw them.

The large black ant walking on the side of the caterpillar in our image treats the *S. molina* caterpillars as if they were just another part of the acacia foliage. The ant is known as *Pseudomyrmex belti* in the older literature and *Pseudomyrmex flavicola* (Formicidae: Pseudomyrmecinae) in the recent literature. The acacia is saturated with the odors of the ant colony, just as is the caterpillar. The uptake of ant odors happens as early as in the four to six eggs newly glued to an ant-acacia leaf. By the time the caterpillar hatches six days later, the first instar has acquired enough colony odor from the ants attacking the eggs and walking over them that it is only mildly attacked (by that particular ant colony). It is also hairier than are most ceratocampine saturniid first instars, suggesting that the hairs may be a partial defense as well, serving until it has fully acquired the colony odor. It also may be that the hairs serve as a sponge for retaining the ant odors on such a small body. The caterpillar eats mature leaves and elicits almost no response from the patrolling ants. As the caterpillar gradually defoliates the tree, only the shoot tips of growing branches remain. To the ant colony, these are the most valuable part of this fast-growing early successional treelet, and the part patrolled and most viciously protected by the oldest and most aggressive ants. In the end, the older ants do indeed drive a hungry caterpillar away from these shoots.

Ant protection is not absolute. Even *S. mexicana* is occasionally parasitized by ichneumonid wasps and tachinid flies, though it is also possible that these particular records came from caterpillars found in ant-acacia crowns with a weak or dying ant colony. A large predatory wasp, *Polistes carnifex* (Vespidae), has been observed to repeatedly enter an ant-acacia crown, find a last-instar *S. mexicana*, kill it by biting off chunks of caterpillar meat, and fly off with these large portions of food. It then returned to do this to two other conspecifics in the same tree. The ants are reliable guards against only certain species of predators.

CATERPILLAR VOUCHER: 83-SRNP-13462; DHJ
ADULT VOUCHER: 81-SRNP-824.31; JCM

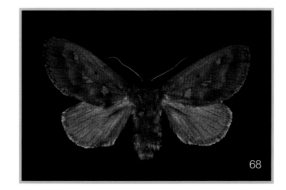

68

68. *EUCLEA NORBA* – LIMACODIDAE

Looking like a piece of slow-walking, shaggy lichen, or perhaps a disorderly Ming Dynasty pot, the *Euclea norba* caterpillar has followed one of the two primary tactics that Limacodidae have evolved in the ever-present challenge of avoiding vertebrate predators (see *Acharia hyperoche*, #44, for the other tactic). Resembling a piece of lichen has its advantages—after all, how fast do pieces of lichen move? Appearing to be lichen is a slam dunk for a limacodid caterpillar, arguably the slowest-moving family of caterpillars. They don't even have proper extensible and visible prolegs. The prolegs have been reduced to a blur on the undulating ventral surface, which moves smoothly over the leaf surface more like a miniature tank than a jerky camel. But if a vertebrate predator does see through the crypsis, those same urticating spines that are sported by many species in the family are a second line of defense.

Euclea norba is a dry-forest caterpillar, and conspicuously a caterpillar eating the mature leaves of large trees as well as the mistletoe parasites of these trees. It is definitely not a caterpillar that feeds on herbs and fast-growing vines and shrubs. In fact, none of the limacodids are. It requires nearly two months for a caterpillar to grow to the size of your thumbnail. Likely it is getting only a small portion of the nutrients present in the leaves it consumes, nutrients that remain in unchewed leaf chips or are bound to the digestion inhibitors (tannins, resins) for which the foliage of many of *E. norba* food plants are famous, including *Spondias*, *Cedrela*, and *Sweitenia*. This caterpillar, like others in the Limacodidae and their close relatives the Megalopygidae and the Dalceridae, produces distinctive, strongly dimpled or even cup-shaped excrement, in contrast to the deeply grooved pellets characteristic of the Saturniidae that feed on the same set of food plants. These cup-shaped pellets may well be a by-product of hindgut morphology that is adapted to recover as much water as possible from the processed food at the end of its digestive journey through the caterpillar gut.

The beauty of the caterpillar of this species is so grand that Janzen presented, in 1997, a print of its photograph to the Emperor of Japan as a gift. Knowing his love of marine invertebrates, this caterpillar looks so much like it belongs stuck to a rock in an intertidal pool that it seemed an appropriate connection between the Kyoto Prize ceremonies for the ACG and the ACG itself, which does, in fact, include marine habitat.

CATERPILLAR VOUCHER: 94-SRNP-5178; DHJ
ADULT VOUCHER: 01-SRNP-15388; JCM

69. ARCHAEOPREPONA DEMOPHOON – NYMPHALIDAE

The most annoying thing about *Archaeoprepona demophoon* is that it has a look-alike close relative named *Archaeoprepona demophon*. The caterpillar of the former is present throughout the ACG dry forest and rain forest, feeding on Lauraceae. The caterpillar of *A. demophon* feeds on select species of rain-forest Annonaceae, Connaraceae, Meliaceae, Fabaceae, Flacourtiaceae, and probably others, including one record from Lauraceae.

The first and second instars of *A. demophoon* are quite easy to find. Just look for a leaf of *Ocotea veraguensis* (Lauraceae) in the dry forest that has had the leaf blade eaten at the very tip, leaving just the midrib. Closer inspection reveals that the caterpillar is indeed there, hiding next to a few tiny leaf chips tied with silk to the newly stripped midrib. The larger later instars are much harder to find, scattered among the foliage, looking from a distance like a slender, dead, brown leaf with petiole intact, draped across a twig, slowly shivering and bobbing in the breeze when disturbed. Look closely and the magnificent false snake eye on each shoulder warns off small avian predators. Yet there is more to this story about defenses against natural enemies. The tiny white dots on the thorax of the penultimate instar look precisely like a smattering of tachinid fly eggs. It is the exact appearance of a last-instar larva with actual tachinid eggs glued (lethally) to its thorax by an undescribed species of *Winthemia* (Tachinidae) fly that specializes at parasitizing this caterpillar. Only an unknowable history can tell us why the last instar does not sport the same visual defense.

Adults of *A. demophoon,* among the largest and most magnificent of the ACG's heavily diurnal Nymphalidae, perch high on tree trunks with their bright pink-red tongues deep in a spoiling fruit or a yeast-infested, sap-rich wound. The silvery gray undersides of the wing, which we show here, look like a flap of peeling bark complete with fine dark reticulations. When disturbed, they launch into a rapid flapping-sailing flight that displays the brilliant iridescent blue stripes on the upper side of the wings. This blue is not to be confused with the blue colors of the wings of *Morpho* butterflies (Nymphalidae), a blue that covers most of the upper side of the wing. In flight, the bright blue colors of *A. demophoon* are easy to see and they probably say to the calculating hawking bird, "I am so fast and agile that it is a waste of your time to try and catch me." When the adult abruptly perches again, the bright blue flag immediately disappears, rendering the butterfly quite difficult to find again. This defense may also be at work when the females descend to taste leaves on low bushes to find oviposition sites, only one or two meters above the ground.

CATERPILLAR VOUCHER: 04-SRNP-46746; JCM
ADULT VOUCHER: 00-SRNP-1608; JCM

70. *SYNARGIS MYCONE* – RIODINIDAE

There are ant plants, such as *Acacia, Cecropia, Cordia,* and *Triplaris,* and there are ant caterpillars. *Synargis mycone,* a medium-sized riodinid butterfly, is an ant caterpillar. This brown (sometimes green), slug-like, slow-moving caterpillar is a specialist at eating the new foliage of *Licania arboreus* (Chrysobalanaceae), and is very commonly tended by ants. In the ACG dry forest these ants are often, but by no means always, the stocky brown *Camponotus planatus* (Formicidae, Formicinae) here perched on the caterpillar. In contrast to other more spindly and delicate-appearing species of *Camponotus, C. planatus* is active day and night and makes highly divided nests in hollow twigs rather than larger cavities in logs as preferred by classical carpenter ants. The ants are constantly collecting sugary material from a dorsal tail-end gland that actively secretes sweet carbohydrates. In effect the ants milk and protect the caterpillar

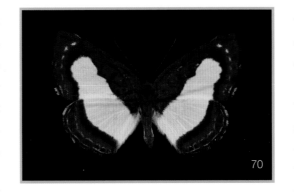

70

"cows" that feed them. The particular worker ant shown in the image was so intent on her caterpillar that she tolerated being brought back to the laboratory in a bouncing plastic bag, and stayed right on or next to her caterpillar the entire time. Gaining this kind of protection from ants of many genera is commonplace among species of Lycaenidae and Riodinidae around the world. In certain cases the relationship has taken a turn by the caterpillar preying on the ant larvae once taken inside the nest by the ants themselves.

Since *S. mycone* is apparently host-specific to *L. arboreus,* at least in the ACG dry forest, it is not likely to require *C. planatus,* or perhaps any other species of ant, as obligatory attendants. In fact, when brought in from nature and reared in the laboratory without attendant ants, *S. mycone* survives about as well as does any species of riodinid. The caterpillar of another common ACG dry-forest riodinid, *Theope virgilius,* in contrast, often dies without its attendant arboreal *Azteca* ants. *Theope virgilius* eats many species of plants. The trade-off is that since the female *T. virgilius* oviposits on foliage patrolled by *Azteca* ants, whatever species of plant that is, the caterpillars suffer whatever the penalties are of having to eat many kinds of plants. Ant behavior is the key to this relationship. *Azteca* are a vicious and aggressive ant, whereas *C. planatus* is a relatively passive ant.

Synargis mycone butterflies are sexually dimorphic. The males and females do not resemble each other in the slightest.

Although the numbers have not been assessed, strong sexual dimorphism in color pattern appears to be more commonplace in riodinid butterflies than in many other butterfly groups. The benefits, risks, trade-offs, and life-history correlates are not obvious. Perhaps the adaptive nature of this phenomenon will emerge when the adults are studied more intensively, as has been the case with the more conspicuous cases of sexual dimorphism in other families of Lepidoptera.

CATERPILLAR VOUCHER: 03-SRNP-789; DHJ
ADULT VOUCHER: 04-SRNP-10640; JCM

71. *PROTAMBULYX STRIGILIS* – SPHINGIDAE

The large, green caterpillars of *Protambulyx strigilis,* with its distinctive posterior single side slash and pointed top to the head, can be reliably found on the two dry-forest Anacardiaceae, *Astronium graveolens* and *Spondias mombin,* throughout the rainy season. They are also very rarely on *Simarouba glauca* (Simaroubaceae). In the ACG rain forest they eat *Tapirira brenesii; Mosquitoxylum jamaicense; Anacardium excelsum;* and the introduced *Anacardium occidentale,* the cashew, all Anacardiaceae; and *Simarouba amara.* With just this information in hand, it is not clear whether there are two species of moths occupying these two major ecosystems, each feeding on a different family of plants, or whether members of a single population circulate over the entire area and feed on two very different plant families.

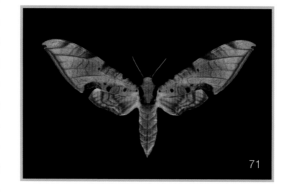

71

The extraordinary pair of *P. strigilis* food plants, Anacardiaceae and Simaroubaceae, are not considered to be related to each other taxonomically or in their defensive chemistry. It was unknown that *P. strigilis* fed on Simaroubaceae when the ACG inventory began. When the first caterpillar of *P. strigilis* was found on *S. glauca* in Santa Rosa, it appeared to be a strange oviposition error by the mother, or a recording error by the *gusaneros.* Gradually, more food-plant records accumulated, and then in 1997 it was commonly found feeding on *S. amara,* a very similar rain-forest tree.

The question of whether there was just one or two species of moths utilizing these two very different food plants remained a puzzle until 2003, when we DNA barcoded a series of adults reared from wild-caught caterpillars on Anacardiaceae and Simaroubaceae. We found them to be genetically identical. There is now simply no reason to question that *P. strigilis* is more than one species in the ACG. It is easy to imagine how having two such very different food plants could lead to speciation. All it would take is a dry area, such as the uplands of the Santa Elena Peninsula with just its resident *Simarouba glauca* trees and no Anacardiaceae, to select for a population that is adapted morphologically and behaviorally to this food plant and to this very dry ecosystem. Why does it not happen? Adult sphingids in general fly long distances in search of adult food and oviposition sites, being one of the more migratory groups of moths. The *P. strigilis* in Santa Elena are constantly bombarded with genes from incoming adults from moister parts of the ACG, and their offspring leave the dry hills to seek their fortune in both taller dry forest and lowland rain forest only a few kilometers distant. If Santa Elena was still an island, as it was for many tens of millions of years before hitting the newly forming Central America about 16 million years ago, the story could be quite different with the arrival of a single gravid female. This scenario is not far-fetched. Eons ago a mainland population of *Manduca* served as the ancestor of *Manduca blackburni* in Hawaii, and similarly, a mainland population of *Manduca rustica* was the source for the endemic subspecies *Manduca rustica galapagensis* in the Galápagos Islands.

Among the three species of ACG *Protambulyx—eurycles, goeldi,* and *strigilis*—only *P. strigilis* occurs in the dry forest. All three occur in ACG rain forest, however. The whereabouts of the caterpillars of the other two species is a total mystery. *Protambulyx strigilis,* or at least what appears to be one species, has a very broad range, occurring from the southern United States to Argentina. This is one of those well-known and widely distributed species that might turn out to be a complex of species once the DNA sequences are revealed. Alternatively, the species may be a broadly distributed, cohesive population.

CATERPILLAR VOUCHER: 04-SRNP-22801; JCM
ADULT VOUCHER: 02-SRNP-17997; JCM

72. *MANDUCA LANUGINOSA* – SPHINGIDAE

Notice the long, strong, hooked protuberance on the tail end. That "horn" is what gives the name "the hornworms" to the

72

caterpillars of the Sphingidae. The familiar tomato hornworm, *Manduca sexta,* graces backyard gardens in much of North America. Many of the caterpillars of this widespread family lose the horn as they molt into later instars. *Manduca lanuginosa* usually has the green body color commonplace for sphingids and the equally commonplace lateral diagonal slash marks of a contrasting color. However, the white slashes taper out into a thin archipelago of black-rimmed white dots extending onto the back of the caterpillar. This feature distinguishes *M. lanuginosa* caterpillars from the other fourteen species of ACG *Manduca.*

During the end of the first month of the rainy season, *M. lanuginosa* caterpillars are extraordinarily abundant on their usual food plant, the secondary successional woody vine, *Cydista heterophylla* (Bignoniaceae). Following this single generation, the pupae remain dormant in the soil throughout the remainder of the six-month rainy season and the following six months of dry season. The coming of the rains in the middle of May causes the daily temperature to plummet from as high as 37°C down to 28°C (Janzen 1993a). This temperature drop then cues the pupae to activate development. The adult ecloses within a few days. There can be hundreds of *M. lanuginosa* attracted to a single light in one night during the first several weeks of the rainy season. The females come first in the early evening and the males later in the night as they search for newly eclosed females and end up at the light instead.

Manduca lanuginosa has become almost like a saturniid in its adult biology. It lives only a few weeks and visits few flowers (there are very few to visit at the time of its flight period). It lays its eggs rapidly, perhaps by the tens per female per night. From the viewpoint of a visually orienting predator, there must be years when, in the early rainy season, the forest is heavily dotted with adult *M. lanuginosa*. This is the perfect circumstance for selection for adult polymorphism, or at least strong variation in color pattern. The predator forms a search image for the particular color pattern that it first encounters and does not notice the others. This favors the other morph through natural selection. Another interpretation is that there are many kinds of bark-colored backgrounds against which the adults may hide during the day, and the mother that produces a mixed brood of colors has a higher chance of some offspring surviving than does one that produces only a single color. Whatever the cause, *M. lanuginosa* is conspicuous for its adult colors ranging from pale slate-gray to strongly mottled tweed to almost dark black-brown. Such extreme variation in adult appearance in one site is commonplace in short-lived Saturniidae (Janzen 1984a), but rare in Sphingidae and not displayed by any other species of ACG sphingid.

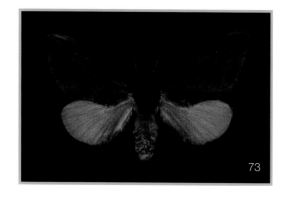

73

Despite their extreme but narrow seasonal abundance, *M. lanuginosa* caterpillars have no specialist parasitoid. From a total of 865 rearings of wild-caught caterpillars almost no generalist parasitoids have been reared (Janzen et al. 2003). They are eaten by birds and preyed upon by generalist predaceous insects, but one wonders why they do not build up to sufficient numbers to cause total defoliation of their common food plant. Perhaps there is substantial predation on the pupae. The pupae are shallowly buried in the upper layers of the soil, where they must survive for eleven months, perhaps serving as easy prey for mice, armadillos, and other soil-bound predators.

CATERPILLAR VOUCHER: 03-SRNP-12447; JCM
ADULT VOUCHER: 03-SRNP-13028; JCM

73. *ACHARIA HORRIDA* – LIMACODIDAE

Acharia horrida and *Acharia ophelians* are the only two heavily gregarious limacodid caterpillars known in the ACG. Each species lays long strings of eggs in a single oviposition bout, and the caterpillars continue to feed side by side all the way through the last instar, assuming the group is not broken up by predators, parasitoids, or physical challenges. The caterpillars even spin their cocoons side by side. The old empty cocoons look like a batch of white gecko eggs glued in a flat patch on the tree trunk.

As the name implies, *A. horrida* inflicts an extraordinarily painful sting when touched. Since comparative pain assessment has not been conducted, however, it is not clear if its urticating spines pack a punch that is any worse than that of the other four species of ACG *Acharia*—*sarans, nesea, hyperoche,* and *ophelians.* Based on appearances, *A. nesea* looks like it could be even more painful, but that is only because its urticating spines are borne on fierce-looking extended tubercles. Based on morphological similarities in their caterpillars and the fact that the adults are quite difficult to distinguish, *A. horrida* and *A. ophelians* would appear to be quite closely related and a bit distant from the other three *Acharia.* Indeed, several decades ago they were often considered to be just different color morphs of the same species.

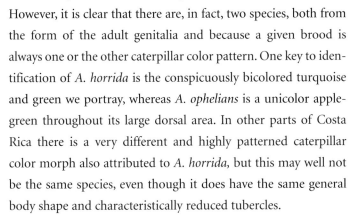

74

However, it is clear that there are, in fact, two species, both from the form of the adult genitalia and because a given brood is always one or the other caterpillar color pattern. One key to identification of *A. horrida* is the conspicuously bicolored turquoise and green we portray, whereas *A. ophelians* is a unicolor apple-green throughout its large dorsal area. In other parts of Costa Rica there is a very different and highly patterned caterpillar color morph also attributed to *A. horrida,* but this may well not be the same species, even though it does have the same general body shape and characteristically reduced tubercles.

We have only 102 rearing records of *A. horrida,* and a number of these are siblings feeding side by side. Yet they are recorded from fifteen very different plant families. Once more records are accumulated, this species will probably be known to

be among the champion generalists, just as are the other *Acharia.* Having noted that, it would be a definite error to assume that they can eat everything, however. In fact, a set of experiments are long overdue. An experiment of value would be to acquire gravid females of these "generalists" from a light trap and test their caterpillars against a truly large array of the species of plants available in the ACG. Such a test would probably reveal that many species of plants are indeed not available to them, and that within those that are available, there are wildly different growth rates of the surviving caterpillars with quite different body weights of the resulting pupae and adults. Such data would illustrate the dietary effects on fitness among siblings, which could be compared to patterns of food-plant use in the wild (for an example of this type of feeding study based on the gypsy moth in the United States, see Miller and Hanson 1989a,b; Miller et al. 1991).

CATERPILLAR VOUCHER: 04-SRNP-2780; JCM
ADULT VOUCHER: 01-SRNP-997; JCM

74. *TARCHON FELDERI* – APATELODIDAE

The first photograph Janzen took of a moth caterpillar in Costa Rica was of *Tarchon felderi* as it walked down the finger of Sally Richards in the now-extinguished rain forest near Rincon de Osa in southwestern Costa Rica in 1965. We all knew it as some sort of "maybe arctiid." It seemed absurdly gaudy and presumably possessed of a gallant stinging or toxic trick as its mechanism for defense. It was often encountered walking along the top side of rain-forest understory plants of every imaginable species. Thirty years later we connected the caterpillar to its adult, allowing us to give it a name. Then we found that the scarcer gold-sided version of the caterpillar is apparently the same species. The adult looks exactly like the adult produced from the red, black, and white version we feature here. Yet it remains to be seen if DNA sequencing shows that these two entities are different color morphs of the same species or two species that are look-alikes.

A masterful food-plant generalist, *T. felderi*, like many species of Apatelodidae, has a horrendously long list of food plants. This species is among the champion generalists with some sixty-five species in more than thirty families. Despite this breadth in diet, it is a rain-forest and lower cloud-forest species, not venturing into ACG dry forest. It will not be surprising, however, to find that it has many species of plants that it cannot eat, just as is the case with the other super-generalists: *Hylesia lineata* (#26), *Automeris zugana* (#3), *Acharia horrida* (#73), *Hypercompe icasia*, *Hypercompe albescens*, *Spodoptera latifascia*, *Tiracola grandirena*, and others. *Tarchon felderi* has an extremely active caterpillar, leading one to believe that in nature it probably eats a bit of something, and then walks on to eat a bit of something else. When the *gusaneros* find it, they give it whatever it was on at the time as its food for the remainder of its life, but that does not mean that it would have remained on that food plant in nature. What kind of gut system and physiology, including the chemistry of polysubstrate mono-oxygenase enzymes, does it take to handle such a variety of plant foods and their secondary compound defensive chemistry?

An equally challenging question is: "Why isn't the world blanketed with *T. felderi* caterpillars eating everything?" Given the brilliant display of colors and the behavior of diurnal perching on the upper surfaces of plants, which also makes them very easy to find by the *gusaneros*, it can hardly be that birds and similar predators do them in. Only 10 percent of the 119 wild-caught caterpillars have been parasitized, and of these, more than half were generalists that parasitize an array of species of caterpillars. In fact, there is only one very low-density ichneumonid that is a candidate for being a host-specific parasitoid on *T. felderi*. About the only visible obstacle to *T. felderi* population growth is that the caterpillars grow very slowly, with the result that the late instars found in the forest are the very few survivors of a long attrition of each clutch from random acts of mortality by predators and climate.

CATERPILLAR VOUCHER: 04-SRNP-3176; JCM
ADULT VOUCHER: 02-SRNP-9476; JCM

75. *DIPTERYGIA ORDINARIUS* – NOCTUIDAE

Dipterygia ordinarius adults are exactly what the species epithet suggests. Resembling rough bark, they are small and unexceptionally ordinary noctuids. They have been selected to be cryptic to avoid being discovered by a searching bird. The caterpillars have taken a very different approach to life. They specialize in feeding on the new, young, and very young foliage of the occasional secondary successional dry-forest vine *Securidaca sylvestris*. This is the only ACG dry-forest Polygalaceae. The vine becomes particularly evident in the mid-dry season, its crown covered with small lavender flowers that attract bees. The caterpillars of *D. ordinarius* come in two color morphs. One is light green, exactly the same color as the newly expanded leaf and nearly invisible when viewed from above. It has a light yellow lateral line, presumably to add a bit of contour or depth to the view. The other morph has a brilliant red head and an orange lateral stripe, and is ringed or checkered dorsally in black and white. The multi-colored morph is clearly advertising itself and can be seen by any and all passers-by. The proportions of the two *D. ordinarius* color morphs have never been recorded. Our records cannot serve as an indicator of the frequency of color forms because the collector is much more likely to notice the ostentatious morph rather than the cryptic morph. The green morph, which would be viewed as "probably highly edible" by birds, might be good evidence that the ostentatious morph is itself quite edible and that there are at least some birds that will eat it. Both morphs can be found perched on the upper- and undersides of the small oval leaves of *S. sylvestris*. The multi-colored morph is a very good mimic of the caterpillar of *Dipthera festiva*, a common noctuid caterpillar on weedy Sterculiaceae that is most decidedly not eaten by birds. Additionally, in the

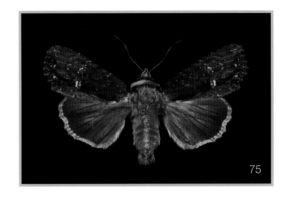

75

morning when birds come and eat the remaining sleeping moths off the sheet from a light trap hung in the forest, it is the brightly colored *D. festiva* adults that always remain sleeping peacefully, untouched by the harvesting birds.

There are easily another fifty species of ACG dry-forest caterpillars that look like the aposematic morph of *D. ordinarius,* and many more in the ACG rain forest. While there are some evident models such as *D. festiva,* it is not at all clear which are models and which are mimics, or even if those terms really should be used at this stage in the evolution of these relationships. Just as birds can be, and some ACG birds definitely are, genetically programmed to avoid brightly ringed caterpillars (Smith 1975), it is plausible that the color pattern of *D. ordinarius* is also instinctively avoided. Or, perhaps the three striking colors—black, white, and orange-red—presented in a pattern with some elements of rings and stripes blurs into a hard-wired perception of "danger" or "inedible" that provides protection to any caterpillar displaying these elements. It is quite striking that on leaves of the same ACG dry-forest *S. sylvestris* plants there is a host-specific caterpillar in the Immidae that is multi-colored in a similar manner. In the cloud forest there is yet another species of Immidae feeding on *Securidaca micheliana*. Its caterpillar color pattern is also a very good approximation of that of the aposematic morph of *D. ordinarius* (see image 99-SRNP-539 on the ACG Web site).

In the cloud forest, *D. ordinarius* adults come to light traps, though the caterpillars have not been found, so they may be migrants rather than residents.

CATERPILLAR VOUCHER: 92-SRNP-2778.1; DHJ
ADULT VOUCHER: 84-SRNP-193; JCM

76. *SOROCABA* JANZEN01 – APATELODIDAE

This is one of those distinctive yet taxonomically challenging species that is distinctive as an adult and distinctive as a caterpillar, yet we have not been able to match it up with a species name.

For many years *Sorocaba* and *Phiditia* were placed in the Lymantriidae. They are now considered to belong in an unusual subfamily, the Phiditinae, within the Apatelodidae. It will be most interesting to see where sequencing their DNA places them in the higher classification of moths. It is difficult to believe that *Sorocaba,* being obviously quite hairless, belongs in either

76

Apatelodidae or Lymantriidae, since the classic members of these two families are typically very hairy caterpillars. *Sorocaba* JANZEN01 is the only member of the genus known from the ACG, or Costa Rica for that matter. It appears to be a true rain-forest moth. It should be noted that several specimens were collected in a light trap in the 1980s in the dry forest at Santa Rosa, however. Although it is a rain-forest moth, its population can creep into adjacent dry forest in wet years.

The brilliant orange, black, and white caterpillars are easily visualized as relatives of *Phiditia lucernaria* (#57) and *Phiditia cuprea,* also phiditine apatelodids. They occur in gregarious groups, presumably derived from a single egg mass laid by a single female. She is nonfeeding, as are all Apatelodidae, and probably lives only five to ten days (as though she is a miniature saturniid). Identifying their food plant is a bit problematic because the *gusaneros* in the early days of the ACG rain-forest inventory had a tendency to confuse *Vitex cooperi* (Verbenaceae) with *Godmania aesculifolia, Tabebuia impetiginosa,* and *Tabebuia guayacan* (Bignoniaceae). The latter two food-plant records probably were *V. cooperi,* and the *G. aesculifolia* record may be as well. All of these plants have palmate compound leaves with strong drip tips on the ends of the leaflets. All of these food-plant records will be confirmed by re-collecting from the actual individual food plants. Species of Bignoniaceae and Verbenaceae are the food plants for *Phiditia* as well.

It is very likely that the brightly ringed and gregarious caterpillars are aposematic models for a large number of less toxic caterpillars. Really, how could they be anything but toxic if they are to survive vertebrate predators with their brightly colored beacon-like facies. *Sorocaba* JANZEN01 is also nearly free of parasitoids. There is just a single record of an incredibly generalist tachinid, *Patelloa xanthura,* from more than 300 wild-caught caterpillars.

CATERPILLAR VOUCHER: 03-SRNP-4767; JCM
ADULT VOUCHER: 02-SRNP-168121; JCM

77. *PARASA SANDRAE* – LIMACODIDAE

Parasa sandrae is perhaps the most frequently encountered limacodid caterpillar in the ACG rain-forest understory. Nevertheless, its scientific description was just published by Epstein and Corrales in 2004. One does wonder how this very common limacodid escaped detection by the rain-forest moth collectors for so long. The ACG inventory database contains 238 rearing records representing about eighty species of plants in over twenty-five families. Its long food-plant list is testimony to its ability to feed and successfully develop on a tremendous variety of food plants while confronting an amazing array of plant defense molecules. The moth does come to lights hung in the forest, but the males, the most common gender to arrive at lights, are relatively small and are easily overlooked among the larger moths. In nature, these moths are almost impossible to find. Their brown wings display a minute green patch, looking like a dead leaf with a small chunk of moss or lichen stuck to it.

The small, urticating spiny caterpillar, marked with neon blue, bears a superficial resemblance to the caterpillar of *Parasa wellesca,* which occurs in the rain forest but is more commonly encountered in the ACG dry forest. Both species unhesitatingly march across the upper sides of leaves as well as the undersides, grow very slowly, and spin their nearly spherical silk cocoons, laden with excrement, tightly to either a green leaf on the plant or a dead leaf among the ground litter. Neither species is quick to eclose as an adult, even in the rain forest. For instance, *P. wellesca* passes the six-month dry season as a prepupa inside a cocoon. In the process of adult emergence, the pupa wiggles part of the way out of the top of the cocoon via a previously formed escape hatch. The moth then crawls directly into the open air and up a stem to hang, expand, and harden its initially moist and crumpled wings. Hardening of the wings is not only drying, but also involves an enzyme-driven solidification of the fluids in the veins of the wings, the same fluid that was pumped into the wings to expand them. Even though *P. sandrae* is one of the smallest ACG limacodids, there are several yet smaller species, *Vipsophobetron marisa* being one of those.

Parasa sandrae is not immune to, or ignored by, parasitoids. Rearing its caterpillars has demonstrated that three species of *Uramya* tachinid flies and two species of ichneumonid wasps use this small caterpillar. There is an interesting single parasitoid record of a species of *Systrophus* (Bombyliidae). This genus of bombyliid is an unusual, wasp-like fly whose host records consist entirely of species in the Limacodidae. This is in stark contrast to the other bombyliids, parasitoids of nesting bees.

CATERPILLAR VOUCHER: 00-SRNP-23634; DHJ
ADULT VOUCHER: 04-SRNP-438; JCM

Dalceridae caterpillars are a natural history mystery. In their slug-like shape, gliding-walking motion, and overall appearance, they are reminiscent of Limacodidae, to which they are closely related. Dalceridae are also closely related to Megalopygidae. In contrast to Limacodidae, whose species are in their own right a study in slow motion, dalcerids zip right along, especially when being attacked, or even photographed. Also, in contrast to limacodids, dalcerids have no urticating spines or other form of physical-chemical defense. They have something that no other caterpillar possesses, however—a copious number of break-away lumpy and sticky body parts. This layer of surface gelatinous material is well developed in all dalcerids, resembling a layer of clear ice. Some, such as *A. hamata,* have a particularly well-developed icing. The white and clear "gelatinous warts" that cover the caterpillar of *A. hamata* are apparently secreted by modified hairs (setae) that are visible as a white rod in the center of the wart. The "warts" break off readily when the caterpillar is grabbed, and can be secreted again. If you pick up a caterpillar in a rough manner, all you get is a gooey mass stuck to your fingers, or a beak, with the caterpillar escaping by quickly walking away. Presumably this is a defense against grasping predators, such as birds, wasps, and ants.

Dalcerid caterpillars occur at very low density in the ACG—one here, one there—in rain forest, dry forest, and cloud forest. They appear to be generalists. The food-plant records for *A. hamata* include nine species in six families (based on eighty-five field-collected caterpillars). We do not have enough feeding records for enough dalcerid caterpillars that were successfully reared to an adult to make a definitive statement about the species in the family as a whole, however.

Adult dalcerids are small, soft-bodied, and somewhat hairy. They may be white, yellow, orange, brown, or a combination of these colors and are often overlooked when they are perched on the sheet of a light trap hung in the forest. This is because they hold their flimsy wings vertically erect in a tent-like form straight over their back, making them appear very small indeed when one is looking straight down on them. In nature they perch on leaves and bark, looking like a flap of discolored leaf. In this position, they wait out the day, avoiding searching predators. Like other bombycoids, the adults do not feed and live only five to ten days. In effect, they are ecologically like tiny saturniids.

The parasitoid fauna associated with *A. hamata* seems to be unique to them. There is a single record of *Houghia* sp. 17 and *Thelairaporia* sp. 01, tachinid flies, and a rogadine braconid wasp. In all these cases, if the parasitoid attacks the caterpillar directly, it perhaps employs a specialized behavior or morphology that can penetrate the curious gelatinous layer covering the caterpillar.

CATERPILLAR VOUCHER: 01-SRNP-6494; DHJ
ADULT VOUCHER: 02-SRNP-8617; JCM

79. *HETEROCHROMA SAREPTA* – NOCTUIDAE

Heterochroma sarepta is in the running for being the dullest of the adults produced from one of the gaudiest of caterpillars. If you saw the adult buzzing around a gas station light in California, Illinois, or Pennsylvania, where this tropical moth does not occur, you would not give it a second glance unless you were one of the perhaps three people among the world's 5.5 billion inhabitants who are fanatics on the taxonomy of Costa Rican Noctuidae. Its food plants, four species of *Smilax* (Smilacaceae) in the ACG, are green-briar, the evergreen thorny vine well known to U.S. field biologists and wildlife aficionados. It is really just a woody, evergreen climbing lily. The different species of *Smilax* occur across the ACG, and *H. sarepta* are found on it in all three major ACG ecosystems: dry forest, rain forest, and cloud forest.

79

The brilliant orange, black, and white caterpillar is unambiguously part of the mimicry complex involving patterns with red/orange head, red/orange rear, black and white ringed/checkered body, red/orange feet, and miscellaneous side markings thrown in for good measure. There are more than 100 species of ACG caterpillars with this general color pattern spread across at least seven families: Hesperiidae, Epiplemidae, Geometridae, Noctuidae, Nymphalidae, Sphingidae, and Saturniidae. Take a moment and glance at the images of *Lycorea cleobaea* (#50), *Phiditia lucernaria* (#57), *Dipterygia ordinarius* (#75), *Sorocaba* JANZEN01 (#76), and *Chrysoplectrum* BURNS01 (#90) to compare nuances in the patterns of these shared traits. There is no way yet to determine which are the models and which are the mimics. Indeed, perhaps all of them are mimics of a generalized genetically programmed pattern that is avoided by vertebrate predators. Yet it is striking that in this case, four of the five species of noctuid caterpillars that feed on *Smilax* in the ACG are colored in this manner. The fifth, as yet not identified to species or even genus, is colored a pure young-leaf green. In keeping with the suite of characters that typify brightly colored and obvious caterpillars, *H. sarepta* generally perches on the upper sides of the leaves, about as conspicuous as it can possibly be.

Although the bright colors of *H. sarepta* must surely be part of a warning system to visually orienting predators, they certainly do not protect this caterpillar from a quite distinctive and very host-specific species of microgastrine braconid, an undescribed species of *Glyptapanteles*. The larvae of this gregarious braconid, in striking contrast to nearly all other Microgastrinae wasps, do not spin white silk cocoons next to the "living" host from which they have just emerged. Rather, they spin hard, orange-brown cocoons next to and partly below the caterpillar body, which is still visually protective. As a side note regarding parasitoid-host relationships, understand that the parasitized caterpillar is considered "physiologically alive" but not "ecologically alive." This is because it is still a physiologically functioning mass, not yet decomposed, but it is reproductively (ecologically) dead because it will not complete development. Its final, physiological death will occur about the same time the wasps are emerging from their cocoons. One cannot help but wonder if the cocoons are gaining protection by displaying a bright color and remaining in the proximity of the gaudy, moribund caterpillar.

CATERPILLAR VOUCHER: 04-SRNP-55967; JCM
ADULT VOUCHER: 98-SRNP-3227; JCM

80. *NYCERYX MAGNA* – SPHINGIDAE

The very gaudy caterpillar of *Nyceryx magna* is a coloration enigma. The early instars are green and well hidden, even with their faint traces of the color pattern soon to be the dominant dress in later instars. The penultimate and ultimate instars are practically gaudy. They are evident to anyone looking at the undersides of the very large leaves of *Pentagonia donnell-smithii* (Rubiaceae). The most reasonable working hypothesis is that the colors are some approximation of aposematism (warning colors) or that they are in fact cryptic if seen from the viewpoint of a bird that is foliage-gleaning in the deeply shady rain-forest understory. Only experimentation will tell.

80

What confounds experimental studies of this sort is, of course, that the process or agent that selected for those colors may be long gone from the scene, and the caterpillar just survives in spite of the "energetic costs" implied by their continued presen-

tation. In this sense, *N. magna* fits well eco-evolutionarily with the bright-yellow caterpillar of the sphingid *Oryba kadeni*, likewise ostentatiously feeding on the underside of huge rain-forest rubiaceous leaves in both the ACG and South America.

Among the sphingids, *N. magna* is one of a few species that simply never appear at a light trap in the forest where they live. Between 1978 and the mid-1990s, Winifred Hallwachs, Daniel Janzen, and nearly seventy-five parataxonomists put out light traps all over the Costa Rican rain forest for literally thousands of trap-nights. A "trap-night" is one light trap hung for one night. We saw and collected tens of thousands of adult sphingids at these lights, and never once did a *N. magna* appear. We even placed the lights for hundreds of trap-nights in the very forest where we later found hundreds of *N. magna* caterpillars, some only a few meters from the lights—the mid-elevation rain forest in Sector San Cristobal of the ACG. Previously, this moth was known only from Ecuador and Peru (D'Abrera 1986), but the finding that it does not visit lights suggests that it may occur very widely. All the records appear to be either moths caught while visiting flowers or moths that happened to wander into a building, which serves then as a giant Malaise trap. All of the other six Costa Rican species of *Nyceryx* are also only rarely, if at all, caught at lights. What is not clear is whether they do not come under the light trap's spell when males are seeking females, or whether these moths fly at dusk and dawn and are settled down during the dark hours of the night. If it were only the latter, one would think that they should occasionally end up in a collector's net or at a light just by chance.

Nyceryx magna escapes the night moth collectors, but it does not escape an ichneumonid wasp, Cryptophion espinozai, which oviposits in the first- to third-instar caterpillars. This is the only species of parasitoid recorded from 251 wild-caught N. magna caterpillars. The wasp larva emerges from the eviscerated third-instar N. magna caterpillar and spins a fat, cylindrical cocoon, white with black markings, glued firmly to the leaf. The wasp larva positions itself such that the caterpillar cadaver, basically an empty cuticle, is draped (and glued) over its dorsal side. This gives the impression of a shriveled and dead (worthless to a bird) caterpillar with a bulge in the middle. This wasp has been reared from fourteen species of sphingid caterpillars throughout all the lower- to mid-elevation dry forest and rain forest of the ACG.

CATERPILLAR VOUCHER: 99-SRNP-1276.3; DHJ
ADULT VOUCHER: 99-SRNP-13023; JCM

81

81. *MORPHO PELEIDES* – NYMPHALIDAE

Many people think they know the caterpillar of that big, iridescent blue butterfly that you see flopping through the air following trails and streambeds, along roadsides through the rain forest, which sits feeding on rotting fruit behind houses or under trees in the forest. But the last instar of *Morpho peleides* occurs in two color morphs and a few in-between individuals. Some are well festooned with yellow (as is the one we show), and without looking closely they are difficult to discern from the caterpillar of *Morpho amathonte*. The other color morph of *M. peleides* looks like brown, grooved tree bark. They are extremely cryptic when sitting on brown stems. This brown morph also has a look-alike, the caterpillar of *Morpho granadensis*. In fact, this later species has been accused of being just a "form" or "variety" of *M. peleides*. *Morpho granadensis* is a perfectly good species with many facies differences from *M. peleides*, however. Furthermore, *M. granadensis* is largely restricted to one species of rain-forest food plant in the ACG, *Machaerium seemannii* (Fabaceae). Whereas there is no mystery in the cryptic morph of *M. peleides*, the bright-yellow-adorned morph could be a mimic of *M. amathonte*. The two of them could be cryptic in the context of some aspect of light, fungi, and rotting fruit. Like *Lirimiris* (#97), they display very bright colors combined with disruptive margins of dark lines and hairs, a pattern that is open to interpretation regarding adaptive functions.

The food-plant list for *M. peleides* is amazing. First, it eats about twenty-three species of dry-forest, rain-forest, and lower cloud-forest woody saplings and vines in the Fabaceae. No surprise there. The surprises are the few records from Dichapetalaceae: *Dichapetalum grayumii* and *D. morenoi*; Malpighiaceae: *Heteropterys latifolia*; Ochnaceae: *Ouratea lucens,* and most recently, in 2004, some lower cloud-forest palms. The latter is a nice bridge to the past since some South American species of *Morpho* eat palms (and the ACG inventory database contains two records of *M. granadensis* from palms), and because close relatives such as *Caligo* and *Miltiades* are palm eaters. *Morpho peleides* finds itself in the same habitat with four other species of *Morpho*. It shares food plants with *M. amathonte* and *M. granadensis,* but not with *Morpho theseus,* whose caterpillars feed on Menispermaceae, and not with *Morpho polyphemus,* whose caterpillars feed on *Inga punctata* (Fabaceae) and *Forchhammeria trifoliate* (Capparidaceae).

In the rainy season *M. peleides* breeds throughout the dry forest. It also breeds throughout the year in rain forest and lower cloud forest. In the dry forest, the adults appear to wait out the dry season feeding on fruit in local shady and dark places, or actually disperse into the volcanic foothills, and then perhaps fly back to the rainy-season dry forest after an unknown number of generations. There are even *M. peleides* breeding in

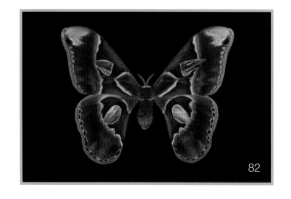

82

the wooded gullies of the very dry Santa Elena Peninsula.

Because of the congeneric relationships and type of overlap in food plants, the parasitoid records for *Morpho* are surprising. In brief, *M. peleides* and *M. polyphemus* share a parasitoid (but not food plants), a tachinid fly, *Hyphantrophaga* sp. 05. However, this parasitoid does not attack *M. amathonte,* a congeneric species that shares food plants with *M. peleides.*

Furthermore, the fly does not attack either of the other congeners, *M. granadensis* and *M. theseus.*

CATERPILLAR VOUCHER: 03-SRNP-6510; JCM
ADULT VOUCHER: 00-SRNP-305; JCM

82. *ROTHSCHILDIA LEBEAU* – SATURNIIDAE

The caterpillar of *Rothschildia lebeau* has become the test-tube *Drosophila melanogaster,* laboratory rat, and guinea pig of the ACG. Among the very first large caterpillars encountered when the ACG inventory began in 1978, it quickly proved itself easy to rear on its four usual food plants in diverse families, easy to transport in its fascinating silk cocoon suspended from a twig, and easy to manipulate as an adult. A drawing of the adult was initially meant to be the emblem of the ACG, but an artist's mix-up led to the more beautiful and more difficult to find *Rothschildia erycina* occupying this place of honor. In the early days of ACG dry-forest succession, when there were clean pastures bordered by saplings and forest edge, a short search at night in June could easily result in finding one of the large *R. lebeau* caterpillars in the tree crown of *Xanthoxylum setulosum* (Rutaceae), *Spondias mombin* (Anacardiaceae), *Casearia nitida* (Flacourtiaceae), or *Exostema mexicanum* (Rubiaceae). Their apple-green bodies are covered with a thin coat of wax that is nearly invisible in daylight but reflects a beam from a flashlight or spotlight like a green-white bicycle reflector.

The caterpillar is a Batesian mimic throughout its life. The first three instars fall somewhere in the group that looks like Limacodidae and hemileucine Saturniidae patterned green, yellow, and black, nearly all possessing nasty urticating spines. By the time it is a large fourth instar, the green caterpillar, with gaudy, spine-tipped scoli, appears to be an *Automeris* or other medium-large hemileucine caterpillar. The fifth instar, portrayed here, simply takes the white and lavender warning-color side stripe of something like *Periphoba arcaei* (#88), a truly nasty hemileucine saturniid, breaks the color pattern into long segments, and arrays it vertically along one side of each segment. How much protection is lost (the spines are gone) by this arrangement is anyone's guess, but the warning message is clear. The last instar is also bedecked with a stubble of white hair that signals "don't touch my spines," even though no spines exist. Throughout, the caterpillar is totally harmless. Perhaps these visual defenses are most effective against something like a monkey, for they clearly will not work against adept nasty-caterpillar killers such as trogons and squirrel cuckoos.

We know too much about this caterpillar to do it justice in this account (e.g., Janzen 1984c), so here is just one story. Research on the guts of *R. lebeau* caterpillars by the Microbial Observatory in Santa Rosa has led to the hypothesis that the amazingly high pH of a caterpillar gut may have more purpose than just to detoxify secondary defensive compounds. Caterpillar guts are famous for being extremely alkaline, with a pH of 10–12, sort of like that of commercial plumbing cleansers. The project on microbes indicates the gut of *R. lebeau* is an "extreme microhabitat on legs." What selected for this?

Caterpillars eat filthy food, namely leaves that are literally and liberally spread with a jam consisting of thousands of species of bacteria and other microbes that have been secreted, excreted, dripped, washed, dusted, and fallen out of or off other plants, animals, cadavers, and the environment in general. The one thing that could really wreck a good diet is to have any of these microbes establish a raging population in the caterpillar gut. After all, a vessel containing masticated plant tissues, and the associated water and nutrients, create a highly suitable soup for microbial growth. The caterpillar passes the chewed leaf bits through its foregut (a holding tank), past the proventriculus (a valve), and into the midgut (what appears to be the digestive center), where it is enveloped in a thin "sausage skin"—the peritrophic membrane. Macro-nutrients pass through the peritrophic membrane into an area next to the midgut wall, where the pH is lower and where the caterpillar and its desirable mutualistic microbes can further digest it. The original food bolus, still within the peritrophic membrane, is passed on through the midgut to the hindgut (an excretory and water reclamation chamber) at a very high pH, blocking the development of all those unwanted contaminants. Of course, the immediate prediction is that there will be some microbial extremophiles that live and thrive only in this alkaline microhabitat, but we have not yet discovered them. We humans do it differently. We drop our food into a stomach full of acid, at a low pH, and then pass it along as a seething compost heap for what will be a digestion process founded on microbes in our intestine.

CATERPILLAR VOUCHER: 03-SRNP-ACGLAB; JCM
ADULT VOUCHER: 03-SRNP-15491; JCM

83. *EUMORPHA LABRUSCAE* – SPHINGIDAE

This strange adult sphingid belongs to a select subset of green adult Lepidoptera. Whereas a vast number of species of caterpillars are green, for obvious camouflage reasons, green is proportionally a quite rare color among adults. Furthermore, the larger the adult of a species, the less likely that species is to be green. The genus *Eumorpha* contains two green members, the dark-green, rain-forest *Eumorpha phorbas* and the omnipresent, apple-green *Eumorpha labruscae*. Although *E. labruscae* seems to be able to live just about anywhere between tropical Mexico and Brazil, its numbers are always low. The caterpillar has been found in the ACG only nine times, although its *Cissus* food-plant vines have yielded thousands of *Eumorpha satellitia* and *Eumorpha vitis* over the decades of the ACG inventory.

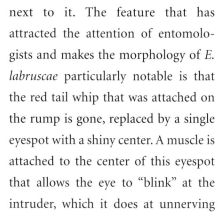

In contrast to the other known *Eumorpha,* which start out looking like Vitaceae-eating tenthredinid sawfly larvae, the early instars of *E. labruscae* resemble cryptic brown twigs, though they do have the classical *Eumorpha* angled side slashes that are displayed by *E. vitis, E. satellitia, E. anchemola, E. megaeacus, E. fasciata,* and *E. triangulum.* The trait equally unique to early-instar *E. labruscae* is the lateral false eyespot on the thorax. After the molt into the last instar, the side slashes have transformed into part of the cryptic snake-like pattern.

The entire caterpillar now looks like a snake that looks like a rotten stem. When disturbed, it puffs up the thorax and displays a magnificent false eye on each side with face-like markings next to it. The feature that has attracted the attention of entomologists and makes the morphology of *E. labruscae* particularly notable is that the red tail whip that was attached on the rump is gone, replaced by a single eyespot with a shiny center. A muscle is attached to the center of this eyespot that allows the eye to "blink" at the intruder, which it does at unnerving intervals. If you are a tiny foraging bird, and suddenly there is an eye blinking at you, what do you do? If you wait to inspect, you are a meal for the bearer of the eye, if indeed it is an eye on a real predator and not on a caterpillar's rear.

The other known *Eumorpha* are much more plebian in their last instars, being nothing more complex than brown, green, or pink with bright white, angled side slashes, and the ability to pull the head firmly back into the thorax where it cannot be grabbed easily. They also vomit great gobs of sticky, gooey gut regurgitate onto the attacker. It is noteworthy that out of 4,515 large insects brought to trogon nestlings in the ACG dry forest, only ten were *Eumorpha* caterpillars—nine *E. satellitia* and one *E. labruscae.* Because this occurred in a habitat and time of year when *E. satellitia* caterpillars were very common, it reveals just how undesirable this caterpillar is to vertebrate predators and suggests that the much less common *E. labruscae,* if found, may be ignored. This conclusion depends, of course, on using trogons as a general proxy species for understanding predatory behavior on caterpillars.

CATERPILLAR VOUCHER: 78-SRNP-35; DHJ
ADULT VOUCHER: 87-SRNP-560; JCM

84. *SELENISA SUEROIDES* – NOCTUIDAE

This unusual caterpillar, *Selenisa sueroides,* looks most decidedly not like the noctuid that it is. For many years, we unsuccessfully attempted to rear these fast-running and food-finicky caterpillars, thinking that they were some strange member of the Notodontidae. This is because it is commonplace for notodontids to elevate the rear part of the abdomen when posing and even sometimes when walking, and *S. sueroides* does exactly this, looking like a thin, young notodontid caterpillar. It is easy to find *S. sueroides* caterpillars. They are everywhere in the dry forest,

84

but a careful examination of the eighty-seven rearing records shows that all of their eighteen recorded food plants are in fact Fabaceae, the bean family. *Selenisa sueroides* does occur in both dry forest and rain forest (and the intergrades), but only in the dry forest are we beginning to understand this species. Its caterpillars simply must have fresh food, and have it frequently. Instead of sitting patiently and consuming much of the leaf it

sits on, it eats a bit of a young to medium-aged leaf and then runs rapidly along the branch to do the same elsewhere. Its color pattern is certainly not that of a sluggard sitting on the same leaf all day, or pressing itself stolidly against a bark-colored twig, motionless to avoid notice by a foraging bird. It boldly feeds and moves, feeds and moves, and when it perceives it is being chased or inspected, commonly drops off the foliage, to later feed some more. In short, *S. sueroides* are very active caterpillars and finicky in food choice, but able, apparently, to eat quite a few species of Fabaceae—perhaps many more than we know.

The caterpillar pupates naked in the litter, meaning without silk, thus no cocoon. The adult will eclose within two weeks. There appear to be multiple generations per rainy season in the dry forest and year-round generations in the rain forest. Either the adult migrates at the end of the rainy season or the pupae pass the dry season dormant in the litter. Many small noctuids do this. There is a third possible behavior, however, which is displayed by another set of small to medium-sized dry-forest noctuids. They simply turn off reproductively as the rainy season comes to an end and hide as passive (but capable of moving if disturbed) adults waiting in some crack or crevice for the six months of dry season to pass. These will, on occasion, visit dry-season flowers, such as those of the guanacaste tree, *Enterolobium cyclocarpum,* but they are not reproductive. If there is a strong rain marking the end of the long dry season, they will come to the light that very same night rather than showing up various days later, as is the case with species that pass the dry season as dormant pupae. So, which is it, pupal dormancy, adult quiescence, or both?

CATERPILLAR VOUCHER: 83-SRNP-142; DHJ
ADULT VOUCHER: 97-SRNP-9623; JCM

85. *JEMADIA PSEUDOGNETUS* – HESPERIIDAE

Jemadia pseudognetus is a caterpillar look-alike of *Yanguna cosyra* (#48), a very distantly related species. In other words, it is quite likely that these two nearly identical caterpillar color patterns are convergently evolved, driven by predators at some time in this caterpillar's history that did not like to eat black hairy caterpillars with orange stripes or spots on their sides. This conclusion is reinforced by the fact that these two genera have quite different DNA sequences, to say nothing of the strong differences in

85

adult facies. In the field there is no danger of confusing these two species. Caterpillars of *J. pseudognetus* feed only on Lauraceae, at least five species of *Nectandra*, three species of *Ocotea*, and *Persea povedae*. On the other hand, *Y. cosyra* caterpillars feed on Clusiaceae. The *J. pseudognetus* caterpillar has another rain-forest look-alike, *Jemadia* BURNS01, but again, in the field, there is no danger of confusion since *J.* BURNS01 caterpillars feed exclusively on leaves of *Casearia arborea* (Flacourtiaceae) and

are extremely rare and locally distributed, whereas *J. pseudognetus* caterpillars are quite common and found throughout ACG rain forest.

The adult of *J. pseudognetus* is part of a very large adult mimicry complex in the ACG. These black, white, and iridescent blue Hesperiidae—*Jemadia, Myscelus, Phocides, Parelbella*, involving eight species in four genera in two subfamilies—are part of a color pattern shared with at least another thirty-five species of Neotropical skippers. The mimicry is best explained by the suggestion that the colors are a flag that says to the bird, "Don't bother. I am agile and as fast as lightning." Adults of *J. pseudognetus* can be distinguished from those of *J.* BURNS01 by the angled blue bands in the central and inner side of the upper side hind wing. The latter has a vertical blue band in the center of this area, whereas this area is black in *J. pseudognetus*. The adult of *Y. cosyra*, incidentally, looks nothing like this, being a black and orange skipper with white dots on the forewings, a pattern that matches the mimicry pattern of the adults of *Heliconius hecale*, ithomiines, *Chlosyne spp.* (Nymphalidae) and other quite unrelated Hesperiidae, such as two species of *Erythropyge* and *Phareas coeleste*.

Among the 134 rearing records from wild-caught caterpillars, *J. pseudognetus* has no parasitoids. Moreover, *Dyscophellus ramon*, a large pyrgine hesperiid caterpillar, looking much like *Dyscophellus* BURNS02 (#59) and found on the same *Nectandra* rain-forest food plants strongly favored by *J. pseudognetus,* likewise has no parasitoids based on 167 rearing records. Rather than view this as exceptional, as one is inclined to do, it needs to be recognized that there are many species of caterpillars in the ACG that are attacked by either no parasitoids (so far) or only the occasional "generalist" parasitoid.

CATERPILLAR VOUCHER: 03-SRNP-6411; JCM
ADULT VOUCHER: 01-SRNP-1937; JCM

86. *PYRRHOPYGE ZENODORUS* – HESPERIIDAE

There must be at least 100 species of caterpillars in the ACG with "segmental" body-rings in colors shading from bright white, to yellow, to orange, to red, similar to those of the caterpillar of *Pyrrhopyge zenodorus.* This rain-forest skipper belongs to a subfamily, Pyrrhopyginae, whose members are given to black bodies with bright pale yellow to deep orange rings, broken rings, or even side spots (Burns and Janzen 2001). Their punk-hairdo heads depart from the commonplace face with fierce false eyespots so com-

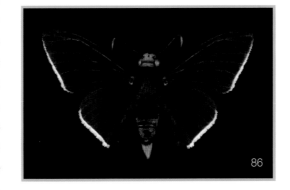

86

mon on hundreds of medium-sized ACG skipper caterpillars that feed on broad-leafed woody plants. It has already been shown experimentally that birds are genetically programmed to avoid brightly ringed objects while not avoiding objects with longitudinal stripes (Smith 1975). This may well be to avoid a lethal encounter with a coral snake, a classic focal organism in the literature regarding "models" and aposematic coloration. However, it might also be that the avoidance behavior became established in evolutionary time based on these caterpillars, and the coral snake may have evolutionarily piggybacked onto an already established caterpillar defense as a Mullerian mimic.

The caterpillar of *P. zenodorus* spends the day in its nest on the large leaves of its sole food plant, *Vismia baccifera* (Clusiaceae), an abundant, early-secondary succession shrubby treelet in the rain forest. At night the caterpillar ventures from the leaf nest to feed. The upper side of the leaf is dark green and the underside is bright beige. The variation in leaf colors results in the nests, made of a cut and folded leaf, being quite conspicuous to a dedicated caterpillar hunter. But the nest, standard for hesperiid caterpillars, is probably as much or more to protect the caterpillar from parasitoids and predaceous wasps as from birds.

Whereas a caterpillar of *P. zenodorus* can be found within several hours of diligent search, we have never seen an adult in the field. They must visit flowers somewhere to obtain nectar, probably high in the canopy and perhaps at dawn and dusk rather than in full daylight. The large adults are deep velvet-black with a slight white border fringe and a bright orange tip to the abdomen. This is evidently part of a massive mimetic complex of black butterflies with some red and white.

But *P. zenodorus* is outstanding among pyrrhopygine caterpillars in having one species of tachinid fly that apparently is a specialist on it. The other seventeen species of ACG pyrrhopygines seem to lack such a specialist. About 10 percent of *P. zenodorus* caterpillars are killed by *Houghia* sp. 09. The last-instar maggots of this fly emerge from the host pupa many weeks after the moment of initial parasitization when the caterpillar was living in its leaf nest. A different undescribed species of parasitoid, an *Apanteles* (Braconidae), also attacks *P. zenodorus,* albeit at a lower frequency. This wasp appears to specialize on just a few species of medium-large skipper caterpillars.

CATERPILLAR VOUCHER: 03-SRNP-6460; JCM
ADULT VOUCHER: 97-SRNP-6008; JCM

87. *COPAXA RUFINANS* – SATURNIIDAE

Copaxa rufinans caterpillars are particularly difficult caterpillars even though they are unambiguously *Copaxa* and very conveniently always feeding on Lauraceae. The caterpillars of two congeneric species, *C. moinieri* and *C. curvilinea,* are essentially identical to those of *C. rufinans.* Thankfully, they are very different from those of two more congeners, *C. escalantei* and *C. multifenestrata.* Complicating matters even more, however, the adults of *C. rufinans* and *C. moinieri* are so similar that they cannot be distinguished reliably unless the genitalia are examined, a tedious and destructive process, or they are subjected to DNA sequencing. The saving grace is that *C. moinieri* occurs exclusively in the dry forest in the ACG and *C. rufinans* only in

87

the rain forest and cloud forest. But this is of little help where the two major lowland ecosystems grade into each other. For example, both species can be found at Estacion Pailas on the western and southern intermediate elevation slopes of Volcan Rincon de la Vieja and in the Del Oro forests on the northern slopes of Volcan Orosi. If there are caterpillars to be reared, the diagnostic trait is that *C. rufinans* spins a stiffly netted cocoon with holes in it and then a shaggy, golden, ruffled layer of silk outside of that. In contrast, *C. moinieri* spins only an inner stiff netting for its cocoon. Unfortunately, this does not help in the rain forest, where both *C. rufinans* and *C. curvilinea* spin shaggy, double-layer cocoons. If the caterpillar develops through to an adult, or an adult comes to a light trap, then the adult of *C. curvilinea* can be identified by the strongly curved line down the center of the forewing, the basis for its specific epithet, and by the strongly beige anterior margin of the forewing.

The short-lived and heavy-bodied female *C. rufinans* lays strings of ten to twenty red, flattened oval eggs with a white equatorial ring. The eggs are glued side by side and flat onto the leaf. In about eight days the small, yellowish, spiny but harmless first instars, looking like batches of highly urticating Limacodidae or hemileucine saturniids, are out munching mature leaves, still side by side. *Copaxa rufinans* lives in a habitat that is rich in species and genera of Lauraceae. The female oviposits on at least twenty species in the genera *Nectandra, Ocotea, Persea, Licaria,* and

Cinnamomum. Although there are more than 400 rearings of wild-caught *C. rufinans* caterpillars in the ACG upper-elevation cloud forest and the lowland rain forest combined, it will take a different kind of study to know if there really are any preferences (ovipositional or feeding) for food plants among these genera or species. On the other hand, *C. moinieri* has only one native Lauraceae on which to oviposit in the dry forest, though it does eat introduced avocado, *Persea americana.*

Caterpillars of *C. rufinans,* like those of the other *Copaxa,* are adept at eating entire leaves, leaving only a stub of the petiole. If it eats just part of the leaf, it often cuts off the remainder, again leaving just a stub. The adaptive nature of this behavior remains to be understood. The classical explanation is that it renders the slow-moving and stay-at-home caterpillar harder to find by vertebrate, visually orienting predators. What is clear is that the conspicuous scoli and long, spine-like setae, coupled with a red, dashed lateral stripe, render the antepenultimate, penultimate, and ultimate (fifth) instars into strong general mimics of highly urticating *Automeris* caterpillars. The first two instars, and to some degree the third instar, are good Batesian mimics of Limacodidae and young hemileucine Saturniidae, both having memorable pain-inflicting spines. *Copaxa* caterpillars in general appear to be highly edible to the species of birds and monkeys that penetrate these defenses. Quetzals in the Monteverde cloud forest have been seen bringing them to

nestlings, presumably either *C. rufinans* or *C. syntheratoides* (the latter species also occurs in the ACG cloud forest but has not yet been reared there). Caterpillars of *C. moinieri* are a common prey item of *Trogon melanocephalus* and *Trogon elegans* foraging for food for their nestlings in the ACG dry forest. Also, *C. rufinans* is noteworthy for having no large parasitic wasps feeding on its caterpillars. This is especially curious because *C. moinieri* is parasitized by the host-specific *Enicospilus bozai* (Ichneumonidae) in adjacent ACG dry forest.

CATERPILLAR VOUCHER: 04-SRNP-2910; JCM
ADULT VOUCHER: 01-SRNP-2350; JCM

88. *PERIPHOBA ARCAEI* – SATURNIIDAE

This moth stinks. Both males and females emit a very strong garlic-musk odor when grabbed. Adults even "play possum"— the motionless moth thus avoids eliciting a killing strike by a predator. They also curl the brightly orange-and-black-ringed abdomen into an obvious warning sign. Drop an adult *Periphoba arcaei* into a raiding swarm of *Eciton burchelli* army ants and there is immediately an eight-centimeter ring around the motionless moth that is clear of the ants. Despite all its chemical defenses, when undisturbed this medium-sized saturniid rests motionless on a branch or foliage in the daytime. It looks like a dull, beige dead leaf.

Newly mated females of *P. arcaei* glue white, spherical eggs in neat patches of ten to twenty eggs on the undersides of their many species of caterpillar food plants. The eggs hatch twelve to fifteen days later. The black, spiny first instars soon molt to red with black spines. Next they molt to green with white and red side stripes and ostentatious, dense, and highly urticating spines. Each spine is a hollow syringe filled with liquid rich in acetylcholine and histamine, two major nerve stimulants. When they stick into you, the tip breaks off and you do remember the injection experience, as do monkeys and birds. Green nearly all over, they are relatively cryptic among the foliage, but viewed up close, the spines and the white and red lateral racing stripe are quite visible warning signals. As expected, the red and white stripe is mimicked by a number of other caterpillars that are probably not nearly as well protected, if at all.

Caterpillars of *P. arcaei,* as is the case with many saturniids and their relatives that are well protected individually, grow quite slowly on their many food plants. Rather than being extremely well camouflaged on a single species of food plant, they blend with their food plant in a general manner and feed on numerous species of woody plants. However, not by any means do they feed on all the species in the ACG. They are quite inefficient at putting on body weight with their more generalist diet, as compared to those species of large caterpillars that feed on just one or a few closely related species of food plants and grow twice as fast (Janzen 1984a).

Most common in the ACG dry forest, *P. arcaei* is also found in the rain forest, though one does not know if it followed man and his open fields and pastures into the rain forest or if it is a true rain-forest denizen.

CATERPILLAR VOUCHER: 04-SRNP-32780; JCM
ADULT VOUCHER: 81-SRNP-1081; JCM

89. *ASTRAPTES* LOHAMP – HESPERIIDAE

Astraptes fulgerator is a very widely distributed diurnal skipper found from Texas to Argentina and in about every ecosystem from the edge of near desert to cloud forest, from dry forest to the deepest, wettest rain forest. Sound suspicious? There is cause to be. In the ACG we reared hundreds of these conspicuous skippers from their brightly colored caterpillars and found them eating more than fifty food-plant species in seventeen families of plants. The adults were all approximately the same, if slightly variable. The caterpillars were more than slightly variable, but a pattern of association with the many food plants was not immediately obvious. John Burns at the Smithsonian Institution, the ACG inventory project's taxonomist for Hesperiidae, could not find any genitalic differences among the adults. Typically, differences in genitalia are usually quite diagnostic for species and, in a morphological sense, are considered critical in determining species boundaries. Still, he felt that given the variation present in the appearance of the adults, there might be as many as seven species present, and he also found that he could accu-

89

rately pick out one species from the great mass of reared specimens. It turned out that the caterpillars of this "one" species fed on *Trigonia rugosa* (Trigoniaceae) in the ACG dry forest and an unidentified Malpighiaceae in the ACG rain forest. Revisiting the plant taxonomy revealed that the unidentified "Malpighiaceae" was misidentified and was really *Trigonia laevis,* a rain-forest congener to *T. rugosa.* It turned out that all the caterpillars of *A. fulgerator* from this food plant looked the same, and not like any of the others. One down and many more morphs to go.

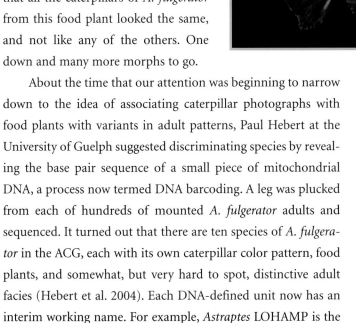

90

About the time that our attention was beginning to narrow down to the idea of associating caterpillar photographs with food plants with variants in adult patterns, Paul Hebert at the University of Guelph suggested discriminating species by revealing the base pair sequence of a small piece of mitochondrial DNA, a process now termed DNA barcoding. A leg was plucked from each of hundreds of mounted *A. fulgerator* adults and sequenced. It turned out that there are ten species of *A. fulgerator* in the ACG, each with its own caterpillar color pattern, food plants, and somewhat, but very hard to spot, distinctive adult facies (Hebert et al. 2004). Each DNA-defined unit now has an interim working name. For example, *Astraptes* LOHAMP is the taxon we feature. It has the interim name LOHAMP because its caterpillar feeds on the lower foliage and seedlings (LO) and because the food plant is *Hampea appendiculata* (Malvaceae) (HAMP). Similarly, *Astraptes* HIHAMP feeds on older, more

mature leaves in the crowns of large trees of *H. appendiculata.* The brilliant orange-ringed caterpillar of *A.* HIHAMP is in striking contrast to the caterpillar with yellow lateral spots—*A.* LOHAMP. The caterpillar of *A.* LOHAMP is, however, a very close approximation of the color pattern of *A.* LONCHO, which feeds mostly on sympatric cloud-forest *Lonchocarpus* (Fabaceae), and of *A.* YESENN, which feeds mostly on lowland to mid-elevation rain-forest *Senna papillosa* and *Senna hayesiana* (Fabaceae). The single "species" of *Astraptes fulgerator* is now expanded into ten. We do not even know which of the ten, if any, actually matches the type specimen for *A. fulgerator*—scientifically described in 1775 and so far not to be found in any of the world's major collections.

CATERPILLAR VOUCHER: 04-SRNP-41644; JCM
ADULT VOUCHER: 01-SRNP-21069; JCM

90. *CHRYSOPLECTRUM* BURNS01 – HESPERIIDAE

Chrysoplectrum BURNS01, still an undescribed species, appears to be a very common caterpillar. The *gusaneros* have found more than 240 caterpillars in the wet lower parts of the ACG rain forest. It is present wherever there are saplings of their sole food plant, *Sclerolobium costaricense* (Fabaceae). The *gusaneros* have been told, perhaps mistakenly, to stop looking. The seemingly "high" abundance of these caterpillars may well be something of an artifact, however. First, the huge leaves and large leaflets of sapling are very evident at a distance. It is therefore tempting to go straight to them as the search begins for caterpillars. Second, since the leaflets are arranged very neatly and are somewhat widely spaced along the midrib, it is easy to notice when a caterpillar has silked two leaflets together. Third, the caterpillars make no effort to escape, but rather brightly display their colors when exposed. Of course, all of these traits should make them easy for birds to find as well.

Each time the *gusaneros* collect and rear another of these brightly ringed caterpillars that are black, white, and red, the mimicry puzzle deepens. The bright colors of *C.* BURNS01 are part of a general pattern that recurs all over the ACG (see the account of *Dipterygia ordinarius,* #75, for an overall view). *Chrysoplectrum* BURNS01 may be a mimic, a model, or neither. Nonetheless, it surely is one of the most ostentatious caterpillars in the ACG. However, to see this caterpillar you must open up its leafy nest by pulling apart the two large leaflets of *S. costaricense* that have been tied together with silk. Otherwise, it is invisible in its green house. When exposed, it is apparent that the closest look-alike caterpillars are two pyrgine hesperiids. *Chrysoplectrum pervivax* is not a surprise. Common ancestry is probably the cause, though it begs the question of why they have remained looking so much alike as they have diverged in habitat, food plant, and adult facies. *Polythrix caunus* is more startling, given that *Polythrix* and *Chrysoplectrum* are two quite dif-

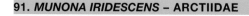

91

ferent genera. But again, there may be more than meets the eye. The very distinctive and complexly patterned pupa of *P. caunus,* in contrast to that of the pupa of other *Polythrix,* is a dead-on facsimile of the pupa of both species of *Chrysoplectrum.* It is possible that *P. caunus* is really a *Chrysoplectrum* with an adult masquerading as a *Polythrix.* Once we conduct the DNA sequencing of the ACG *Polythrix* and *Chrysoplectrum,* relationships among the species in these two genera should become more apparent.

This species certainly lacks a specialist parasitoid. The ACG inventory has been able to rear hundreds of caterpillars, and the sole parasitoid record is that of *Patelloa xanthura,* a tachinid fly that attacks hundreds if not thousands of species of caterpillars.

CATERPILLAR VOUCHER: 04-SRNP-41322; JCM
ADULT VOUCHER: 01-SRNP-5049; JCM

91. *MUNONA IRIDESCENS* – ARCTIIDAE

The strange caterpillar you see is showing a morphological condition that is ephemeral. The caterpillar of *Munona iridescens* is covered with snow-white hairs throughout almost all of its life. But just when the last instar has finished feeding on its *Cordia alliodora* (Bignoniaceae) leaves, the hairs abruptly turn gunmetal gray-black for the day that it walks about off the food plant in search of a place to spin its gray-black cocoon. The cocoon is a mix of these gray hairs and silk. It is not at all obvious how these apparently inanimate hairs can change color, since arctiid hairs are simply dead elongate scales like our own hair. The change is abrupt—one afternoon a white caterpillar, the next morning a dark one.

If rearing the caterpillar in a plastic bag, another change is notable. When feeding, the caterpillar is not active, jumpy, or restless, unusual behavior for the commonly quite restless arctiids. It is doing its best to mimic the hairy, white (and very painful with their urticating spines under the white, fluffy, harmless hairs), slow caterpillars of Megalopygidae in the same habitat. But when it changes to its prepupal dark colors, it suddenly becomes a runner, steadily marching around and around the bag, in its mind covering many tens of meters away from its natal food plant before finally settling down to spin its cocoon. A minority of the adults eclose within a few weeks, and a majority wait until the beginning of the rains next year.

Munona iridescens is one of many ACG caterpillars that are attacked by just a single species of host-specific parasitoid. This specialist is an undescribed species of the big, black, fuzzy tachinid fly *Leschenaultia*. It parasitizes the caterpillars at a high frequency. Roughly, 10–30 percent of the caterpillars contain this fly maggot. The fly glues its eggs to the leaf (we believe near the caterpillar) and the caterpillar swallows the eggs while biting off leaf chips. Eggs then hatch in the caterpillar gut. The young maggot goes to some unknown place in the caterpillar

92

(unknown to us, but see Ichiki and Shima 2003) where it is free of its hosts' encapsulating cells. There it waits to develop until the caterpillar has grown to full size, then eats the contents of the pupa, makes its own puparium inside the host pupa, and ecloses one to several months later. That the adult fly ecloses in the same rainy season as it pupates implies that it has a second generation within the same rainy season. This in turn implies that there are enough *M. iridescens* caterpillars to support them. We have yet to find caterpillars of *M. iridescens* in the second half of the rainy season, however. The other possibility is that the fly migrates to some other place to wait until the next May to return and may or may not have another generation in that place. Given the very large number of arctiid caterpillars reared without evidence to the contrary, it is unlikely that this parasitoid is using some other species of caterpillar for a second generation.

CATERPILLAR VOUCHER: 04-SRNP-ACGFIELD; JCM
ADULT VOUCHER: 04-SRNP-46354; JCM

92. *GAMELIA MUSTA* – SATURNIIDAE

When you find a caterpillar like this—festooned with small, white braconid wasp cocoons of *Cotesia* sp.—you really come to appreciate being a big mammal. The tiny, black mother wasp found this particular last-instar *Gamelia musta* caterpillar (Saturniidae) when it was an earlier instar and literally injected several dozen eggs into it. The first-instar parasitoids remained dormant until the caterpillar was fully grown but not yet in the prepupal phase. The larvae then ate much of the blood and other tissues of the host. Once fully developed, the parasitoid larvae burrowed out through the cuticle and spun their loosely attached, white cocoons among the spines. Curiously, the parasitoid larvae did not consume all of the host's tissues. The caterpillar was still walking, but ecologically dead.

The adult wasps will eclose in about twelve days after spinning their cocoons. During that time, the caterpillar will not feed and will remain motionless. Most spectacular of all, somehow the wasp larvae modify the caterpillar's behavior so that it will attempt to bite any intruder that approaches the wasp cocoons. In this manner the *Cotesia* wasps presumably avoid being parasitized as well. Entomologists are inclined to call this phenomenon hyperparasitism. The caterpillar eventually becomes moribund and then dies shortly after the wasps emerge. This parasitoid-host relationship is extremely common among caterpillars parasitized by braconid wasps, but not those parasitized by ichneumonids or tachinids.

When the foreleg of an adult *G. musta* was removed for DNA barcoding we found this well-known species to actually be at least two species in the ACG, one at high elevations on the volcanoes and one in the lowlands on the rain-forest side of the ACG. The upper-elevation specimens tend to have darker and larger males than the somewhat brown lowland species. It is not clear to which of these different species we should apply the name *G. musta.* That will require comparing both "genotypes" with the holotype specimen for *G. musta,* and likely DNA bar-

coding it as well. A second described species of *Gamelia, G. septentrionalis,* is a *G. musta* look-alike found in the rain-forest lowlands of Costa Rica but not yet found in the ACG. *Gamelia* is a close relative to *Automeris,* from which the adults are most easily distinguished by the presence of bright-red false eyespots on the upper side of the hind wings in *Gamelia.* The caterpillar of *Gamelia* also resembles an *Automeris* caterpillar, but lacks a distinctive array of warning colors on its sides, being rather a stark but boldly patterned whitish green. Not surprisingly, it hurts as much as an *Automeris* when picked up.

CATERPILLAR VOUCHER: 03-SRNP-3702; DHJ
ADULT VOUCHER: 01-SRNP-7803; JCM

93. *CAIO CHAMPIONI* – SATURNIIDAE

Costa Rica's equivalent of old-growth white pine wood is *Bombacopsis quinatum* (Bombacaceae), or *pochote* in the vernacular. It is a very large dry-forest tree that grows quickly and whose seeds are dispersed by the wind. This tree was one of the first species to be logged out of the forest. Among the dense foliage of its large, palmate compound leaves are oversized *Caio championi* caterpillars. This saturniid begins life at the start of the rainy season as a flat, ovoid egg glued singly or in pairs to the underside of the leaf by the mother while she is situated on top of the leaf. Initially green, the eggs turn red by the sixth day and upon hatching produce classically spiny arsenurine saturniid first instars. The caterpillars perch on the underside of a leaflet midrib and proceed to eat a tiny and very characteristic deep notch out of the tip of the leaflet as their first meal. The notch gets larger with subsequent meals, and the caterpillar grows through four instars looking like a ragged, damaged leaf, gradually transforming from a tiny purple and white caterpillar to a larger caterpillar that is primarily leaf green.

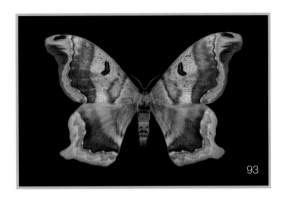

The last instar molts into the ubiquitous pattern of green with white and purple side slashes also prominently displayed in other large last instars, such as *Manduca rustica* (#30), *Manduca dilucida,* and *Rothschildia lebeau* (#82). Presumably the caterpillar is a Batesian mimic of *Periphoba arcaei* (#88), in particular, and other well-endowed urticating hemileucine saturniids. At any distance, the green caterpillar is largely invisible, except at night when it reflects brilliantly in the beam of a flashlight directed high into the canopy. Close up, the red-and-white side stripe flashes a highly visible warning. The value of crypsis, as well as aposematism, becomes evident via an examination of diets of nestling *Trogon elegans* and *Trogon melanocephala.* Eighty out of 4,515 large insects brought by the parents were last-instar *C. championi.* They are clearly edible to baby birds, though there still remains the question of whether all birds can eat the same caterpillars as young trogons can.

We have reared several hundred wild-caught *C. championi* caterpillars as well as hundreds placed out in the foliage as parasitoid-trap caterpillars, sacrificial lambs so to speak. Only two species of parasitoids have been documented. One is an unde-

scribed *Cotesia* known from only nine records. This tiny, black microgastrine braconid wasp lays hundreds of minute eggs in some earlier instar. During the host's last instar, well before the prepupal phase, the wasp larvae mature and, in near unison, burrow out through the cuticle to spin a solitary, yellow-white cocoon shaped like an elongate oval and stuck at one end to the caterpillar, but very easily dislodged. The caterpillar wanders aimlessly and is still alive but on its deathbed when the wasps eclose some ten days later. The same species of wasp, or at least what looks like it, also very rarely attacks *Rothschildia lebeau* in the ACG dry forest. The other recorded parasitoid of *C. championi* is the tachinid fly *Winthemia subpicea,* known from only four records. This fly was believed to attack only one of the other two pochote-eating arsenurines, *Arsenura armida* (#18), while its large caterpillars are clustered on the sides of pochote trees (Costa et al. 2004). However, the fly does on very rare occasions find a *C. championi* caterpillar as well. The fly eggs are glued directly to the cuticle of the last instar, but the maggots wait until the pupa is fully formed before consuming the pupal contents, then they pupate in the soil. If parasitism occurs during the full rainy season, the fly completes a generation in three to four weeks. If the parasitism is within the *C. championi* generation at the end of the rainy season, however, then the maggots sometimes remain undeveloped and do not initiate development until the moth pupa has passed the long dry season. Adult flies emerge almost exactly when last instars are available as hosts for the next generation.

CATERPILLAR VOUCHER: 03-SRNP-12882; JCM
ADULT VOUCHER: 01-SRNP-14650; JCM

94. *EUMORPHA SATELLITIA* – SPHINGIDAE

Eumorpha satellitia is arguably the most abundant and most easily located of the large sphingid caterpillars in early successional ACG dry forest. During June, the first full month of the rainy season, walk into the edges of five- to twenty-year-old secondary succession and find a plant of *Cissus alata* (*Cissus rhombifolia* in old literature) or *Cissus pseudosicyoides* (*Cissus sicyoides* in old literature). These are the two common dry-forest wild "grape vines" (Vitaceae). There is a good chance that an *E. satellitia* caterpillar will be on any vine with more than a few dozen leaves on it. By late June, most of these caterpillars have walked down into the litter to pupate. Adults emerge a few weeks later. By early August the new adults largely migrate out of the ACG dry forest, so that there are only a very few caterpillars of *E. satellitia* remaining in the ACG dry forest during the second half of the rainy season. Only a very few pupae remain in the litter as well. Adults emerge from these with the first rains in the following year, after a dormant period through the preceding long dry season.

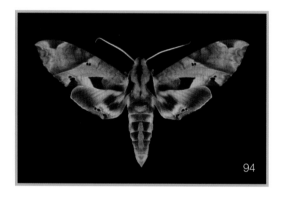

94

The great majority of the parents of the next year's generation immigrate into the dry forest from the wetter rain forest in the east, the Caribbean lowlands. The massive migration out of the dry forest in July, and the much more diffuse migration into the dry forest in mid-May with the first rains, is the reason why these moths are commonly encountered in mountain passes between the Pacific and Atlantic sides of Costa Rica. What is so striking in collections from lights placed in a mountain pass are the equal sex ratios. Most of the adult Lepidoptera to arrive at a light in the breeding grounds are males. This is because the males are using the lights as guidance points in their search for females in the breeding habitat, and females end up at the light only if they happen to pass nearby.

Adults of *E. satellitia,* as with many sphingids, have only a medium-length tongue and so visit relatively shallow flowers. *Crescentia alata* (Bignoniaceae), a relative of the *Catalpa* tree, is a common mega-fauna fruit tree that is now on its way to extinction in the ACG dry forest because of the absence of mega-faunal dispersal agents (with the removal of the Pleistocene horse, Janzen 1982a,b; Janzen and Martin 1982). Its cauliflorous yellow and purple large flowers open at night and are widely labeled as bat pollinated. Indeed, they are definitely visited and probably pollinated by *Glossophaga* bats. However, Hallwachs noticed with an infrared video camera that the flowers were also heavily visited, and presumably pollinated, by *E.*

satellitia moths. Whereas the bats were tolerant of a flashlight, but not of the infrared camera, the sphingids were oppositely affected. This is probably why no one has seen them at these flowers before. Showing the moths visiting flower after flower, the video also revealed several times that the hovering sphingids were captured by bats of an unidentified species. The bats came from above, snatching the moths in midair. It is a rough and dangerous world out there.

CATERPILLAR VOUCHER: 03-SRNP-12594; JCM
ADULT VOUCHER: 02-SRNP-16655; JCM

95. *SYSSPHINX MOLINA* – SATURNIIDAE

Find a large *Pithecellobium saman* tree in Santa Rosa in June, and just about any other rainy-season month, and scrutinize the

ground below for bright (new) to dull (older) fecal pellets that resemble short cylinders about four millimeters long with six longitudinal grooves. Pick up a pellet and crush or smear it between your fingers to better see the hundreds of tiny leaf chips that have passed through the digestive system. This excrement from *Syssphinx molina,* and sometimes *Syssphinx colla,* is a classical

95

fecal pellet from leaf feeders that are "chippers" or "snippers" of leaves. The caterpillar mandibles operate somewhat like a pair of scissors, snipping off pieces of leaf and swallowing them without further mastication. As they pass through the digestive system of the caterpillar, nutrients leach out of the cut edges and that is

about all the caterpillar gets. For the most part, the nasty tannins in leaf-tissue vacuoles and, probably, most other secondary compounds for plant defense remain inside the leaf fragments. Caterpillars, in particular the Saturniidae and Limacodidae, with this feeding strategy (Bernays and Janzen 1988) tend to grow slowly and feed on plants classically defended by large-molecule digestion-inhibiting tannins and resins (Janzen 1984a). The opposing feeding strategy is employed by "mushers." These caterpillars, Sphingidae being the archetypical case, have mandibles that work by grabbing a leaf blade as with a pair of pliers and crushing or ripping off the leaf piece. The material that is swallowed is more a puree than a bolus of large leaf fragments. The result is that all of the secondary defensive compounds, which in their food plants tend to be nasty, small, and very toxic molecules, are loose in the gut lumen along with all the nutrients in the leaf. These caterpillars are resistant to the toxins, tend to be very food-plant specific, and grow nearly twice as fast as do the "chippers." The caterpillar of *S. molina* was the example that first led to investigating this way of looking at the world of herbivory through the mouth of a caterpillar.

Caterpillars of *S. molina* have a second distinctive trait. They are, along with *S. colla* and other ceratocampines, the host for a large, black ichneumonid wasp, *Thyreodon santarosae.* This diurnal wasp is known only from the ACG, but probably extends throughout the range of *S. molina* and *S. colla* (and perhaps other similar *Syssphinx*) in the Neotropics (Gauld and Janzen 2004). The wasp places a single egg in the caterpillar. The wasp larva remains dormant, hidden somewhere in the caterpillar until the caterpillar has fed fully and descended (or dropped?) to the ground to burrow into the litter to pupate. Then the parasitoid larva initiates development, eats the insides of the caterpillar, and emerges through the cuticle. It spins a black, blunt, fat, tough cocoon in the chamber that the caterpillar made for its own pupa. The wasp either ecloses one to two months later or eleven months later, indicating that there are both bivoltine and univoltine generations occurring concurrently. Although first reared from caterpillars of *S. molina*, this wasp parasitizes seven species of ACG dry-forest cerato-campine Saturniidae. The wasp is of interest to more than the ecologists. The genus *Thyreodon,* and its close relative *Rhyncophion,* are parasitoids of sphingids, with wasp natural histories like those described above for *T. santarosae*. The host associations of *T. santarosae* represent a major evolutionary jump from being a sphingid parasitoid to being a saturniid parasitoid. It is from a species-level lineage like this that a new genus or other kind of species complex may evolve. The *T. santarosae* lineage is now poised to evolutionarily explore the huge number of *Thyreodon*-free Saturniidae in the Neotropics.

CATERPILLAR VOUCHER: 82-SRNP-428; DHJ
ADULT VOUCHER: 89-SRNP-348; JCM

96. *MANDUCA FLORESTAN* – SPHINGIDAE

The leaf-green first four instars of *Manduca florestan* (our image depicts a fourth instar) display just a trace of the white to lemon-yellow lateral and dorsal slash marks that become so well-developed in the last (fifth) instars, which also look like *Manduca pellenia* (#56), a rain-forest Solanaceae eater. Caterpillars perched in the daytime on the undersides of the large leaves they eat, displaying their small white or yellow markings, give the impression of holes punched through the leaf. The colors break up the obvious "caterpillar contour" as well as look somewhat like the venation of the leaf. The last instar, a finger-sized caterpillar as long as nine centimeters, is much more evident hanging under a leaf or on a petiole. In the same way as the earlier instars, however, it is more strikingly broken up into green and white or yellow. It appears that there is a yellow morph and a white morph. Such a caterpillar polymorphism is common among species of sphingids that may occur at high abundance, thus attracting the attention of smart vertebrate predators capable of forming a search image for one morph or the other. This in turn selects for genes that lead to the mother producing broods with both colors.

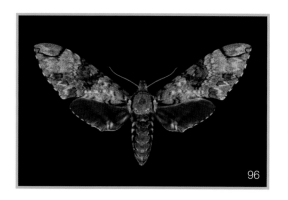

96

Although the green and white last instar of *M. florestan* looks just like the caterpillar of *M. pellenia*, the latter appears to feed only on Solanaceae and does not occur in the ACG dry forest. Also, the green and yellowish caterpillar of *M. florestan* is very similar to the caterpillar of the dry-forest *Manduca barnesi* (no rain-forest incursion, to date), which even eats the same food plants as *M. florestan* in ACG dry forest. But the former is just a bit more roughly covered with small tubercles, has more finely delineated, yellow lateral slash marks, and tends to have strongly yellowish dorsal coloration and darker leaf-green ventral coloration, with the two greens meeting at the yellow lateral slash marks. Furthermore, *M. barnesi* tends to be more often found on the leaves of bignoniaceous trees, such as *Godmania aesculifolia* and *Tabebuia ochracea*. To complicate matters, the adult *M. barnesi* is extremely similar to the adult of *M. florestan*, but the latter invariably has a slight brownish patch in the center of the forewing. This patch is lacking in the more gray-white *M. barnesi*. Also, *M. florestan* has a slightly more bluntly rounded forewing apex compared to the relatively more pointed forewing of *M. barnesi*. Fortunately, for the task of identifying moths in collections from the wet parts of Costa Rica, *M. barnesi* appears to be restricted to dry forest.

The adults of *M. florestan* share the honor, along with *Manduca rustica* (#30), of being the most ecologically and geographically widespread and the most commonly encountered of the seventeen species of *Manduca* in Costa Rica. It is hard to place a moth light trap in the rain forest, the dry forest in the wet season, and the mountain passes in August and December, without getting one of these large lichen-gray moths at the light. The caterpillars of *M. florestan* have one of the longest food-plant lists for an ACG sphingid (*M. rustica* holds the record for ACG sphingids). It appears that the female *M. florestan* deposits one egg at a time on the young foliage of several dozen species of trees and vines in the Bignoniaceae and of trees and shrubs in the Verbenaceae in ACG dry forest, where the moth is common. It does the same in the rain forest, where it is quite rare, and even into the lower edges of cloud forest on Volcan Cacao at about 1,000 meters elevation. However, in the cloud forest it appears that the species is creeping up Volcan Cacao and presumably the other volcanoes as well, along with many other lowland species, as the cloud layer retreats upward with global warming. We are still discovering its "native" hosts in the ACG rain forest, but these include Olacaceae and Boraginaceae, as well as bignones and verbenas.

In the same vein, the widespread occurrence of *M. florestan* in the pastures, along roadsides, and along field edges of Costa Rican rain-forest ecosystems may indeed be at least in part an invasion and ecological population increase by a largely dry-forest species. As such *M. florestan* appears to be part of a suite of anthropogenic species such as coyotes, white-tailed deer, *Automeris io*, *Epargyreus* "sp2" (and its food plant, *Gliricidia sepium*), *Carystoides basoches* (and its food plant, *Acrocomia aculeata*), and *Guazuma ulmifolia*. All of these species and more are part of the general human-driven dynamic that is transforming Costa Rican rain forests toward some dry-forest characteristics. They are members of the cosmopolitan agroscape community that originated as dry-forest species, both as ruderals and denizens of old-growth forest.

CATERPILLAR VOUCHER: 81-SRNP-461; DHJ
ADULT VOUCHER: 81-SRNP-708; JCM

97. *LIRIMIRIS GIGANTEA* – NOTODONTIDAE

Intense lobbying on the part of Jeffrey Miller resulted in the presentation of this species to act as a proxy for representing the other incredible caterpillars of *Lirimiris*. The other species are not included here because they have boring natural histories, and they are very hard to understand with respect to the ecology of their color patterns. In the final species ledger for the book, we simply could not pass up this ridiculous caterpillar, *Lirimiris gigantea*. As its name implies it is, relatively speaking, gigantic. The adult is among the largest of the *Lirimiris* and thus among the largest of the ACG Notodontidae, along with *Naprepa, Hapigia,* and *Anurocampa*. One can talk oneself blue in the face trying to figure out what could possibly have selected for this amazing yet absurd combination of colors and hairs. We show a penultimate instar, the colors of which simply become more ostentatious in the last instar. Were it an adult moth, these ornaments would of course be immediately attributed to the courtship display and placed in the bucket of peacock story lines. However, caterpillars do not court, so that is out. The old fallback of aposematism just might apply to *Lirimiris* caterpillars. In general, they are all gaudy but gaudy in different ways, although there is a general *Lirimiris* aspect that works for the genus if you let your mind be open. But this is a very uncomfortable explanation for all of them, including *L. gigantea,* since the plants that they eat are among the oatmeal types of food plants, and therefore the caterpillars would have to make their own nasty defensive toxins. Notodontidae are not known for that in general. Really, *L. gigantea* could hardly be more ostentatious. Perhaps it falls in the category of "really gross decomposing fungus stuck to the underside of a leaf"?

97

Serious efforts toward resolving the why of *L. gigantea* colors will have to await another phase of ACG caterpillar studies. All signals are that it is a denizen of the crowns of its food plant, *Coussapoa nymphaefolia,* and perhaps other species of *Coussapoa,* rain-forest trees in secondary succession. The leaves of *Coussapoa* are among the largest of rain-forest tree leaves, and the colors of *L. gigantea* may relate to this as well. The ACG inventory has found the caterpillar only four times. The single adult reared from those caterpillars is the one shown here. The definitive caterpillar-adult connection was accomplished from associating a prepupal larva walking across the ground below its *C. nymphaefolia* food plant with an adult reared from another unphotographed caterpillar. This scarcity in the ACG inventory makes it virtually impossible to say anything about its natural history. The species ranges from Mexico to South America, as does its food plant, as evidenced by adult specimens collected at lights and preserved in the moth collections at the National Museum of Natural History of the Smithsonian

Institution. Incidentally, the strikingly colored adult is quite invisible with its wings folded down and over its back, clinging to a branch stem and waiting throughout the day.

CATERPILLAR VOUCHER: 04-SRNP-3015; JCM
ADULT VOUCHER: 00-SRNP-21593; JCM

98. *EUGLYPHIS* JANZEN01 – LASIOCAMPIDAE

The genus *Euglyphis* is an amazingly species-rich taxon, occurring in the rain forest and cloud forest, and characterized by medium-sized, bark-colored bombycoid moths. Crypsis appears to be their only mode of defense during their short adult lives. As is the case with Saturniidae, Limacodidae, Apatelodidae, Lymantriidae, and Bombycidae, adult Lasiocampidae do not feed as adults and live only five to ten days. The females mate only once, and that on the night of eclosion. During the next few nights, they are totally dedicated to laying eggs. They live off the reserves of nutrients and water accumulated as a caterpillar. The male is essentially a nocturnal flying set of testes, frantically following pheromone odor plumes upwind in search of virgin females. Individuals of both sexes perch on tree bark during the day, blending into the environs to escape the attention of a bird or monkey.

The caterpillars, however, are not at all above being involved in both crypsis and mimicry. The bright caterpillar of

98

Euglyphis JANZEN01 stands out strongly at the mimicry end of the spectrum. As evident from its interim name, this rain-forest critter is apparently an undescribed species. There are no specimens of this very dark brown and sexually dimorphic moth in any of the world's large collections of *Euglyphis*. When you stare at the foliage of its food plants, some twenty species of Lauraceae, you do not see the last instars of this caterpillar. It constructs a very cryptic nest by silking one leaf on top of another. But tear open the nest, and you are confronted by a bright, yellow-on-black-ringed caterpillar, some having cherry-red patches down the back between the rings, and all having orange feet and orange-ornamented rears. This caterpillar fits very nicely with the big and brightly ringed and spotted caterpillars of several species of large skipper butterflies, most notably the color morphs of *Astraptes fulgerator* (which we now know to be many species (Hebert et al. 2004; see *Astraptes* LOHAMP, #89), but also including many others. In truth, which is the mimic, which is the model, and what type of mimicry is involved are all unknown. Models and mimics may be spurious issues if the birds and monkeys are simply genetically programmed to reject brightly ringed caterpillars without even sampling them in the first place.

Other species of *Euglyphis* caterpillars show various degrees of aposematism. Commonly, last instars are hairy and solitary, dorsally cryptically dressed in various combinations of greens, browns, and grays, very unlike the punkish and ostentatious sorts of extremely aposematic, hairy caterpillars (see *Lirimiris gigantea*, #97). However, when disturbed violently, they roll and display red, yellow, orange, or white spots on the ventral or lateral sides and on the head or rear. The species that are brightly colored overall, such as *E.* JANZEN01, tend to make leaf nests in which to hide. The younger instars of many species are often gregarious in small groups, and yet more brightly colored, presumably emphasizing the aposematic flag through their group display.

CATERPILLAR VOUCHER: 04-SRNP-35610; JCM
ADULT VOUCHER: 03-SRNP-4191; JCM

99. *ELYMIOTIS ALATA* – NOCTUIDAE

The four species of ACG dry-forest *Elymiotis* caterpillars and their adults—*E. attenuata, E.* JANZEN01, *E.* JANZEN02, and *E.* JANZEN03—are not easy to identify, in great part because they share many traits in their facies. The males and females are very different in appearance, and all of the over 270 rearing records are from the Malpighiaceae. Happily, the rare caterpillars of the rain-forest *Elymiotis alata* have the aspect of the Malpighiaceae-eaters, which also occur in the ACG rain forest, but their food plants are in the Malvales, *Pavonia schiedeana* (Malvaceae) and *Pachira aquatica* (Bombacaceae). The adults are also distinctive due to the greenish wash over their bark-colored front wings. This produces the appearance of a thin film of green algae over tree bark, or perhaps a green chlorophyll layer peeking through the thin, dead brown of the bark. The caterpillars of a fifth species, *Elymiotis tlotzin,* eating *Zyziphus guatemalensis* (Rhamnaceae), which grows next to the coastal mangroves, strongly resemble their food plant's spiny branches and are therefore not difficult to identify.

Viewed at any distance, *E. alata* caterpillars appear to be a twisted, dead piece of vegetation stuck to a leaf or twig. The slight yellow and white markings on a purplish brown background suggest nothing but rotting tissue. The caterpillar, as is usual for caterpillars with this general appearance, freezes when approached, arching its head and tail-end off the substrate, even further distorting a classical caterpillar profile. It may not invariably fool a professional foliage gleaner, but it probably deceives many more generalist birds and, perhaps through its motionless stance, lizards and monkeys as well. The latter is moot, however, since we have to date found the few caterpillars only near ground level, where rain-forest monkeys, scarce as they are, never forage.

99

Our image is a lateral one, not permitting a view of the other defense of this caterpillar. Seen from the side, there is a yellow fattened slash on the upper side of the rear. Seen from the rear itself, and especially up close, this is the right eye of a face looking straight at you. It even has a nose and a mouth. This "face-on-the-rear" pattern is strikingly presented by the four dry-forest look-alike *Elymiotis* mentioned above, whereas *E. tlotzin* has dropped this defense in favor of rendering the entire posterior end into looking like a massive stem spine of its rhamnaceous food plant. The false eyes of the rear of these *Elymiotis* are not as perfect a match for the vertebrate eye as found in some of the better snake mimics. But when seen in the mottled semi-dark of dense and tangled vegetation, they give the definite impression of a vertebrate looking at you. Starting with this raw material, it is easy to see how selection, driven by the "right" predators, could transform these eyespots and facial patterns into something much more accurately snake-like, such as seen on the thorax of *Hemeroplanes triptolemus* (#53), the pupa of *Dynastor darius* (#54), and

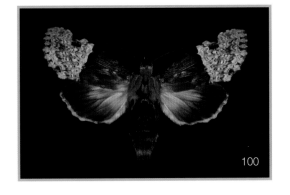

100

even the posterior end of another notodontid, *Nystalea aequipars* (#100), which certainly derived its false face quite independently, in an evolutionary sense, from that of *Elymiotis*.

CATERPILLAR VOUCHER: 02-SRNP-16; DHJ
ADULT VOUCHER: 00-SRNP-1141; JCM

100. *NYSTALEA AEQUIPARS* – NOTODONTIDAE

This caterpillar starts out as a classical *Nystalea*, appearing to be a fragment of dead, green-brown leaf margin draped or wound along a twig. In contrast to the other *Nystalea*, which just become larger and larger twisted leaf margins, the rear end of

Nystalea aequipars begins to assume a snake-like appearance in the fourth (penultimate) instar, which we show here. By the fifth instar it is really hard to convince yourself that the rear of this caterpillar is not some kind of strange beast out of the movies, peering ever so intently at you. The caterpillar raises its rear and somewhat aggressively turns it toward you. If you are a small bird, and you flee quickly, rather than stop to ponder such a creature, then you might escape becoming a meal just enough times to have long ago selected for your species to be wary first, ask questions later.

Nystalea aequipars is basically a rain-forest insect, yet if its five or six species of *Clusia* food plants (ground-rooted to epiphytes in the Clusiaceae, or Guttiferae of old) were to extend generally into dry forest, it would probably be a lowland dry-forest species as well. We have found it, and its distinctive feeding damage to the large, fleshy evergreen *Clusia* leaves, wherever this plant genus grows. This includes a few very isolated *Clusia rosea* growing in exceptionally wet ravines in some of the driest parts of the ACG, the barren upper hills of the Santa Elena Peninsula. The *N. aequipars* in these isolated pockets of *Clusia* could be maintained through annual replenishment by the occasional wandering female from the rain forest in the east, and thus really not be a dry-forest insect, or they could be a true self-maintaining population, only to be extinguished with the local extinction of the *Clusia* population during an exceptionally dry spell. The

Clusia then would probably be re-established through the movement of seeds when the climate moistens up again. Its seeds are bird-dispersed from the wetter areas in the east. It is easy to see how an isolated population of *N. aequipars* could become established quite far from the parental population and then be subject to different selective pressures than in the rain forest. It could quickly evolve a dry-forest daughter species. In this way, it would be re-enacting the biology that has through history given us new species.

Known from specimens taken at lights all over Costa Rica, *N. aequipars* is suspected, based on very slight differences in male genitalia, to be perhaps made up of two sibling species. We hope to resolve this puzzle through DNA barcoding.

Based on thirty-two wild-caught caterpillars (they are hard to find), *N. aequipars* is free from parasitoids other than a single species (two records) of *Hypomicrogaster* wasp (Braconidae, Microgastrinae) that feeds on an array of medium-large notodontid caterpillars, including *Nystalea, Pentobesa, Elasmia, Poresta,* and *Tachuda,* but mostly *Nystalea.* The parasitoid occurs in both ACG dry and rain forest, but not in the cloud forest.

CATERPILLAR VOUCHER: 03-SRNP-6474; JCM
ADULT VOUCHER: 95-SRNP-6071; JCM

DANIEL JANZEN started the ACG caterpillar inventory in the early rainy season of 1978 after fifteen years of studying animal-plant interactions in the tropics, mostly in Costa Rica. He was walking down the Quebrada Guapote in eastern Sector Santa Rosa of the ACG, censusing the fruit crops of a large tree (*Hymenaea courbaril*). When he jumped off a small ledge into the stream, his feet slipped on the algae-covered rocks, and he fell on top of his Nikon camera, which broke one or two of his lower ribs. He made it back to the Santa Rosa headquarters and sat for a month strapped in a rocking chair at the front door while the pain gradually subsided. The camera survived. Stuck sitting under a single 60-watt light bulb, he was thoroughly bored. He started collecting and spreading the moths that came to the light, just to see how many there were. The number of species impressed him. Curiously, no year since then has experienced as high a density of adult moths or caterpillars in the ACG dry forest. When he could walk freely again, he went back into the forest and found caterpillars everywhere. Even though he was at that time being supported by an NSF ecology grant to study dry-forest seed dispersal and seed predation, he decided to shift from bruchid beetles (Janzen 1980a,b) to caterpillars.

WINIFRED HALLWACHS came onto the ACG scene in January 1978. After graduating and spending a year in Sweden and Africa, Hallwachs signed up for a course at the University of Pennsylvania. Finding that class dull, she wandered across the hall into Janzen's Habitats and Organisms course, in which he was showing slides—all sun, tropics, and exotic organisms. She signed up. On the last day, she knocked on his office door and asked about fieldwork opportunities in tropical biology. He said that if she paid all expenses, he could use her as a volunteer in the late summer, and then he left for Costa Rica, broke his rib, and started pinning moths. By the time she arrived, he had decided that the adult moths had to be inventoried, and on her second night in Costa Rica she set to work spreading moths. A year and tens of thousands of pins later they could have won the mixed doubles of moth spreading at any Olympics. For years they collected in assembly-line style from a light-trap sheet at night and then spent all day sorting, spreading, and oven-drying them. Meanwhile Hallwachs became fascinated with the wild Santa Rosa agoutis and wrote her doctoral dissertation at Cornell on that subject (see Hallwachs 1986). She feels at home living in a tin-roofed shack in the forest with *Liomys* mice foraging for scattered rice on the living-room floor, bats hanging under the bed, frog-eating snakes in the kitchen sink, and water always dripping somewhere through the roof.

IN JANUARY 1980, Janzen and Hallwachs drove up to Poas National Park—at about 1,800 meters elevation—outside San Jose and put up the light for fun. They were dumbfounded to meet, at that high elevation and in a soupy, wet, cold habitat, many tens of species of moths that they had come to think of as dry-forest moths (many of these were migrants from Pacific dry forest on their way over the mountains to Atlantic rain forest; Janzen 1987a, b). If the moths in Poas National Park are not so different from those in northwestern Costa Rica dry forest, they reasoned, then it would be possible to inventory the entire country. The increased size of the collection would give taxonomists more data to work with and result in more definite identification of new and existing species.

The National Moth Inventory was born from that serendipitous seed of a few hours on the side of a Costa Rican volcano. The project grew in many directions and precipitated a number of developments, including the creation of the ACG, which grew from the 10,000 ha dry-forest Parque Nacional Santa Rosa to the 153,000 ha ACG covering 2 percent of the country and four major ecosystems—marine, dry forest, rain forest, and cloud forest. In 1989, INBio was created as an extension of Rodrigo Gamez's Biodiversity Office in the Ministerio de Recursos Naturales y Energia (MINAE, called MIRENEM in those years), and the first six-month parataxonomist course was taught in the ACG to introduce the ACG way of thinking about conservation into the entire Costa Rican national park system (Janzen 1991, 1992, 1993b, 1996, 2000, 2004; Janzen et al. 1993; Reid et al. 1993; Nielsen et al. 2004). The moth inventory resulted in a huge collection gradually accumulated through 1989 that was stored at the University of Pennsylvania and the Philadelphia Academy of Natural Sciences. With the emergence of INBio in 1989, two things happened. First, the large number of INBio parataxonomists, the first three courses of whom cut their biodiversity teeth on moth collecting and pinning in the ACG (1989, 1990, 1992), took over national-level moth and other insect collecting and built the massive inventory collections now at INBio. In 1996 Janzen and Hallwachs drove the entire moth collection amassed in Philadelphia (3,000+ Bioquip Redwood insect boxes) to Miami in a U-Haul truck, and LACSA (at the time, the national airlines of Costa Rica) flew the entire package pro bono to San Jose, where INBio then integrated them with the growing parataxonomist-collected collections. At that time, Janzen and Hallwachs officially bowed out of the national moth inventory to focus on the caterpillars of the ACG.

JEFFREY MILLER came out of the Pacific Northwest forests and into the ACG with his camera and a scientific background in insect ecology and natural history (Miller 1993, 2004a,b) with a specialty in Lepidoptera—in particular, caterpillars (Miller 1995; Miller and Hammond 2000, 2003; Parsons et al. 1991). In late June 2003, about when the rainy season's first generation of caterpillars were most abundant, Miller attended an international workshop in Santa Rosa held by the ACG inventory program. The goal was to introduce the world's workers on caterpillars to the inventory and the ACG. This book is one of the products of the contacts formed at that workshop.

Before Miller visited the ACG, he had been studying caterpillars of one sort or another in agroecosystems (Miller 1980, 1983, 1996; Miller and West 1987; Kimberling and Miller 1988;

Miller and Ehler 1990) and, more recently, forests (Hammond and Miller 1998; Miller 1990a,b, 1999; Lattin and Miller 1997; Muir et al. 2002; Miller et al. 2003) in Oregon. He became a self-taught photographer because he needed images of hundreds of species of field-collected caterpillars before they pupated.

Following the 2003 ACG workshop, during which Miller visited three of the then seven ACG rearing barns, he processed his digital images. He was truly in awe of the detailed beauty of forms, colors, and patterns. Never before had he seen such magnificent creatures. He surfed the ACG Web site for names and to see what he had missed and contacted Janzen and Hallwachs to discuss the possibility of this book.

Photographing Caterpillars

So, what does a photographer of tropical caterpillars bring into the field? First, if at all possible, bring an assistant. Also, invest in a camera bag or pack. A backpack made specifically for storing a laptop computer with cameras and accessories is very handy for getting around airports and moving from place to place once you have arrived at your destination. It goes without saying that cameras, laptops, and other expensive equipment are strictly carry-on items.

The camera pack of a professional photographer is usually a bit heavier than that of the ecotourist. It might contain: two digital cameras, one with a 90mm macro lens, the other with a 180mm macro lens; possibly two additional lenses—a 40–70mm wide angle (great for landscapes) and a 200–400mm telephoto (ideal for birds and mammals); a backup battery and charger unit for each camera; two 1-gigabyte flash disks; a USB (or firewire) flash disk reader; a laptop computer (with 110v power cord); one 40-gigabyte external USB hard drive; a dozen blank compact discs; one dual flash unit that attaches to the end of the lens; four individual flash units equipped with a slave trigger; two custom-made six-inch stands for the flash units; sixteen rechargeable AA batteries; one six-foot tripod; one six-inch tripod equipped with a custom spring-steel clamp; one jewelers' forceps; up to three cloth panels; one fine-tipped camel-hair brush; notebooks and pens; and last but not least, a list of "must get" shots.

Some of the items listed above have an obvious function, but a few of them require an explanation. When working with a long macro lens, a tremendous amount of light is needed, especially when the subject is dark in color and not amenable to staying perfectly still. A live subject requires relatively fast shutter speeds, in turn requiring even more light than ambient conditions can provide. Thus, four slaved flash units are very useful. They do, however, use battery power rapidly, hence the need for batteries that can be recharged on a daily basis. The miniature tripod is the focal point of the staging area. With a custom clamp, it is used to hold the twig, stem, or leaf that, in turn, is the prop upon which the caterpillar is situated. The jewelers' forceps and camel-hair brush are the prod and tickler, respectively, to persuade the caterpillar to move into a position suitable for a portrait. Do not tease the caterpillar excessively—it will respond negatively, either by curling up for hours on end, fainting and falling off the prop, breaking into a running bout, or worse, spitting up gut contents.

A clean, open surface that is at least waist high makes a good field studio, if the black backdrops are placed correctly. Direct sunlight on the backdrop can result in an uneven, gray background that can prove difficult to correct once the image is captured. Two additional cloth panels are useful to block wind and sun from the side. The staging area, the zone immediately surrounding the six-inch tripod, should be in front of the backdrop by a distance that puts the backdrop out of focus, typically two to three feet. The slaved flashes can then be placed as desired.

Always be prepared for the unexpected. Creativity and a few supplies can salvage a difficult set-up situation. Heavy string, clothespins, duct tape, electricians' tape, push pins, and elastic cords with hooks on each end have saved a shoot on more than one occasion. Most of these supplies will help secure backdrops and side panels on a windy day.

Capturing caterpillar images is the fun part of the entire expedition. It is also the activity that determines success or failure. The number of acceptable final images can be maximized by following certain rules, practices, and precautions. The first step is to check that the camera is set for taking raw files under manual control of aperture and shutter speed.

Selection and documentation of the specimen are next. If only one specimen is available to represent a given species, then this step is very simple. If many individuals of a given species are available, however, an assistant is enormously helpful. By screening the specimens and recording data, an assistant can increase the number of captured images by a factor of two and a half to three times. Once a particular caterpillar is chosen to be photographed, it is essential to record the camera-image number and a very short description of the specimen.

Staging the specimen requires a cautious approach. It is very important to handle the caterpillar with care to avoid disturbing a resting pose or a feeding posture. The photographer may encounter caterpillars that are runners, such as many of the arctiids. In these cases, the staging tripod is useless and the assistant is invaluable. The running caterpillar, the agile assistant, and the patient photographer must become synchronized in their motion to capture a good image. The assistant turns, spins, and twirls the prop to keep the caterpillar not only in the frame of the picture but in focus—no easy feat. Experience has shown that caterpillars do not tire easily but may stop momentarily, then quickly set out on another bout of running. It is these short pauses that provide the opportunity to get the shot.

A final comment that also serves as a statement of ethics is in order. Do not anesthetize or otherwise treat the caterpillars with chemicals or cold conditions to force them into quiescence. The photograph will reveal such mistreatment through the posture of the caterpillar, and the means do not justify the ends.

The final activity in photographing caterpillars, or anything for that matter, is image processing. It is important to save the original image file and create a backup file for all images prior to any conversion of file formats or editing. Do this daily. Use the laptop computer to house the original files and an external hard drive or a compact disc for storage of the backup files. The raw files can then be converted to tif files for editing, saving a backup of these files as well. Finally, save the edited image under an appropriate name. The filename should relate the edited images to the original raw file and the master tif file. Some forethought into the process of storing and naming files (the taxonomy of the images) will avoid grief by preventing the overwriting of files. At the same time, it will provide a platform for the organization of a portfolio and for future searching and retrieval of images.

THE IMAGES WE HAVE SHOWN were photographed by either Daniel Janzen or Jeffrey Miller. The photographs by Janzen are from Kodachrome 25 slides, taken with a Nikon FM2 stock 50 mm lens and extension tubes and a hand-held Vivitar flash over the years of the inventory. More than 30,000 of these images have been scanned at 2700 dpi, and thumbnail images placed on the inventory Web site (http://janzen.sas.upenn.edu), where the high-resolution digital images can also be downloaded individually by the user. Miller selected images from the Web site for the book and scanned those particular slides using a Nikon "SuperCoolScan 4000" slide scanner. The digital images were imported into PhotoShopCS and manipulated to maximize a black background, framed by cropping, enhanced by adjusting contrast, and sharpened.

Miller's photographs were acquired using a digital camera, either a Nikon D-100 or a Canon EOS-1ds. The Nikon was equipped with a 90mm macro lens whereas the Canon had a 180mm macro lens. In both cases multiple and slaved flash units were used to obtain the required light levels for shooting at a shutter speed of 1/80–1/100 and an f-stop of 16–28, all highly dependent on the color of the caterpillar and its size. A typical working distance (subject to lens) was eight inches when using the Nikon and about thirty inches when using the Canon equipment.

References

Aiello, A. and Silberglied, R. 1978. Life history of *Dynastor darius* (Lepidoptera: Nymphalidae). *Psyche* 85:331–345.

Bernays, E. A. and Janzen, D. H. 1988. Saturniid and sphingid caterpillars: Two ways to eat leaves. *Ecology* 69:1153–1160.

Boettner, G. H., Elkinton, J. S., and Boettner, C. J. 2000. Effects of a biological control introduction on three species of nontarget native species of saturniid moths. *Conservation Biology* 14:1798–1806.

Briscoe, A. D. and White, R. H. 2005. Adult stemmata of the butterfly *Vanessa cardui* express UV and green opsin mRNAs. *Cell Tissue Research* 319:175–179.

Burns, J. M. and Janzen, D. H. 2001. Biodiversity of pyrrhopygine skipper butterflies (Hesperiidae) in the Area de Conservación Guanacaste, Costa Rica. *Journal of the Lepidopterists' Society* 55:15–43.

——— 2005. Pan-Neotropical genus *Venada* (Hesperiidae: Pyrginae) is not monotypic: Four new species occur on one volcano in the *Area de Conservación Guanacaste* Costa Rica. *Journal of the Lepidopterists' Society* 59:19–34.

Casagrande, M. M. 2002. Naropini Stichel, taxonomia e imaturos (Lepidoptera, Nymphalidae, Brassolinae). *Revista Brasileira de Zoologia* 19:467–569.

Costa, J. T., Fitzgerald, T. D., and Janzen, D. H. 2004. Trail-following behavior and natural history of the social caterpillar of *Arsenura armida* in Costa Rica (Lepidoptera: Saturniidae: Arsenurinae). *Tropical Lepidoptera* 12:17–23.

Costa, J. T., Gotzek, D. A., and Janzen, D. H. 2003. Late-instar shift in foraging strategy and trail pheromone use by caterpillars of the neotropical moth *Arsenura armida* (Cramer) (Saturniidae: Arsenurinae). *Journal of the Lepidopterists' Society* 57:220–229.

D'Abrera, B. 1986. *Sphingidae Mundi. Hawk moths of the world.* Faringdon UK: E. W. Classey.

DeVries, P. J. 1987. *The butterflies of Costa Rica and their natural history. Papilionidae, Pieridae, Nymphalidae.* Princeton: Princeton University Press.

Epstein, M. E. and Corrales, J. F. 2004. Twenty-five new species of Costa Rican Limacodidae (Lepidoptera: Zygaenoidea). *Zootaxa* 701:1–86.

Gauld, I. D. 2000. The Ichneumonidae of Costa Rica, 3. *Memoirs of the American Entomological Institute* 63:1–453.

Gauld, I. D. and Janzen, D. H. 2004. The systematics and biology of the Costa Rican species of parasitic wasps in the *Thyreodon* genus-group (Hymenoptera: Ichneumonidae). *Zoological Journal of the Linnean Society* 141:297–351.

Hall, J. P. W., Harvey, D. J., and Janzen, D. H. 2004. Life history of *Calydna sturnula* with a review of larval and pupal balloon setae in the Riodinidae. *Annals of the Entomological Society of America* 97:310–321.

Hallwachs, W. 1986. Agoutis *(Dasyprocta punctata):* the inheritors of guapinol (*Hymenaea courbaril:* Leguminosae). In *Frugivores and Seed Dispersal,* A. Estrada and T. Fleming, eds. Dordrecht: Dr. W. Junk Publishers, pp. 285–304.

Hammond, P. C. and Miller, J. C. 1998. Comparison of the biodiversity of Lepidoptera within three forested ecosystems. *Annals of the Entomological Society of America* 91:323–328.

Haxaire, J. 1996. Les genres Pachygonidia Fletcher, *Nyceryx* Boisduval et *Perigonia* Herrich-Schaeffer en Guyane francaise. (Lepidoptera, Sphingidae). *Lambillionea* 96:342–350.

Hebert, P. D. N., Penton, E. H., Burns, J. M., Janzen, D. H., and Hallwachs, W. 2004. Ten species in one: DNA barcoding reveals cryptic species in the neotropical skipper butterfly *Astraptes fulgerator. Proceedings of the National Academy of Sciences* 101:14812–14817.

Ichiki, R. and Shima, H. 2003. Immature life of *Compsilura concinnata* (Meigen) (Diptera: Tachinidae). *Annals of the Entomological Society of America* 96:161–167.

Janzen, D. H. 1967. Interaction of the bull's-horn acacia (*Acacia cornigera* L.) with an ant inhabitant (*Pseudomyrmex ferruginea* F. Smith) in eastern Mexico. *University of Kansas Science Bulletin* 47:315–558.

——— 1969. Birds and the ant x acacia interaction in Central America, with notes on birds and other myrmecophytes. *Condor* 71:240–256.

——— 1977. Why fruits rot, seeds mold, and meat spoils. *American Naturalist* 111:691–713.

——— 1980a. Two potential coral snake mimics in a tropical deciduous forest. *Biotropica* 12:77–78.

——— 1980b. Specificity of seed-attacking beetles in a Costa Rican deciduous forest. *Journal of Ecology* 68:929–952.

——— 1982a. How and why horses open *Crescentia alata* fruits. *Biotropica* 14:149–152.

——— 1982b. Fruit traits, and seed consumption by rodents, of *Crescentia alata* (Bignoniaceae) in Santa Rosa National Park, Costa Rica. *American Journal of Botany* 69:1258–1268.

——— 1984a. Two ways to be a tropical big moth: Santa Rosa saturniids and sphingids. *Oxford Surveys in Evolutionary Biology* 1:85–140.

——— 1984b. Natural history of *Hylesia lineata* (Saturniidae: Hemileucinae) in Santa Rosa National Park, Costa Rica. *Journal of the Kansas Entomological Society* 57:490–514.

——— 1984c. Weather-related color polymorphism of *Rothschildia lebeau* (Saturniidae). *Bulletin of the Entomological Society of America* 30(2):16–20.

——— 1985a. On ecological fitting. *Oikos* 45:308–310.

——— 1985b. A host plant is more than its chemistry. *Illinois Natural History Bulletin* 33:141–174.

——— 1987a. When, and when not to leave. *Oikos* 49:241–243.

——— 1987b. How moths pass the dry season in a Costa Rican dry forest. *Insect Science and Its Application* 8:489–500.

——— 1991. How to save tropical biodiversity. *American Entomologist* 37:159–171.

——— 1992. A south-north perspective on science in the management, use, and economic development of biodiversity. In *Conservation of biodiversity for sustainable development*, O. T. Sandlund, K. Hindar, and A. H. D. Brown, eds. Oslo: Scandinavian University Press, pp. 27–52.

——— 1993a. Caterpillar seasonality in a Costa Rican dry forest. In *Caterpillars: Ecological and evolutionary constraints on foraging*, N. E. Stamp and T. M. Casey, eds. New York: Chapman and Hall, pp. 448–477.

——— 1993b. Taxonomy: Universal and essential infrastructure for development and management of tropical wildland biodiversity. In *Proceedings of the Norway/UNEP Expert Conference on Biodiversity, Trondheim, Norway*, O. T. Sandlund and P. J. Schei, eds., Trondheim: NINA, pp. 100–113.

———— 1996. Prioritization of major groups of taxa for the All Taxa Biodiversity Inventory (ATBI) of the Guanacaste Conservation Area in northwestern Costa Rica, a biodiversity development project. *ASC Newsletter* 24(4): 45, 49–56.

———— 2000. Costa Rica's Area de Conservación Guanacaste: a long march to survival through non-damaging biodevelopment. *Biodiversity* 1(2): 7–20.

———— 2003. How polyphagous are Costa Rican dry forest saturniid caterpillars? In *Arthropods of tropical forests: Spatio-temporal dynamics and resource use in the canopy.* Y. Basset, V. Novotny, S. E. Miller, and R. L. Kitching, eds. Cambridge: Cambridge University Press, pp. 369–379.

———— 2004. Setting up tropical biodiversity for conservation through non-damaging use: Participation by parataxonomists. *Journal of Applied Ecology* 41:181–187.

Janzen, D. H. and Martin, P. S. 1982. Neotropical anachronisms: The fruits the gomphotheres ate. *Science* 215:19–27.

Janzen, D. H., Hallwachs, W., Jimenez, J., and Gámez, R. 1993. The role of the parataxonomists, inventory managers and taxonomists in Costa Rica's national biodiversity inventory. In *Biodiversity prospecting,* W. V. Reid et al., eds. Washington, D. C.: World Resources Institute, pp. 223–254.

Janzen, D. H., Walker, A. K., Whitfield, J. B., Delvare, G., and Gauld, I. D. 2003. Host-specificity and hyperparasitoids of three new Costa Rican species of *Microplitis* Foerster (Hymenoptera: Braconidae: Microgastrinae), parasitoids of sphingid caterpillars. *Journal of Hymenoptera Research* 12(1): 42–76.

Joyce, F. J. 1993. Nesting success of rufous-naped wrens *(Campylorhynchus rufinucha)* is greater near wasp nests. *Behavioral Ecology and Sociobiology* 32:71–77.

Kimberling, D. N. and Miller, J. C. 1988. Effects of temperature on larval eclosion of the winter moth, *Operophtera brumata.* Entomologica Experimentalis et Applicata 47:249–254.

Kitching, I. J. and Cadiou, J.-M. 2000. Hawkmoths of the world: An annotated and illustrated revisionary checklist (Lepidoptera: Sphingidae). Ithaca: Cornell University Press.

Langham, G. M. 2004. Specialized avian predators repeatedly attack novel color morphs of *Heliconius* butterflies. *Evolution* 58:2783–2787.

Lattin, J. D. and Miller, J. C. 1997. Pacific Northwest arthropods. In J. P Smith and M. W. Collopy, eds. Status and trends of US biota. Washington, D.C.: USDI, National Biological Service, pp. 655–657.

Lemaire, C. 1988. The Saturniidae of America. Ceratocampinae. San Jose, Costa Rica: Museo Nacional de Costa Rica.

——— 2002. The Saturniidae of America. Part 4. Hemileucinae. Keltern, Germany: Goecke & Evers.

Mielke, O. H. H. 2002. Pyrrhopyginae: Generos novos e revalidados (Lepidoptera, Hesperiidae). *Revista Brasileira de Zoologia* 19:217–228.

Miller, J. C. 1980. Niche relationships among parasitic insects occurring in a temporary habitat. *Ecology* 61:270–275.

——— 1983. Ecological relationships among parasites and the practice of biological control. *Environmental Entomology* 12:620–624 (Forum Section).

——— 1990a. Field assessment of the effects of a microbial pest control agent on nontarget Lepidoptera. *American Entomologist* 36:135–139.

——— 1990b. Effects of a microbial insecticide, *Bacillus thuringiensis kurstaki*, on nontarget Lepidoptera in a spruce budworm-infested forest. *Journal of Research on the Lepidoptera* 29:267–276.

——— 1993. Insect natural history, multi-species interactions and biodiversity in ecosystems. *Biodiversity and Conservation* 2:233–241.

——— 1995. Caterpillars of Pacific Northwest forests and woodlands. USDA, USFS, FHM-NC-06-95.

——— 1996. Temperature-dependent development in *Meteorus communis* (Hymenoptera: Braconidae), a parasitoid of the variegated cutworm (Lepidoptera: Noctuidae). *Journal of Economic Entomology* 89:877–880.

——— 1999. Monitoring the effects of *Bacillus thuringiensis kurstaki* on nontarget Lepidoptera in woodlands and forests of western Oregon. In *Nontarget effects of biological control*, P. A. Follett and J. J. Duan, eds. Boston: Kluwer Acad. Publ., pp.°277–286.

——— 2004a. Insect life history strategies: Development and growth. *The encyclopedia of plant and crop science.*

——— 2004b. Insect life history strategies: Reproduction and survival. *The encyclopedia of plant and crop science.*

Miller, J. C. and Ehler, L. E. 1990. The concept of parasitoid guilds and its relevance to biological control. In *Critical issues in biological control*, M. Mackauer and L. E. Ehler, eds. Andover, UK: Intercept Press, pp. 159–169.

Miller, J. C. and Hammond, P. C. 2000. Macromoths of Northwest forests and woodlands. USDA, USFS, FTET 98-18.

————— 2003. Caterpillars and adult Lepidoptera of Northwest forests and woodlands. USDA, USFS, FHTET-2003-03.

Miller, J. C, Hammond, P. C., and Ross, D. N. R. 2003. Distribution and functional roles of rare and uncommon moths (Lepidoptera: Noctuidae: Plusiinae) across a coniferous forest landscape. *Annals of the Entomological Society of America* 96:847–855.

Miller, J. C. and Hanson, P. E. 1989a. Laboratory feeding tests on the development of gypsy moth larvae with reference to plant taxa and allelochemicals. Oregon State University Experiment Station Bulletin no. 674.

————— 1989b. Laboratory studies on development of gypsy moth, *Lymantria dispar* (L) (Lepidoptera: Lymantriidae), larvae on foliage of gymnosperms. *Canadian Entomologist* 121:425–429.

Miller, J. C., Hanson, P. E., and Kimberling, D. N. 1991. Development of the gypsy moth on Garry oak and red alder in western North America. *Environmental Entomology* 20:1097–1101.

Miller, J. C. and West, K. J. 1987. Host specificity of *Cotesia yakutatensis* on Lepidoptera in alfalfa and peppermint. *Entomophaga* 32:227–232.

Miller, J. S., Janzen, D. H., and Franclemont, J. G. 1997. New species of *Euhapigioides*, new genus, and *Hapigiodes* in Hapigiini, new tribe, from Costa Rica, with notes on their life history and immatures (Lepidoptera: Notodontidae). *Tropical Lepidoptera* 8(2): 81–99.

Muir, P. S., Mattingly, R. L., Tappeiner, J. C. II, Bailey, J. D., Elliott, W. E., Hagar, J. C., Miller, J. C., Peterson, E. B., and Starkey, E. E. 2002. Managing for Biodiversity in Young Douglas-fir Forests of Western Oregon. Biological Science Report, USGS/BRD/BSR-2002–0006. USGS, Forest and Rangeland Ecosystem Science Center, Corvallis, OR.

Nielsen, V., Hurtado, P., Janzen, D. H., Tamayo, G., and Sittenfeld, A. 2004. Recolecta de artopodos para prospeccion de la biodiversidad en el Area de Conservacion Guanacaste, Costa Rica. *Revista de Biologia Tropical* 52:119–132.

Parsons, G. L., Cassis, G., Moldenke, A. R., Lattin, J. D., Anderson, N. H., Miller, J. C., Hammond, P., and Schowalter, T. D. 1991. Invertebrates of the H. J. Andrews Experimental Forest, Western Cascade Range, Oregon. V: An annotated list of insects and other arthropods. USDA, USFS, PNW Research Station, General Technical Report, PNW-GTR-290.

Reid, W. V., Laird, S. A., Gámez, R. R., Sittenfeld, A., Janzen, D. H., Gollin, M. A., and Juma, C. 1993. A new lease on life. In *Biodiversity prospecting*, W. V. Reid et al., eds. Washington, D. C.: World Resources Institute, pp. 1–52.

Smith, S. 1975. Innate recognition of coral snake pattern by a possible avian predator. *Science* 187:759–760.

Willmott, K. R. 2003. The genus *Adelpha:* Its systematics, biology and biogeography (Lepidoptera: Nymphalidae: Limenitidini). Gainesville: Scientific Publishers.

Acknowledgments

From the very beginning of the caterpillar inventory in 1978, and for seven years before, the friendliness and help of the administration and infrastructure of the then Parque Nacional Santa Rosa (Santa Rosa National Park, or SRNP) were essential. Equally the support and guidance of the upper echelons of the Servicio de Parques Nacionales in the Ministry of Natural Resources and Energy (MIRENEM, and then MINAE)—and specifically Alvaro Ugalde and Mario Boza—were also essential. Not charging for use of buildings, laboratory and office space, and electricity, water, roads, security, and companionship were key start-up ingredients and perpetual operations support. These gestures made this project politically, sociologically, and economically feasible. The off-the-shelf cost of this support would have easily equaled the dollar support from the various NSF grants along the way. This continues to be the situation today, with the ACG pro-bono maintenance of seven of the eight caterpillar rearing stations for the project, albeit with the project contributing here and there for remodeling and building repair. The greatest contribution is the maintenance and protection of the entire block of living biodiversity on which the inventory is based. The inventory is critically stimulated by the realization that after all this work of finding out what is there, the ACG will ensure that it indeed still exists into perpetuity, to be used and enjoyed by an indefinite number of future generations.

Enter the parataxonomists. The ACG and its immediate neighbors are far more than a hotel and giant garden for the caterpillar inventory. They are the source of the entire parataxonomist team, the *gusaneros,* many of whom have invested the best part of their working lives in the project. The on-site parataxonomists had their start in 1979 with Roberto Espinoza, the first ACG caterpillar parataxonomist. As a late teen-aged fishing boat roustabout, field hand, and high school dropout, he proved to be an immediately capable, humorous, diligent, smart, tough, reliable protoparataxonomist. His predecessor, Gerardo Vega, a research assistant, came from an even rougher background, and by this time had moved back to his profession as sometime gold miner in the Osa Peninsula. Today, reflecting his immediate love of, and ability with, the caterpillar food plants, Roberto is the resident botanist of the ACG, along with Adrian Guadamuz and Maria Marta Chavarria, all of whom lead the small team of plant parataxonomists both inventorying the ACG's over 5,000 species of plants and providing the identification of the caterpillar inventory food plants. About 1990, four more parataxonomists were added to the caterpillar team—Osvaldo Espinoza (Roberto's brother), Roster Moraga, Guillermo Pereira, and Manuel Pereira. Within a year, Harry Ramirez and Gloria Sihezar joined. Shortly after, Mariano Pereira, Elieth Cantillano, Lucia Rios, and Ruth Franco pushed the group up to so large a size that it was time to expand to various stations in the rain forest and cloud forest to the east of Santa Rosa's dry-forest headquarters. Many of the cloud-forest and rain-forest caterpillars died of unknown causes when brought to the dry forest to rear. Then when the anticipated UNOCAL-ACG geothermal project closed down in late 1999, its three parataxonomists, veterans of the third (largely female) parataxonomist course in 1992, Carolina Cano, Freddy Quesada, and Dunia Garcia, were out of work. They were hired by the caterpillar project. In a convulsive fit of government-driven downsizing in 2003, the ACG let go its two parataxonomists, veterans of the first parataxonomist course in 1989, and Calixto Moraga and Petrona Rios joined the caterpillar team. Between 1999 and 2004 the Rincon Rainforest expansion of the ACG into deeper and lower-elevation rain forest established Estacion Caribe, and the caterpillar inventory used this opportunity to hire and train two more new parataxonomists, Freyci Vargas and Jose Perez. In 2003, Minor Carmona became the next fully salaried project parataxonomist. The project has been blessed with more than 150 resident apprentices and international student volunteers as well. Finally, on 16 January 2005, two new apprentice parataxonomists took up the dual role of "Encargado del Sector" and parataxonomist for the new ACG Estacion La Perla in Sector Mundo Nuevo.

Toward the end of this growth of the field parataxonomist team, Waldy Medina, a Liberia resident specializing in GIS, newly graduated with a degree from Montana State University, joined in 1998. He took up the role of project and ACG map-maker, surveyor, explorer, and GIS expert for all kinds of ACG biodiversity maps, aerial photographs, and geopositioning. In 1996, Isidro Chacon took on the task of integrating the newly merged collections of the "Inventory of the Moths of Costa Rica" with the huge moth collections being amassed by the INBio parataxonomists around the country, thereby providing essential taxonomic background. In 2004 he was joined in this task by Bernardo Espinoza, also at INBio.

FROM JEFF MILLER

Jean Miller, my wife and field assistant, has been an integral part of the team from start to finish. She has endured long days in the tropical environment, going places and doing things that appall the staff of our local travel clinic. Her keen record-keeping and eye for detail during editing have contributed to our book in countless ways. William C. Krueger, head of my newly adopted Department of Rangeland Ecology and Management at Oregon State University has given me unconditional support to continue with entomological studies while my career shifts from the context of the now-departed Department of Entomology. Oregon State University awarded me a grant (OSU 2003–2004 General Research Funds Grant Program) covering travel and expenses. For this I am extremely grateful—the financial and administrative support was a substantial morale booster. Joe Scheer of Alfred University hosted me as an artist-in-residence and provided unlimited use of his time and facilities. His book, *Night Visions,* his friendship, and his professional critique of my work have inspired and allowed me to become a better photographer. John Burns, our skipper expert at the Smithsonian Institution, kindly hosted me and my two coauthors the day I took photographs of adults. Jane Lyons, owner of Mindo Bird Tours, based at the Reserva Las Gralarias, Ecuador, was very kind to accommodate me at her reserve and encourage my pursuit of photographing caterpillars and their adults in Ecuador. Her involvement in keeping alive a chain of opportunity is vital to maintaining the energy required to produce a book such as this one. She also provided me with the name of the subspecies of *Manduca rustica* that occurs in the Galápagos Islands. Dave Wagner at the University of Connecticut has been a long-distance friend for many years. He too integrates photography with a scientific pursuit of caterpillar biosystematics and ecology, and has been a partner in publishing caterpillar field guides with the support of Richard Reardon, U.S. Forest Service, West Virginia. Dave is the person that submitted my name to Dan and Winnie as a possible speaker at the 2003 ACG Caterpillar Workshop, thereby introducing me to the ACG caterpillars. Harvard University Press, in particular Ann Downer-Hazell, was trusting in the belief that we could produce these images and their text in a timely manner and at a level of quality worthy of their reputation. Last, and most graciously, Dan and Winnie invited me into their world of tropical caterpillars, a piece of work twenty-eight years in the making, and for this I am in awe.

FROM DANIEL JANZEN AND WINIFRED HALLWACHS

How do we know so much about the caterpillars of the ACG? Because twenty Costa Ricans have invested the best part of their adult lives pretending to be birds and monkeys—and scorpions, and ants, and spiders, and wasps, and frogs, and mice, and all the other things that search for and eat caterpillars—and bringing the caterpillars back with their food plants, babysitting them through to adults, and databasing and photographing them. These are the project parataxonomists, or *gusaneros* (Janzen 2004), with about 200 person-years of field work among them since 1988. They are Carolina Cano Cano, Elieth Cantillano Espinoza, Osvaldo Espinoza Obando, Ana Ruth Franco Guadamúz, Roster Moraga Medina, Guillermo Pereira Espinoza, Manuel Pereira Espinoza, Mariano Pereira Espinoza, Fredy Quesada Quesada, Harry Ramiréz Castillo, Lucia Ríos Castro, Gloria Sihezar Araya, José Manuel Peréz Fernández, Elda Araya Martinez, Petrona Riós

Castro, Dunia García García, José Alberto Sánchez Chavarría, José Cortés Hernández, Mainor Carmona Bonilla, and Jose Manuel Perez Fernandez. They and their collection localities have been guided throughout by the maps and GPS of Waldy Medina, the ACG and project Costa Rican GIS specialist. And all of them have been assisted by a great zoo of volunteers ranging in geography from the same family to many far-away countries.

We also know a great deal about the caterpillars of the ACG because hundreds of Costa Ricans of all social points of life have tolerated, facilitated, encouraged, helped, financed, stimulated, and absorbed this effort to inventory—to set up for all of society to do whatever it wishes with them—the caterpillars of the ACG. We also know because U.S. tax dollars, filtered through the IRS, Congress, and the U.S. National Science Foundation (grants 8307887, 8610149, 9024700, 9306296, 9400829, 9705072, 0072730, and 0515699 to Janzen from Biotic Surveys and Inventories) have paid the lion's share of the bill. It is a fair estimate that the government of Costa Rica through the Ministerio de Recursos Naturales y Energia (MINAE), the Sistema Nacional de Areas de Conservacion (SINAC), the Museo Nacional de Costa Rica, and the ACG itself have contributed as much financial support in-kind as the international community has contributed in dollars. While all of the ACG staff have been invariably encouraging and facilitatory, we wish to thank Roger Blanco, Maria Marta Chavarria, Julio Diaz, Luis Fernando Garita, Jose Jaramillo, Felipe Chavarria, Luz Maria Romero, Magda Rodriguez, Jose Antonio Salazar, Randall Garcia, Johnny Rosales, Guisselle Mendez, and Sigifredo Marin for a multitude of specific acts supporting the inventory. Ranging more widely throughout Costa Rica, we remember and gratefully acknowledge much explicit support for the inventory from Rodrigo Gamez, Luis Diego Gomez, Alvaro Umaña, Rene Castro, Isidro Chacon, Jesus Ugalde, Angel Solis, Jorge Corrales, Bernardo Espinoza, Jorge Jimenez, Jenny Phillips, Raul Solorzano, Mario Boza, and Alvaro Ugalde.

And most of all we know a great deal about the ACG caterpillars because nearly 150 insect and plant taxonomists all over the world have worked long, inconvenient, sweaty, back-aching, dusty, dull, exhilarating hours to help us identify the adult moths and butterflies, their parasitoids, and their food plants. Special thanks are due to particular individuals who were key in the identification of the particular moths and butterflies that we display: John Burns, Claude Lemaire (deceased), Jean-Marie Cadiou, Ian Kitching, Dick Vane-Wright, Keith Willmott, Jason Hall, Don Harvey, Phil DeVries, Jim Miller, Jack Franclemont (deceased), John Rawlins, Isidro Chacon, Bernardo Espinoza, Bob Poole, Vitor Becker, Mike Pogue, Scott Miller, Marc Epstein, William Schaus (deceased), Alan Hayes (deceased), and Bernard D'Abrera. The parasitoid discussions would have been impossible without the identifications provided by Monty Wood, Norm Woodley, Ian Gauld, Rodolfo Zuñiga, Mike Schauff, Mike Sharkey, Carlos Sarmiento, Jim Whitfield, Alejandro Valerio, Josephine Rodriguez, Andy Deans, Won-Young Choi, Scott Shaw, and Nina Zitani. The food plants for the caterpillars displayed here would be just so much green salad without the identification labor freely offered by Nelson Zamora, Roberto Espinoza, Adrian Guadamuz, Maria Marta Chavarria, Luis Diego Gomez, Ron Leisner, Barry Hammel, Mike Grayum, Francisco Morales, Alexander Rodriguez, Luis Poveda, Jose Gonzales, Al Gentry (deceased), Jose Gomez-Laurito, William Haber, and Quirico Jimenez.

Numerical Species List

1. *Automeris postalbida*
2. *Automeris tridens*
3. *Automeris zugana*
4. *Dirphia avia*
5. *Xylophanes juanita*
6. *Nystalea collaris*
7. *Navarcostes limnatis*
8. *Morpho polyphemus*
9. *Citheronia lobesis*
10. *Leucanella hosmera*
11. *Opsiphanes zelotes*
12. *Opsiphanes bogotanus*
13. *Xylophanes guianensis*
14. *Eacles imperialis*
15. *Othorene purpurascens*
16. *Syssphinx quadrilineata*
17. *Eudocima colubra*
18. *Arsenura armida*
19. *Perigonia ilus*
20. *Euhapigiodes hallwachsae*

21. *Talides* BURNS01
22. *Phocides lilea*
23. *Rothschildia triloba*
24. *Lepidodes gallopavo*
25. *Euselasia eubule*
26. *Hylesia lineata*
27. *Phobetron hipparchia*
28. *Mimoides branchus*
29. *Manduca muscosa*
30. *Manduca rustica*
31. *Colax apulus*
32. *Crinodes besckei*
33. *Dyscophellus* BURNS01
34. *Chioides catillus*
35. *Narope* JANZEN01
36. *Archaeoprepona meander*
37. *Erinnyis crameri*
38. *Nyceryx tacita*
39. *Adeloneivaia jason*
40. *Schausiella santarosensis*

41. *Copiopteryx semiramis*
42. *Arsenura batesii*
43. *Adelpha celerio*
44. *Acharia hyperoche*
45. *Anurocampa mingens*
46. *Naprepa houla*
47. *Sosxetra grata*
48. *Yanguna cosyra*
49. *Phoebis sennae*
50. *Lycorea cleobaea*
51. *Xylophanes chiron*
52. *Xylophanes germen*
53. *Hemeroplanes triptolemus*
54. *Dynastor darius*
55. *Cocytius lucifer*
56. *Manduca pellenia*
57. *Phiditia lucernaria*
58. *Memphis pithyusa*
59. *Dyscophellus* BURNS02
60. *Venada daneva*
61. *Rhuda dificilis*
62. *Marpesia petreus*
63. *Erinnyis ello*
64. *Unzela japix*
65. *Callicore pitheas*
66. *Calydna sturnula*
67. *Syssphinx mexicana*
68. *Euclea norba*
69. *Archaeoprepona demophoon*
70. *Synargis mycone*
71. *Protambulyx strigilis*
72. *Manduca lanuginosa*
73. *Acharia horrida*
74. *Tarchon felderi*
75. *Dipterygia ordinarius*
76. *Sorocaba* JANZEN01
77. *Parasa sandrae*
78. *Acraga hamata*
79. *Heterochroma sarepta*
80. *Nyceryx magna*
81. *Morpho peleides*
82. *Rothschildia lebeau*
83. *Eumorpha labruscae*
84. *Selenisa sueroides*
85. *Jemadia pseudognetus*
86. *Pyrrhopyge zenodorus*
87. *Copaxa rufinans*
88. *Periphoba arcaei*
89. *Astraptes* LOHAMP
90. *Chrysoplectrum* BURNS01
91. *Munona iridescens*
92. *Gamelia musta*
93. *Caio championi*
94. *Eumorpha satellitia*
95. *Syssphinx molina*
96. *Manduca florestan*
97. *Lirimiris gigantea*
98. *Euglyphis* JANZEN01
99. *Elymiotis alata*
100. *Nystalea aequipars*

Alphabetical Species List

73. *Acharia horrida*
44. *Acharia hyperoche*
78. *Acraga hamata*
39. *Adeloneivaia jason*
43. *Adelpha celerio*
45. *Anurocampa mingens*
69. *Archaeoprepona demophoon*
36. *Archaeoprepona meander*
18. *Arsenura armida*
42. *Arsenura batesii*
89. *Astraptes* LOHAMP
1. *Automeris postalbida*
2. *Automeris tridens*
3. *Automeris zugana*
93. *Caio championi*
65. *Callicore pitheas*
66. *Calydna sturnula*
34. *Chioides catillus*
90. *Chrysoplectrum* BURNS01
9. *Citheronia lobesis*

55. *Cocytius lucifer*
31. *Colax apulus*
87. *Copaxa rufinans*
41. *Copiopteryx semiramis*
32. *Crinodes besckei*
75. *Dipterygia ordinarius*
4. *Dirphia avia*
54. *Dynastor darius*
33. *Dyscophellus* BURNS01
59. *Dyscophellus* BURNS02
14. *Eacles imperialis*
99. *Elymiotis alata*
37. *Erinnyis crameri*
63. *Erinnyis ello*
68. *Euclea norba*
17. *Eudocima colubra*
98. *Euglyphis* JANZEN01
20. *Euhapigiodes hallwachsae*
83. *Eumorpha labruscae*
94. *Eumorpha satellitia*

25. *Euselasia eubule*

92. *Gamelia musta*

53. *Hemeroplanes triptolemus*

79. *Heterochroma sarepta*

26. *Hylesia lineata*

85. *Jemadia pseudognetus*

24. *Lepidodes gallopavo*

10. *Leucanella hosmera*

97. *Lirimiris gigantea*

50. *Lycorea cleobaea*

96. *Manduca florestan*

72. *Manduca lanuginosa*

29. *Manduca muscosa*

56. *Manduca pellenia*

30. *Manduca rustica*

62. *Marpesia petreus*

58. *Memphis pithyusa*

28. *Mimoides branchus*

81. *Morpho peleides*

8. *Morpho polyphemus*

91. *Munona iridescens*

46. *Naprepa houla*

35. *Narope JANZEN01*

7. *Navarcostes limnatis*

80. *Nyceryx magna*

38. *Nyceryx tacita*

100. *Nystalea aequipars*

6. *Nystalea collaris*

12. *Opsiphanes bogotanus*

11. *Opsiphanes zelotes*

15. *Othorene purpurascens*

77. *Parasa sandrae*

19. *Perigonia ilus*

88. *Periphoba arcaei*

57. *Phiditia lucernaria*

27. *Phobetron hipparchia*

22. *Phocides lilea*

49. *Phoebis sennae*

71. *Protambulyx strigilis*

86. *Pyrrhopyge zenodorus*

61. *Rhuda dificilis*

82. *Rothschildia lebeau*

23. *Rothschildia triloba*

40. *Schausiella santarosensis*

84. *Selenisa sueroides*

76. *Sorocaba JANZEN01*

47. *Sosxetra grata*

70. *Synargis mycone*

67. *Syssphinx mexicana*

95. *Syssphinx molina*

16. *Syssphinx quadrilineata*

21. *Talides BURNS01*

74. *Tarchon felderi*

64. *Unzela japix*

60. *Venada daneva*

51. *Xylophanes chiron*

52. *Xylophanes germen*

13. *Xylophanes guianensis*

5. *Xylophanes juanita*

48. *Yanguna cosyra*